heterosexism in contemporary world religion

heterosexism in contemporary world religion

problem and prospect

Marvin M. Ellison and
Judith Plaskow, editors

THE
PILGRIM
PRESS
Cleveland

The Pilgrim Press
700 Prospect Avenue
Cleveland, Ohio 44115-1100
thepilgrimpress.com

✿ Printed in the United States of America on acid-free paper that contains
post-consumer fiber.

12 11 10 09 08 07   5 4 3 2 1

Library of Congress Cataloging-in-Publication Data

Heterosexism in contemporary world religion : problem and prospect / Marvin M. Ellison
and Judith Plaskow, editors. – 1st ed.
    p. cm.
  ISBN 978-0-8298-1770-6
  1. Sex – Religious aspects. 2. Sexual minorities.   I. Ellison, Marvin Mahan.
II. Plaskow, Judith.
BL65.S4H48 2007
201′.7 – dc22

2007025006

Contents

Contributors

Ghazala Anwar is assistant professor at Islamic International University, Islamabad. Previously she was lecturer in the Religious Studies Department at University Canterbury, Christchurch, New Zealand.

Kelly Brown Douglas is The Elizabeth Connolly Todd Distinguished Professor of Religion at Goucher College, Baltimore, Maryland. She is the author of several books, including *Sexuality in the Black Church: A Womanist Perspective*.

Marvin M. Ellison is Willard S. Bass Professor of Christian Ethics at Bangor Theological Seminary, Maine. Among his publications is *Same Sex Marriage? A Christian Ethical Analysis*.

Ann-Marie Hsiung, associate professor at I-Shou University in Taiwan, teaches gender issues in Confucianism and Taoism. Her research interests relate to translation, culture, and globalization; she has edited *Gender and Boundary*.

Mary E. Hunt is a feminist theologian who is co-founder and co-director of the Women's Alliance for Theology, Ethics and Ritual (WATER) in Silver Spring, Maryland. A Catholic active in the women-church movement, she lectures and writes on theology and ethics. She has written or edited several books, including *Good Sex: Feminist Perspectives from the World's Religions*.

Yu-chen Li is associate professor of Chinese Literature at Tsing Hua University in Taiwan. Having conducted fieldwork at more than sixty Buddhist nunneries worldwide, as well as being an active member of Sakyadhita (the International Association of Buddhist women), her research focuses primarily on Buddhist nuns and gender issues in contemporary religion.

Daniel C. Maguire is professor of ethics at Marquette University and president of The Religious Consultation on Population, Reproductive Health, and Ethics, the organization sponsoring this project. Among his writings is *Sacred Choices: The Right to Contraception and Abortion in Ten World Religions*.

Judith Plaskow is professor of religious studies at Manhattan College, Riverdale, New York, and a Jewish feminist theologian. She is past president of the American Academy of Religion. Her books include *Standing Again at Sinai: Judaism from a Feminist Perspective*.

Anantanand Rambachan is professor of religion and philosophy at Saint Olaf College, Northfield, Minnesota. He is the author of several books, book chapters, and articles in scholarly journals, including *The Advaita Worldview: The Limits of Scripture*.

Introduction

Heterosexism, Not Homosexuality, Is the Problem

DANIEL C. MAGUIRE

Homosexuality is not a problem: heterosexism is a problem, and not just for sexual minorities. To think of homosexuality as "problem" — which even persons of liberal bent can do — is a distraction and a surrender to the unjust and poisonous prejudice of heterosexism.

Homophobia has, in irony, been called "the last respectable prejudice," but, of course, no prejudice merits respect. All prejudice metastasizes into other sites and spreads its malignancy into policy, law, custom, and culture. Any prejudice tolerated makes other prejudices seem more natural. By its nature, prejudice "outgroups" persons, disenfranchising them of their human rights. It marks persons out for special and negative handling simply because of who they are.

Unlike its cousins anti-Semitism, sexism, and racism, heterosexism has enjoyed undue immunity from critique, especially religious critique. Worse yet, religions have been the major offenders in fomenting prejudice against sexual minorities. The pope says gays cannot be priests. As theologian Mary E. Hunt points out in chapter 6, heterosexual Catholics have seven sacraments; gays and lesbians have only six since the sacrament of matrimony is denied them. Some Episcopalians want to split their church apart to prevent same-sex marital bonding. The stress on reproduction in all religions often disparages non-reproductive sex, thus tabooing and insulting all homosexual relationships. Religious prejudices seep deeply

1

into cultures. Thus, sexual minorities not only cannot be clergy, they also cannot be teachers or even soldiers.

Religions are always active and influential in defining the meaning of the bonding called family and have regularly shrunken it into a gated preserve for heterosexuals. This gives religious blessing to a heterosexual monopoly on committed love. It transforms marriage from a human right into an award for being heterosexual. Sexual pleasure itself is put on trial; it must be justified or validated by reproductivity. Sexual joy in its own right is stripped of its natural legitimacy. Sexual minorities are thus not the only victims of heterosexist brutality. The damage is so much broader.

Diversity Phobia

Humanity needs its exuberant diversity, but humans tend to flee from it. William Sloane Coffin writes: "Diversity may be the hardest thing for a society to live with — and perhaps the most dangerous thing to live without."[1] This self-protective hunger for a cowering monism could indeed be the fatal flaw of our species. We either learn to live with and exult in the wealth of our natural and cultural differences — religious, ethnic, racial, sexual — or we perish.

The fervor that animates homophobia seeks ill-fated support from zoology, hoping to show that nature requires heteronormativity. Alas, the desired evidence is not there, and contrary evidence abounds. In his extensive study *Biological Exuberance: Animal Homosexuality and Natural Diversity*, biologist Bruce Bagemihl shows that homosexuality is part of our evolutionary heritage as primates. He reports that more than 450 species regularly engage in a wide range of same-sex activities ranging from copulation to long-term bonding. Even the assumed male/female dimorphism is not fixed in nature. "Many animals live without two distinct genders, or with multiple genders."[2] Finding evidence that our preferred

---

1. William Sloane Coffin, "Diversity and Inclusion," *Mount Holyoke Alumnae Quarterly* (Winter 1999): 23.

2. Bruce Bagemihl, *Biological Exuberance: Animal Homosexuality and Natural Diversity* (New York: St. Martin's Press, 1999), 37.

social arrangements are exemplified in edifying animal conduct is also doomed. The lovely mallards sometimes form "trio-bonds" with one male and two females or one female with two males.[3]

Homophobia and Fear of Change

A similar and related timidity makes us fear change. Extreme conservatives seem to be saying that "nothing should be done for the first time." Yet change is of the essence. From the molecular micro to the macro of the universe, flux is normative and incessant. "First times" are an unending feature of nature. Clearly many changes would come to society if heterosexism with its multiple noxious ramifications were banished from our cultural lexicon and buried with evils of the past, such as cannibalism and the divine right of kings. The extent of change, it seems, is keenly felt.

If the patriarchally conceived model of marriage were changed and more egalitarian forms of marriage and family were legitimated, a lynchpin would be yanked out of current social constructions. As Marvin M. Ellison points out in chapter 2 of this volume, governments might have to support people on the basis of need and not of conformity to a narrow definition of family. His words: "Making marital status the exclusive conduit for these benefits does little to correct the entrenched patterns of social and economic inequities that are rapidly expanding within the global capitalist social order."

Patriarchal marriage has long been the building block of society, and through its symbolic power it finds reflection in governments and corporate structures. It weaves hierarchical assumptions into the expression of power. Heterosexist and biased definitions of normalcy attach to the central nerves in the economic and political arrangements now in place. Change in these matters is not just personal; it is political and important, and powerholders know it. Hence the frenzy and uproar in church and state when regnant notions of marriage and family are threatened by new thought.

---

3. Ibid., 494.

Fear of two persons who love each other and want to bond permanently, legally, and if they choose, religiously, would not, on its face, seem to presage social disaster. Why does it engender such panic?

It does seem to be a rule of life that when an issue becomes suddenly inflamed in society, it rarely has anything to do with the issue. It has everything to do with power. Powerholders, like animals who sense earthquakes before others, first feel the distant tremors that threaten their foundations and their privileges.

All of this helps to explain the shocking enigma of misplaced moral indignation in the political arena and among religious people. One would think that the ongoing starvation of 1.3 billion people in absolute poverty would command our moral attention. If not that, then one would hope that the double basting of the planet in CO_2 with catastrophes of melting polar and glacial ice already happening would focus our minds. How compatible it would be with the peace-passions and empathy traditions of all the world's major religions to mount campaigns against bloated military budgets that suck the blood out of our economies while children starve and wars and illiteracy spread, with health-care needs unforgivably unmet.

But no. In countries such as the United States, a demonic, fear-driven pelvic orthodoxy, with scandalous over-absorption in issues like same-sex marriage, contraception, and abortion, consumes politics, churches, legislatures, and judiciaries.

The widely unappreciated truth is that heterosexism with its attendant assumptions forces us into a closet of fear — terrible, damaging, corrupting fear. This book is written as an invitation to exit that closet.

Religion as Problem; Religion as Cure

The Religious Consultation on Population, Reproductive Health, and Ethics, with support from The Brico Fund, recruited the scholars contributing to this volume, some living as far away as Singapore, Taiwan, and New Zealand. We met twice over two years for four-day meetings. At the table were representatives of Hinduism, Buddhism, Taoism, Confucianism, Judaism, Protestant and Catholic Christianity (including a specialist in Black American Christianity), and Islam. We gathered in the conviction that where heterosexism flourishes, fundamentalist religious inaccuracies dominate public discourse affecting public attitudes, laws, and policies. The ingredients in the world's religions that support same-sex unions are largely hidden, and we set out to correct that. Our goal is to give voice in this volume and in multiple media to the religious resources that are truly antidotal to heterosexism and can bring balance to discussions of the moral rights of sexual minorities. Truth well delivered is the hoped-for solvent of prejudice.

All the scholars in this volume agree, as we do in all the Consultation's projects, that multi-religious collaboration breaks open the lockbox of monocultural ethical analysis. It facilitates what Robert McAfee Brown used to call "caricature assassination."

Meeting twice over two years face to face and not just by e-mail, fax, and phone — though we did that too — makes a qualitative difference in the dialogue. The Jesuit social theorist John Courtney Murray used to say that "disagreement is a rare achievement," and he had a point. Distance from one's interlocutors can breed an undue politeness. We break through that with this methodology. We can agree and disagree, probe and question, and so more effectively pull away the veils of false, culturally ensconced assumptions. Our funder saw the value of this and made it possible for us to build a small collegium through these intense and exhilarating meetings. Parting after our second meeting was "sweet sorrow" since bonds were forged that will continue to bear scholarly fruit.

Each chapter of this volume has a different perspective to offer. There is refreshment in seeing that Chinese cultures did not think of a person as "a homosexual"; they didn't even have a word for it, though the reality was there. This is in chastening contrast to much of Western homophobic culture. In this view, sexual orientation does not constitute personhood. In other religions, too, sexual orientation is not the grounds for either dignity or scorn.

Homosexuality, like heterosexuality, is morally neutral. It is primarily how persons live and relate to other persons and to their parent earth that gives persons their main identity. In healthier cultures, the "is" of a person is not established by sexual orientation or by height, but by moral commitments. The object of one's passion and love does not stigmatize the lover. We know more of what makes a person a person by finding his or her lived-out attraction to compassion and justice. Thus, in Buddhism, the concern is not so much whether a person is homosexual as whether the person observes and embraces celibacy and the other requirements of a moral life as a monk.

This same healing theme appears here and there like an aspiring leit-motif in all those flawed but powerful classics called world religions. The healthy emphasis on the moral character of persons — rather than with whom they fall in love — strips away and embarrasses the moralistic pretensions of heterosexist cultures. Seeing persons through heterosexist lenses is radically distortional.

Realism on Religion

The writers in this volume do not proceed under the illusion that religions are immaculately conceived and free of sin. *Au contraire!* Religions are not only sinners, they are also influential sinners.[4] As already noted, all religions contributed and continue to contribute to heterosexist prejudice. No religion is a complete moral success. There is a Buddhist saying that every belief system is an illness waiting to be cured. That may overstate the case, and it may also out-postmodern the postmodernists, but there is a point there. The goal of our authors is to seek out the renewable moral

---

4. The term *religion* is not univocal and indeed is not tidily mirrored in many other languages. Chinese scholars say there is no word in the Chinese languages that perfectly parallels the common usage in English. In the world of ancient Israel, as Morton Smith writes, there was no "general term for religion"; philosophy of life would come closer to their understanding. (Morton Smith, "Palestinian Judaism in the First Century," in *Israel: Its Role in Civilization* [New York: Jewish Theological Seminary of America, 1956], 67–81.) In The Religious Consultation on Population, Reproductive Health, and Ethics we have worked with the idea of religion as a response to the sacred whether that sacred is theistically or non-theistically explicated. (Cf. Daniel C. Maguire, "Introduction," *Visions of a New Earth: Religious Perspectives on Population, Consumption, and Ecology*, ed. Harold Coward and Daniel C. Maguire [Albany: State University of New York Press, 2000], 1–7).

energies of these classics, however flawed they may be, and direct those energies creatively to contemporary moral crises.

All religions suffer from amnesia. They can forget their better moments in the past when prejudice did not dull their vision. Thus, as John Boswell showed, Christianity was not always heterosexist and homophobic.[5] The task of religious scholarship is to call the religions before the bar of their professed ideals and to show them times when those ideals were better realized. Religions also suffer from contagion. Heterosexist poisons cross borders, and the various scholars in this volume take note of these unhappy imports into their religions.

Some, not all, of authors in this volume bring their own experience as sexual minorities to their scholarship. This was indispensable and appreciated by all participants. Six of the participants are women, two men. Since men tended to write the script for most religions, all of our Consultation projects welcome the newly emergent voices of women scholars.

Judith Plaskow, our scholar in Judaism and co-editor of the book, is no stranger in feminist literature. As past president of the American Academy of Religion, she has been an influential presence, and there are few who are not in debt to her valuable and courageous work. She points out how society tries to shrink sexual expression into a tight binary and then derives sexual norms from this artificial arrangement that do not match the richness of nature. Violations of these norms, she says in chapter 1, quoting Kate Bornstein, "seem to endanger the foundations of the earth, the walls of our only safe and certain home in the universe."[6] It takes courage to challenge these norms. But courage, of course, is the mark of all who struggle against the headwinds of prejudice.

Co-editor Marvin Ellison is a gay man teaching in the venerable Bangor Theological Seminary and author of the recently published *Same-Sex Marriage? A Christian Ethical Analysis*, in which he defends same-sex marriage

---

5. John Boswell, *Christianity, Social Tolerance, and Homosexuality* (Chicago: University of Chicago Press, 1980).

6. Kate Bornstein, *Gender Outlaw: On Men, Women, and the Rest of Us* (New York: Routledge, 1994).

on Christian grounds.[7] Ellison shows how power concerns operate in the effort to make heterosexuality normative for the whole human race and how government conspires with religious prejudice and religious ignorance to dictate narrowly defined "family values."

Ghazala Anwar, a leading Muslim scholar, brings to this volume what most have thought impossible: a defense of same-sex marriage based on the Qur'an and other authoritative Muslim sources. She even shows how this has moved beyond scholarly debate and is being lived out successfully in ways that are virtually unknown in the West by committed and fully faithful Muslim lesbians, the Ṣamadiyyah. Professor Anwar, now teaching in New Zealand, returns frequently to her native Pakistan where she has lectured on "Lesbian Shariah." She reports in her chapter on the surprisingly encouraging reactions she has gotten on her courageous mission to her beloved Muslim community.

Anantanand Rambachan draws from his own Hindu experience and from his life of scholarship on the multiple traditions covered by the general term *Hinduism*. Respect for diversity is at the heart of Hindu cultures. There are many names for God and many embodiments of divinity. Unlike the rigidly monotheistic faiths, there is less stress on tidy categories, more humility, and more openness to surprise. Since early times, the Hindus saw that persons were not divided neatly into male and female; there was also a third sex, and this normalized gender and sexual variety. This reflects the acceptance of "two spirit" people in Native American cultures.[8] There are remedies in these traditions for the dogmatic dimorphism found in other cultures.

Yu-Chen Li, from the National Tsing Hua University in Taiwan, shows how Buddhism relativizes not only gender but sexual orientation. It is the successful management of sexual desire, not the orientation of that desire, that matters. Virtue and enlightenment are possible for anyone in

---

7. Marvin M. Ellison, *Same-Sex Marriage? A Christian Ethical Analysis* (Cleveland: Pilgrim Press, 2004).

8. See Mary Churchill, "Native Americans," 535–38, "Two-Spirit," 779–80, in *Encyclopedia of Lesbian and Gay Histories and Cultures*, vol. 1, ed. Bonnie Zimmerman (New York: Garland Publishing, 2000).

this tradition. Of course, the privileging of males is pandemic and leaves no religion untouched, and so sexual and gender prejudices are present in Buddhist history even to this day. Still, professor Yu-Chen Li shows that there are forces within Buddhism that stress that acceptance of this universe as it is, with all of its natural differences, is the path to true enlightenment. Privileging one sexual orientation over another is not the path of wisdom.

Professor Ann-Marie Hsiung writes of Taoism and Confucianism. In the Chinese religions there is, of course, a strong stress on the need for reproduction, and Professor Hsiung points out how Confucian rigidities were conducive to heterosexism. Still, there is not the homophobic resistance to same-sex romance found so widely in the West. Same-sex relations among males were common, though often in situations where status, power, and wealth gave freedom to privileged males. Women enjoyed more freedom for homoerotic relationships as witnessed in the outpouring of passionate literature. In one play, a young married woman, Cui, falls in love with a beautiful young woman, Cao, in her visit to a Buddhist convent, and Cao reciprocates her feelings. The two seek union as husband and wife and even invoke the Buddha as their witness: "We could share the same bed and afterwards the same tomb and we would be joined, like two butterflies, flitting hither and thither." In some cases a partnered lesbian would take up a simultaneous relationship with a man to fulfill her child-bearing duty and then would return to her true lesbian love. The human desire (more prominent in the West than in the East) to pack sexual and gender reality into tidy fenced-in categories does little justice to human experience more broadly seen.

Professor Kelly Brown Douglas discusses the fact that in the African American church communities there is pronounced homophobia and heterosexism. She points out that this was strategically exploited by the Republican Party with some success in the 2004 presidential election. She explores the multiple reasons for this: a reaction to past charges of African Americans' aberrant hypersexuality, fear that the anti-heterosexist movement is bypassing the enduring justice claims of African Americans, and an overreaction to their past history, when marriage was denied them. Homophobia and heterosexism are also stimulated by fundamentalist interpretations of the Bible's anti-homosexual texts. Professor Douglas counters all of this with a sophisticated Christian theology that better corresponds to the spiritual power and élan of the African American churches.

The biblical "texts of terror" used by popular evangelists are also influential with conservative Catholics newly bonded with fundamentalist Protestants. The texts themselves are their own refutation, and no one could take them literally. Leviticus 20:13 demands capital punishment for sexual minorities. It says of those who have had homosexual sex, "they shall be put to death. Their blood shall be on their own heads." Paul also prescribes capital punishment for same-sex activity: "Those who behave like this deserve to die" (Rom. 1:32). Obviously these texts, like other texts in the Bible permitting slavery, animal sacrifice, and polygamy, are not applicable or applied today. Yet they continue to do mischief, and not just in the African American communities. They also resonate in the chambers of American lawmakers and judges.

Dr. Mary E. Hunt writes "as a Catholic lesbian feminist theologian" and faces up to the enormous problems caused by homophobia and heterosexism in the Roman Catholic Church. She notes the basic irrationality of heterosexism: "Homosexuality is a phenomenon that, absent heterosexism, is no more ethically interesting or relevant than heterosexuality. It is a descriptive category that is morally neutral." Hunt argues that heterosexism has a deviant power mission in Catholicism. She asks why "a religious organization would spend its symbolic capital on sexuality unless it were the lynchpin in its hierarchically dualistic worldview. Paired with the sexism that always accompanies it, heterosexism plays a key role in Catholic kyriarchal thinking, both to discriminate against lgbt people and to prevent especially women from exercising moral and spiritual agency." A truly Catholic theology would call for the celebration of same-sex love, not its condemnation. True Catholicism would extol persons for their virtues and not burn them for their loves. Dr. Hunt's logic would also hold for political heterosexism. There is no state interest in preventing two persons who love one another from bonding for life in secular or religious ceremonies of their choosing. Thus, a not-so-secret power agenda is again afoot.

Religions are never neutral or passive bystanders in public debates on issues of morality and human relations. Nothing so stirs the will as the tincture of the sacred. In the United States and many other countries, simplistic and fundamentalistic theologies that distort the religious traditions have held sway. They have been the loudest voices in the public square. This book seeks to remedy that and to do honor to the racial, ethnic, and sexual variety with which humanity is blessed.

Chapter One

Dismantling the Gender Binary within Judaism

The Challenge of Transgender to Compulsory Heterosexuality

JUDITH PLASKOW

Gender is one of the fundamental categories through which we order and interact with the world. Most people absorb the fundamental "rules" of gender at an early age, and these rules provide the basis for all relationships with others. There are two and only two genders, we are taught, male and female; all human beings who have ever lived are one or the other; gender is determined through visual inspection of a baby's genitals at birth and remains unchanged throughout life; female/male dimorphism is natural, having nothing to do with social criteria or decisions, and so is individual membership in one gender or another.[1] These assumptions are so basic to the way in which we understand reality that anything that threatens them — a baby with ambiguous genitalia, a person on the street whose gender is difficult to determine, a man who is cross-dressed, a butch woman — may evoke both anger and a profound sense of vertigo.

---

1. Harold Garfinkel, *Studies in Ethnomethodology* (Englewood Cliffs, NJ: Prentice Hall, 1967), 122–28. Cited in Suzanne J. Kessler and Wendy McKenna, *Gender: An Ethnomethodological Approach* (Chicago: University of Chicago Press, 1978), 113f. Note that while the distinction between (biological) sex and (cultural) gender was an important contribution of feminist theory, this distinction has come under increasing criticism. I am following Kessler and McKenna (7) and many other recent feminist theorists in including so-called biological sex as part of the gender system.

Violations of gender norms seem to endanger the foundations of the earth, the walls of our only safe and certain home in the universe.[2]

I would argue that we cannot comprehend the virulence of homophobia or the power of compulsory heterosexuality apart from these deep-seated assumptions about gender. Homophobia and a binary understanding of gender are intertwined aspects of the same hierarchical system, and dismantling one requires exploring and attempting to dismantle the other. The very way gender is defined in U.S. society assumes the alignment of gender assignment, gender identity, gender role, and sexual desire. To be female or male is to be recognized as such from birth; to affirm this identity; to behave in certain expected ways in terms of emotional characteristics, interests, activities, and skills; and to be attracted to members of the "opposite" sex.[3] To be a proper woman or a proper man is to be heterosexual — to establish one's own gender through differentiation from the gender of the desired partner.[4] The same complex web of ideologies and institutions, of expectations, rewards, and punishments that teaches us what it means to be a man or a woman also teaches us that we will someday fall in love with someone of the other sex, marry, and create a family.[5] Gender roles guarantee that the smallest viable social unit will consist of one man and one woman whose desire must be directed toward each other, and that men have rights to women's sexuality, time, attention, and labor that women do not have either in relation to men or to one another.[6]

---

2. Kate Bornstein, *Gender Outlaw: On Men, Women, and the Rest of Us* (New York: Routledge, 1994), 72; Judith Shapiro, "Transsexualism: Reflections on the Persistence of Gender and the Mutability of Sex," in *Body Guards: The Cultural Politics of Gender Ambiguity*, ed. Julia Epstein and Kristina Traub (New York: Routledge, 1991), 249; Steven Greenberg, *Wrestling with God and Men: Homosexuality in the Jewish Tradition* (Madison: University of Wisconsin Press, 2004), 138.

3. Kessler and McKenna, *Gender*, 8–12; Kate Bornstein, *My Gender Workbook* (New York: Routledge, 1998), 27; Judith Butler, *Gender Trouble: Feminism and the Subversion of Identity* (New York: Routledge, 1990), 6f., 17.

4. Butler, *Gender Trouble*, 22f.

5. Adrienne Rich, "Compulsory Heterosexuality and Lesbian Existence," *Signs: Journal of Women in Culture and Society* 5, no. 4 (1980): 63–60.

6. Gayle Rubin, "The Traffic in Women: Notes on the 'Political Economy of Sex,'" in *Toward an Anthropology of Women*, ed. Rayna Reiter (New York: Monthly Review Press,

There have always been individuals and groups who have challenged this tightly ordered gender and sexual system, but their existence has often been interpreted in ways that reinforce heterosexuality and the gender binary. When the concepts of homosexuality and heterosexuality emerged in nineteenth-century Europe, for example, homosexuals were understood as inverts — those with marked characteristics of the other sex. The notion of the masculine lesbian and the effeminate homosexual man managed to combine gender and sexual variance into one neat package that preserved a dichotomous view of gender and desire.[7] The concept of homosexuals as wishing they were the other sex still shapes popular stereotypes and images of gays and lesbians and leads people to label and harass as gay those with non-stereotypical gender-role self-presentations. The treatment of intersex infants — those born with ambiguous genitalia — has similarly been aimed at maintaining heterosexuality and a dichotomous understanding of gender. Doctors have been concerned not only to "correct" intersex children's genitals so that they can grow up as clearly female or male, but also to do so in a way that holds out the possibility of their living a "normal" adult heterosexual life. A child assigned as female must have a vagina that can receive a normal-size penis, while a child assigned as male must have a penis that can satisfy a female partner.[8] An analogous set of medical criteria has been used for the past fifty years to treat transsexuals. The protocols for sex-reassignment surgery, like those for intersexuals, assume the existence of two and only two "opposite" genders. Those seeking surgery often find that they must demonstrate a firm commitment to

---

1975), 178–83. See my essays "Sexual Orientation and Human Rights: A Progressive Jewish Perspective" and "Authority, Resistance, and Transformation: Feminist Reflections on Good Sex," in Judith Plaskow, *The Coming of Lilith: Essays on Feminism, Judaism, and Sexual Ethics 1972–2003* (Boston: Beacon Press, 2005), 186–88 and 196–201.

7. Anne Fausto-Sterling, *Sexing the Body: Gender Politics and the Construction of Sexuality* (New York: Basic Books, 2000), 14; Judith Halberstam, *Female Masculinity* (Durham, NC: Duke University Press, 1998), 76, 82.

8. Fausto-Sterling, *Sexing the Body*, 71–72; Suzanne J. Kessler, "The Medical Construction of Gender: Case Management of Intersexed Infants," *Signs: Journal of Women in Culture and Society* 16, no. 1 (1990): 19–20; Suzanne J. Kessler, *Lessons from the Intersexed* (New Brunswick, NJ: Rutgers University Press, 1998), 105–6.

heterosexuality by constructing compelling and "authentic" personal histories of exclusively heterosexual desire, whether or not these accord with their experiences.[9]

In each of these cases, a potential threat to a binary gender and sexual system is integrated back into the system, demonstrating its enormous power and flexibility and the stake of medical and other social institutions in maintaining it. But at the same time that these exceptions have been used to bolster the system, they still have the capacity to complicate and ultimately to undermine it, particularly as various social movements over the last four decades have explicitly challenged the naturalness of both gender and heterosexuality. The feminist movement has demonstrated the socially constructed and damaging nature of gender roles, and certain strands within feminism have attacked the very notion of two genders as a tool for the oppression of women.[10] The lesbian, gay, and bisexual liberation movement has rejected the notion of inversion, claiming that there is no necessary correlation between gender and the contours of desire. A growing intersexual rights movement has called for an end to infant surgery and demanded that intersexed persons be able to make up their own minds about gender identity and surgery as they mature.[11] Increasing numbers of transsexuals, by refusing to live seamlessly and invisibly in their new gender identities, are rejecting the demand that they uphold the two-gender system. A new "transgender" movement is emerging that highlights the kinship among gender-variant identities and celebrates a multiplicity of ways of challenging the gender and sexual binaries.[12] This movement

---

9. Bernice L. Hausman, *Changing Sex: Transsexualism, Technology, and the Idea of Gender* (Durham, NC: Duke University Press, 1995), 6–7, 146, 460. This demand is not part of the Benjamin Standards of Care for Gender Identity Disorders, but it has been the reality at many clinics.

10. See Monique Wittig, "One Is Not Born a Woman," *Feminist Issues* 1, no. 2 (Winter 1981) for an early and important example of this position.

11. See the Intersex Society of North America (ISNA) website.

12. Kate Bornstein is an important spokesperson for this movement (see Bornstein, *Gender Outlaw*; idem, *My Gender Workbook*). See also Anne Bolin, "Transcending and Transgendering: Male-to-Female Transsexuals, Dichotomy, and Diversity," in *Third Sex, Third Gender: Beyond Sexual Dimorphism in Culture and History*, ed. Gilbert Herdt (New York: Zone Books, 1994), 260–85.

has the capacity to extend and deepen the feminist critique of gender roles and gender hierarchy by enacting and embodying the disruption of gender dimorphism.

In the rest of this chapter I explore the relationship between moving beyond the gender binary and dismantling compulsory heterosexuality in the Jewish context. While rabbinic Judaism definitely maintains a hierarchical, dichotomous gender system and a notion of male/female marriage as a universal norm, the rabbis also seem to have been aware of the existence of gender-variant persons who threatened the stability of this system. Contemporary Jews committed to a nonsexist and non-heterosexist vision of Jewish life may be able to use rabbinic discussions of gender variance as a jumping off point for a radical critique of gender and the compulsory heterosexuality with which it is intertwined.

Judaism, Gender, and Heteronormativity

Until the invention of the concept of heterosexuality in the modern era, Jewish culture was certainly heteronormative, but it was not explicitly homophobic. Male/male anal intercourse was forbidden and regarded as an "abomination," but it was the sexual *act* that was proscribed, not intimacy or attraction between men, which was in fact an important part of rabbinic culture.[13] Sex between women was also prohibited but was seen as a minor infraction. There is no evidence that the rabbis categorized people on the basis of the gender of their sexual-object choice.[14] The relatively sparse legal literature dealing with same-sex sexual relations manifests none of the anxiety or horror that marks modern debates. It is clear that some Jews engaged in same-sex sex, and it seems that they were treated in the same way as those who violated any other legal prohibition. Contemporary statements that condemn "homosexuality" as prima facie disgusting and

---

13. Daniel Boyarin, *Unheroic Conduct: The Rise of Heterosexuality and the Invention of the Jewish Man* (Berkeley and Los Angeles: University of California Press, 1997), 14, 16–17.

14. Michael Satlow, "'They Abused Him Like a Woman': Homoeroticism, Gender Blurring, and the Rabbis in Late Antiquity," *Journal of the History of Sexuality* 5, no. 1 (1994): 18, 24.

unnatural and that depict gays as threatening the Jewish family and all of civilization should be read in the context of recent gay demands for legitimacy and equality rather than as expressions of an unchanging Jewish position.[15]

While Jewish tradition has not necessarily singled out same-sex sex for special opprobrium, it has been thoroughly heteronormative in that it prescribes highly differentiated gender roles, develops elaborate legislation for preventing illicit sexual contact between women and men as if heterosexual sex were the primary temptation for everyone, and assumes that all Jews should marry. As one feminist scholar of rabbinics points out, "Jewish law is based on a fundamental assumption of gender duality."[16] Although there are many commandments, especially negative commandments or "thou shalt nots," incumbent on both women and men, it is virtually impossible to talk about Jewish legal obligations without talking about gender. The Mishnah, the second-century code of Jewish law that is the foundational text of rabbinic Judaism, frames and attempts to categorize individual laws in terms of a tightly gendered schema. The general principle it enunciates is that women are exempt from positive commandments that must be performed at particular times. While this principle is riddled with exceptions and contradictions, the rule holds that women are excused from certain crucial religious duties, such as praying three times daily and wearing *tzitzit* (fringes) and phylacteries, while adult men are never excused. The reason for women's exemption is not stated in the Mishnah and has been the subject of extensive interpretation and debate, but its effect is to release women from many of the ritual practices that constitute the center of a positive Jewish religious identity. It is possibly for this reason that the traditional Jewish man recites the infamous morning

---

15. Greenberg, *Wrestling with God and Men,* 129–30, 133–34, 136. For examples of the contemporary homophobic position, see Greenberg's discussion on 137–38, and Norman Lamm, "Judaism and the Modern Attitude toward Homosexuality," in *Jewish Bioethics,* ed. Fred Rosner and J. David Bleich (New York: Sanhedrin Press, 1979), esp. 204.

16. Charlotte Fonrobert, "Gender Identity in Halakhic Discourse," in *Jewish Women: A Comprehensive Encyclopedia,* ed. Paula Hyman and Dalia Ofer (Jerusalem: Shalvi Publishing Company, forthcoming).

blessing thanking God for not making him a woman — because he carries the full burden and benefit of obligation while women do not.

Even the briefest consideration of the gendered nature of Jewish law makes clear that the gender binary is asymmetrical. Indeed, it is impossible to talk about *halakha* (Jewish law) and gender without talking about hierarchy. Because those obligated to perform any commandment have a higher status in its performance than those who are not obligated, people who are exempt cannot perform religious acts on behalf of others, even should they choose to take on particular commandments for themselves. Thus, according to *halakha,* women cannot lead religious services or read publicly from the Torah when men are present. They are also exempt from Torah study, the quintessential form of Jewish religious expression. Traditional Jewish law views women as "enablers": they perform the tasks that allow men and boys to engage in regular prayer, observe numerous special rituals connected with the holidays, and have time to study, but women themselves are "peripheral Jews."[17] Not only are they secondary in the public realm, but they are also subordinate within marriage. A woman "is taken" or acquired in marriage, but she herself does not "take" or acquire a husband. Her sexuality is sanctified to her husband, but his is not set apart to her. He has the right to divorce her by writing a bill of divorce, and, according to rabbinic law, he has the right to take other wives, but these rights are not reciprocal. Women's sexuality and reproductive functions constitute a central, though not exclusive, locus of anxiety for the Mishnah, which is deeply concerned to regulate and control these functions in the interests of a patriarchal system.[18]

---

17. This is Rachel Adler's language in her classic essay "The Jew Who Wasn't There: *Halakhah* and the Jewish Woman," in *On Being a Jewish Feminist: A Reader*, ed. Susannah Heschel (New York: Schocken Books, 1983), 13–14. See also Paula Hyman, "The Other Half: Women in the Jewish Tradition," in *The Jewish Woman: New Perspectives*, ed. Elizabeth Koltun (New York: Schocken Books, 1976), 105–13. Contemporary liberal Judaism no longer follows any of these laws.

18. Fonrobert, "Gender Identity in Halakhic Discourse"; Judith Romney Wegner, *Chattel or Person? The Status of Women in the Mishnah* (New York and Oxford: Oxford University Press, 1988). Cf. Miriam Peskowitz, *Spinning Fantasies: Rabbis, Gender, and History* (Berkeley and Los Angeles: University of California Press, 1997); Peskowitz points out that there are many loci of rabbinic control in addition to sexuality.

Several recent articles on the Jewish prohibition of male/male intercourse have argued that one of its key purposes is to maintain gender
hierarchy. Leviticus 18:22 condemns the active partner in male anal intercourse, while Leviticus 20:13 sentences both the active and passive
partners to death. As the rabbis elaborated on the laws of Leviticus, they
dwelled on the humiliation of the man penetrated "like a woman," but
they also continued to see the penetrator as guilty of a transgression.[19]
His fault seems to lie in mixing or confusing kinds: a man who pene-
trates another man violates the gender binary, treating another man as
one should treat only a woman, and thus moving a male body into the
category of female. Like cross-dressing, which Leviticus also forbids, sex
between men confuses borders that are meant to be kept clear as part
of the order of creation. The weight of this violation is underscored by
the fact that very word for female in biblical and rabbinic Hebrew means
"one with an orifice," as if being penetrated is natural to females but not
to males.[20] Thus male/male intercourse endangers gender boundaries in
two different ways: it "unmans" the particular man who is the penetrated
partner, but it also threatens the notion of penetrative intercourse as a
defining aspect of gender difference.[21]

The rabbis may have regarded sex between women as a less serious infraction than sex between men both because it is not explicitly prohibited
by the Torah and because they did not see it as intrinsically threatening
gender hierarchy. The brief Talmudic discussion of female homoeroticism
revolves around whether women who "rub against each other" have lost
their status as virgins and are forbidden to marry priests. The majority
opinion is that such behavior is "mere indecency" and does not count
as a disqualification. The argument assumes that "lewdness" (*mesolelot*)
between women is not incompatible with marriage to men. Indeed, the
one other Talmudic passage that touches on sex between women concerns

---

19. Satlow, " 'They Abused Him Like a Woman,' " 9–15.

20. Daniel Boyarin, "Are There Any Jews in 'The History of Sexuality?' " *Journal of the History of Sexuality* 5 (1995): 340–47. See also Greenberg, *Wrestling with God and Men*, 178–79.

21. Greenberg, *Wrestling with God and Men*, 179.

a rabbi who forbids his daughters to sleep in the same bed together lest they become accustomed to a foreign body. His worry seems to be either that the daughters are not yet ready for marriage or that they need to get used to sleeping alone during the period of menstrual impurity when married sex is forbidden. But unlike female homoeroticism, which evokes only mild anxiety, the possibility of marriage between women is roundly condemned by later sources. A midrashic commentary on the book of Leviticus interprets the "practices of the land of Egypt and the land of Canaan" referred to Leviticus 18:3 as a man marrying a man and a woman marrying a woman. As medieval codifiers understood this text, marriage between women is forbidden by the Torah. The possibility of a woman taking on the role of husband is as unacceptable as a man taking on the role of wife because it threatens gender hierarchy and the institution of heterosexual marriage.[22]

The prohibition of male anal intercourse and marriage between women makes the relationship between heteronormativity and sharply differentiated gender roles very clear. But even where same-sex sex is not the explicit topic of rabbinic discussion, there is still a mutually constitutive relationship between dichotomized gender roles and the cultural insistence on male-dominated marriage. Whether we look at the work roles and obligations of women and men, the religious division of labor, issues of property rights, or the rabbinic conception of marriage, gender differentiation is part of a system in which the very meaning of being a woman or a man depends on taking certain roles within a heteronormative framework. The Mishnah's principle of exempting women from positive, time-bound commandments both presupposes and helps create a social structure in which women's primary obligations are to fathers, husbands, and children. In caring for small children, observing the dietary laws, and preparing for holy days by readying their homes and cooking special foods, women free

---

22. For discussion of rabbinic sources on lesbianism, see Rebecca Alpert, *Like Bread on the Seder Plate: Jewish Lesbians and the Transformation of Tradition* (New York: Columbia University Press, 1997), 29–33; Rachel Biale, *Women and Jewish Law: An Exploration of Women's Issues in Halakhic Sources* (New York: Schocken Books, 1984), 192–97; Greenberg, *Wrestling with God and Men,* 86–89; Satlow, " 'They Abused Him Like a Woman,' " 15–17.

men for their own prayer and Torah study and enable them to observe the
dietary laws and the Sabbath and holidays fully. At the same time, women
need men to take on ritual roles in the home that they themselves are neither obligated nor educated to assume. Thus, laws that seem to concern
only religious obligations are also an important node in the construction of
heterosexual marriage. The same point applies to other aspects of gender
role division that appear only peripherally connected to the compulsion
toward marriage. Just as a man is forbidden to violate gender boundaries
by having sex with another man, so he is advised not to transgress gender
norms by teaching his son a craft that is practiced among women. The rabbis seem to have been concerned both with preventing men from laboring
alongside women and thus being tempted by illicit (heterosexual) sex, and
with protecting men from becoming like women by doing labor coded as
feminine. The ultimate male work was Torah study, work that was limited
to men by definition and that marriage allowed them to pursue.[23]

Hermaphroditic Disruptions

Given the fundamental place of the gender binary in rabbinic thought and
legislation, it is both surprising and understandable that the rabbis were
fascinated by "exceptions" that might potentially disrupt the dichotomized
gender system. Like the Hindu texts described by Anantanand Rambachan
in his contribution to this volume,[24] rabbinic texts describe a number of
categories of persons who in some way extend or challenge the dominant
schema of gender roles or gender dualism. The rabbinic classifications of
aylonit (barren woman) and *saris* (eunuch), for example, refer to persons
who are clearly female or male, but who confound gender role expectations
by being unable to reproduce and who thereby stand in a complicated
relationship to the elaborate laws of marriage. The *aylonit* is defined as
a woman who fails to produce two pubic hairs by a certain age, who

---

23. Peskowitz, *Spinning Fantasies*, 60–74.
24. See Anantanand Rambachan, "'There Are Many Branches on the Tree of Life':
The Incompatibility of Hinduism and Homophobia," esp. 213–21.

never develops breasts, who finds sexual intercourse difficult, who does not have the lower abdominal curve of a normal woman (the meaning of the Hebrew is uncertain), and who has a deep voice that is indistinguishable from a man's. The *saris* is a man who likewise fails to produce two pubic hairs by a certain age; who has soft, smooth skin and no beard; whose urine does not froth, ferment, or form an arc; whose body does not steam when he bathes during rainy season; and whose voice is so thin, it is hard to tell whether he is male or female.[25] Within the Jewish legal framework, it was crucial that families be aware of these signs of infertility before arranging a marriage, because the reproductive status of the partners affects important areas of marriage law. Both the *aylonit* and *saris* are exempted from Levirate marriage, for instance (marriage with a deceased brother's wife, as specified in Deuteronomy 25:5–10), because the purpose of such a marriage is to ensure progeny for a deceased man who has left no children. Similarly, since a man is legally required to have children, he should not marry a barren woman unless he already has children or has another wife who is fertile.[26]

In Roman culture, which generally had a profound impact on rabbinic Judaism, the eunuch was often depicted as less than male and associated with all kinds of vices. It is interesting, therefore, that the rabbis never ask whether the *saris* or the *aylonit* is a "real" man or woman; nor do they generally regard them as untrustworthy. The laws that refer to the eunuch and the barren woman treat them in almost all cases as having the same rights and responsibilities as anyone else of their gender, save where their infertility becomes important for the laws of marriage.[27] This

---

25. Charlotte Fonrobert, "The Semiotics of the Sexed Body in Early Halakhic Discourse," in *Closed and Open: Readings of Rabbinic Texts*, ed. Matthew Kraus (Piscataway, NJ: Gorgias Press, forthcoming); *The Code of Maimonides, The Book of Women*, trans. Isaac Klein (New Haven, CT: Yale University Press, 1979), chap. 2. On the *saris*, see Sarra Lev's doctoral dissertation, "Genital Trouble: The Figure of the Eunuch in Rabbinical Literature and the Surrounding Cultures of the Period" (Ph.D. diss.: New York University, 2004).

26. Fonrobert, "The Semiotics of the Sexed Body"; "Eylonith," in *Encyclopedia Talmudica* (Jerusalem: Talmudic Encyclopedia Institute, 1972), 1:642.

27. Sarra Lev, "Excerpt from *Genital Trouble*" (paper delivered to the Jewish Feminist Research Group, January 2005), 3–5, 14. While Lev focuses on the eunuch, the same applies to the *aylonit*. See Fonrobert, "The Semiotics of the Sexed Body." The *saris* is

suggests that the rabbis read gender off the basic morphology of the body. Just as in U.S. culture gender is assigned on the basis of a baby's genitals at birth, so, for the rabbis, the genitals were "the place from which it can be recognized whether s/he is male or female."[28] The presence or absence of secondary sex characteristics, such as breasts or body hair, in no way affected the status of the individual in Jewish law. Thus, it seems that the rabbis preferred tolerating a certain range of gender ambiguity to challenging gender dimorphism. They were willing to stretch the boundaries of femaleness and maleness to accommodate a deep voice in a woman or the absence of a beard in a male, and even to accept the maleness of a eunuch, rather than to entertain the notion of a multiplicity of genders.[29]

The rabbis also discussed two other categories of persons whose bodies presented different and more ambiguous gender possibilities. The *tumtum* and *androgynus* (hermaphrodite), whom today we would label "intersexed" persons, are categories that often appear together in rabbinic literature.[30] The rabbis defined the *tumtum* as an individual who is actually a man or a woman, but who appears to have no genital organs because his or her genital area is covered over at birth. If the covering is later opened and the person is found to be male, then he is considered a full male, or if she is found to be female, then she is considered a female in every respect. The *tumtum* raised a practical problem for the rabbis, but not a theoretical one because s/he fell within the binary system, even though the rabbis might not know where. The *androgynus* is the more interesting category because s/he has the genitals of both sexes, and it can never be determined whether s/he is male or female.[31] S/he thus posed a serious challenge to

---

forbidden to judge capital cases, but Lev thinks the reasons for this are related to his absence of parental responsibility rather than gender (22–24).

28. Genesis Rabbah 46:5, 13. Cited in Fonrobert, "Gender Identity in Halakhic Discourse."

29. Fonrobert, "The Semiotics of the Sexed Body." See J. David Bleich, *Judaism and Healing: Halakhic Perspectives* (Jersey City, NJ: KTAV Publishing House, 1981), 76.

30. Fonrobert, "The Semiotics of the Sexed Body." Fonrobert sees the notion of the *androgynus* as a "figure of thought" that allowed the rabbis to elaborate the gender binary. While it certainly served that function, I see no reason to believe that the rabbis were unfamiliar with people who exhibited a range of primary and secondary sex characteristics.

31. *The Code of Maimonides*, chap. 2, 24–25.

a legal system thoroughly structured around a dichotomized understanding of gender. If one can hardly say anything about the obligations of a Jew without immediately talking about gender, then what happens to a Jew whose gender is in principle undeterminable? Rabbinic debates about the hermaphrodite shed interesting light on the rabbis' understandings of gender, gender hierarchy, and heteronormativity.

There are several different views of the *androgynus* in rabbinic literature. The majority position was that s/he is of uncertain sex, either male or female. Others argued, however, that s/he is part male and part female, others that s/he is definitely male, and still others that s/he is a creature sui generis. Some sages suggested that there are three doubts about the hermaphrodite: whether s/he is a distinct creature, a man, or a woman.[32] The question for the rabbis, then, when discussing any particular area of legal obligation, was how to define the hermaphrodite in such a way that, whatever the person's "true" status might be, no laws would be violated.[33] One passage in the Mishnah, for example, lists the ways in which the *androgynus* falls into the *halakhic* (legal) category of men, the ways s/he falls into the category of women, the ways s/he straddles the two, and the ways s/he fits neither. The most important way in which s/he functions legally like men is that s/he can take a wife but cannot be taken (note the passive) as a wife. Also like men, s/he must perform all the commandments of the Torah and dress like a man.[34] S/he functions like women in that s/he contaminates with per[35] menstrual flow, must not be alone in the company of men, does not need to perform Levirate marriage, and does not receive a share in inheritances with sons. S/he fits both categories in that anyone who maims per incurs guilt or who kills per is subject to punishment; per mother must bring an offering at the time of the birth, and s/he receives a share of sacrifices to be consumed outside the Temple. Unlike men and women, however, s/he incurs no penalty for entering the Temple unclean;

---

32. "Hermaphrodite," *Encyclopedia Talmudica*, 2:386.
33. Thanks to Sarra Lev for this important point. Conversation, January 2005.
34. Mishnah Bikkurim 4:1–5. I am listing only a few of the ways in which the *androgynus* fits each category for purposes of illustration.
35. I am using *per* as a neutral pronoun to avoid cumbersome phraseology.

s/he cannot be sold as a Hebrew slave, and s/he cannot be evaluated for the purpose of making an offering (see Lev. 27:2–7).[36] Clearly, the rabbis struggled to fit a doubly sexed person into the limits of a binary system without undermining any rules of that system.

The ingenuity with which they addressed this task can be seen from a couple of specific examples. According to Jewish law, girls reach maturity at twelve years and a day, while boys reach maturity at thirteen. Thus, in case s/he is a woman, the hermaphrodite is obligated to any precepts incumbent on women from twelve years and one day. S/he is exempt from any precepts not incumbent on women until the age of thirteen, however, because if s/he is a man, s/he is still a minor, and if s/he is a woman, s/he is exempt from these laws altogether. Rules of inheritance pose especially complicated issues for the rabbis because these rules depend on overall family configuration as well as the size of the estate. The majority view is that an only child who is a hermaphrodite inherits the father's whole estate. If an estate is large and the father leaves a son and a hermaphrodite, the son inherits because he is clearly an heir, whereas the hermaphrodite is doubtful, but the hermaphrodite has a right to be maintained with the daughters. If the estate is small enough that everything would normally go for the daughters' maintenance, the daughters can relegate the hermaphrodite to the category of sons and say s/he has no right to share. If a man leaves daughters and a hermaphrodite, they share the estate equally. The rabbi or rabbis (the texts are unclear) who see the hermaphrodite as sui generis, on the other hand, rule that s/he is not maintained with the daughters because s/he is not a daughter, whereas those who see the hermaphrodite as a definite male say s/he inherits equally with a son.[37] Because the rabbis insist on fitting the hermaphrodite into the available (gendered) legal categories rather than questioning those categories, the laws concerning the hermaphrodite help to clarify the ways that gender distinctions operate in relation to various areas of *halakha*.[38]

---

36. Mishnah Bikkurim 4:1–5.
37. "Hermaphrodite," 2:388, 395.
38. Fonrobert, "The Semiotics of the Sexed Body."

The gender ambiguity of the *androgynus* produces numerous shifts in per status, but where the rabbis must make a choice as to whether the *androgynus* is male or female, per default status seems to be male. This is suggested by the fact that the *androgynus* can marry a woman but cannot be taken as a wife and that, in a culture in which cross-dressing was a serious violation, s/he must dress as a man. Of all the ways in which the hermaphrodite is in some ways like men and in others like women, these are the ways that would have the greatest impact on daily life. The presence of testes carries more signifying weight than the presence of a vagina, or, as one contemporary Orthodox authority says in discussing the treatment of intersexed infants, "The presence of testes, either external or internal, is an absolute indication that the child is not a female."[39] It is interesting to compare the default maleness of the *androgynus* with the "one-drop rule" for determining race in many states in the American South. Light-skinned Americans with African ancestry have been defined and generally raised as black, as if "one drop" of so-called black blood were sufficient to contaminate their lineage. In the case of the hermaphrodite, however, the dominant status trumps the subordinate status. It would be unthinkable to treat as female someone who might be male or to make such a person into a wife.[40]

A central reason to treat the hermaphrodite as male has to do with the issue of preventing *halakhic* violations. Because men are fully obligated to all the commandments and women are not, to treat a potential male as female is to run the risk that the *androgynus* might incur a long list of legal transgressions. Among the laws that the hermaphrodite must not infringe is the commandment not to lie with a man as one lies with a woman. A hermaphrodite cannot be taken as a wife because in the event s/he is male, marriage with per would constitute lying with a man. The rabbis are clear that men are liable for stoning for intercourse with a hermaphrodite, just as for intercourse with a male, but they debated whether men incur this penalty for intercourse with a hermaphrodite or just through the male

39. Bleich, *Judaism and Healing*, 78.
40. Satlow, " 'They Abused Him Like a Woman,' " 18.

orifice.[41] According to one view, the hermaphrodite is counted as a male for sexual purposes, so any intercourse with per is forbidden. Indeed, one rabbi interprets Leviticus 18:22's prohibition on lying with a man as with a woman as referring specifically to the hermaphrodite since only the hermaphrodite has two places of cohabitation.[42] The opposing view is that a man incurs the penalty for lying with a man only "when he comes upon him [the *androgynus*] in the way of males, but if he does not come upon him in the way of males, he is not liable."[43] For the rabbis who hold this position, the hermaphrodite is sufficiently male that s/he must not be penetrated by another man, yet per female genitalia retain independent significance. A similar debate about whether the hermaphrodite is fully and completely male occurs around the issue of circumcision and whether one should circumcise a hermaphrodite on the Sabbath if it is the eighth day after birth. While all the sages agree that a hermaphrodite must be circumcised, some argue that circumcision overrides the Sabbath only in the case of a definite male, but not in the case of one whose status is in doubt. The alternative view is that the hermaphrodite should be circumcised on the Sabbath if necessary because Genesis 17:10 reads, "Every male among you shall be circumcised," and "every" includes the hermaphrodite.[44]

Implications

The figure of the hermaphrodite plays a paradoxical role in rabbinic thought, as it does in other cultural contexts. On the one hand, the hermaphrodite poses a problem that a binary gender logic must find a way

---

41. Talmud Yevamot 83b. See Joshua Levinson, "Cultural Androgyny in Rabbinic Literature," in *From Athens to Jerusalem: Medicine in Hellenized Jewish Lore and in Early Christian Literature*, ed. Samuel Kottek, Manfred Horstmanshoff, Gerhard Baader, and Gary Ferngren (Rotterdam: Erasmus Publishing, 2000), 127–28; Satlow, "'They Abused Him Like a Woman,'" 17–18.

42. Talmud Yevamot 83b.

43. Tosefta Yevamot 10:2; Satlow, "'They Abused Him Like a Woman,'" 18.

44. "Hermaphrodite," 2:387.

to erase; it is a "necessary irritant" that ultimately serves to consolidate and stabilize the two-gender system. On the other hand, the hermaphrodite is the "vanishing point" of the gender binary; it "embodies the dissolution of male and female as absolute categories."[45] While the fundamental approach of rabbinic texts is to use the *androgynus* as a kind of thought experiment that serves to clarify and shore up a rigid gender grid, the rabbis differed among themselves in the extent to which they were willing to entertain the notion of a dual-sexed person.[46] For the majority of the rabbis, the hermaphrodite must be either male or female. Because they did not know which, they tried to manage their ignorance by ensuring that the hermaphrodite would transgress as few *halakhic* norms as possible. For practical purposes, s/he was treated as a male except when such female bodily functions as menstruation made this impossible. At least one rabbi, however, understood the hermaphrodite as a third-sex being who was forced to function in a binary system.[47] This dual-sex person was "a creature unto itself" who could be both a prohibited passive male in sex and a permitted passive female, a creature who could exempt others of its own kind from certain legal obligations such as hearing the shofar blown or reading the Megillah, but who could not exempt either men or women.[48] The minority view did not upend the gender grid, but it seemed to presuppose a map of the world that allowed genuine exceptions to it.

The challenge for contemporary Jews is to find ways to use the opening provided by rabbinic categories that potentially extend or undermine a binary understanding of gender to question our own gender dimorphism. Just as the rabbis tried to fit the *androgynus* into a bifurcated system, so

---

45. Ann Rosalind Jones and Peter Stallybrass, "Fetishizing Gender: Constructing the Hermaphrodite in Renaissance Europe," in Epstein and Traub, *Body Guards*, 80.

46. Fonrobert, "The Semiotics of the Sexed Body." In using the phrase "thought experiment," I do not mean to suggest that the *androgynus* was only that, but simply that the rabbis' fascination with *androgynus* serves a particular role in their system.

47. Greenberg, *Wrestling with God and Men*, 188–89; Levinson, "Cultural Androgyny," 128.

48. It is R. Yose who holds that a hermaphrodite is sui generis; Talmud Yevamot 83a. See also, "Hermaphrodite," 2:388.

modern Western culture has found ways to force a range of gender out-
laws — from homosexuals, to intersexuals, to transsexuals — into the same
binary system. It has used a variety of strategies to read the psychology,
experience, and bodies of those who might threaten gender dualism to
reinterpret and restabilize it. As the rabbinic concepts of *aylonit* and *saris*
suggest, the very imprecision and malleability of the concepts of male and
female have aided in this task, helping to sustain a dimorphic understanding of gender. None of the characteristics that supposedly differentiate
males and females is always and without exception found in only one gender. Many, perhaps most, people fail to fit at least some of the stereotypical
expectations concerning their gender. Yet the traits that allow someone
to be labeled a man or woman are so elastic that very few people present
themselves as entirely ambiguous.[49] When we meet someone previously
unknown to us, we generally attribute gender to that person automatically
and at first glance. We then interpret all further evidence to support our
initial ascription and explain away any cues that fail to fit.[50] Like the rabbis, we have a profound stake in maintaining our picture of human beings
as dichotomously gendered.

This picture, which has been under attack by feminists and gays for over
three decades, is now facing criticism from a new angle: that of transgender
activists. The notion of transgender was added to the nomenclature of
the lesbian, gay, and bisexual (glb) rights and liberation movements in the
mid 1990s, and it has a complicated, if short, history. There is not space
here to discuss the "border wars" between different groups within the glbt
coalition or the permutations that the concept of transgender has itself
undergone.[51] Transgendered folks have often been suspicious of gay and
lesbian hegemony within the glbt struggle; being gay does not necessarily
entail openness to people who consider themselves transgendered. Some
gays have seen transgenderism as threatening to "queer" a movement that

---

49. Halberstam, *Female Masculinity*, 20, 27; Kessler and McKenna, *Gender*, 1–2.
50. Kessler and McKenna, *Gender*, 161–62.
51. The term "border wars" is Halberstam's (see *Female Masculinity*, chap. 5). See Bolin,
"Transcending and Transgendering," for a discussion of shifts in the meaning of *transgender*.

has increasingly sought assimilation into the U.S. mainstream. On the other hand, because the term *transgender* has often been identified with transsexuals — people who experience themselves as having been born the "wrong" gender and who seek sex-change surgery — some feminists and gays have criticized transgendered people for buying into traditional gender roles and accepting heteronormativity.[52]

I am interested in the concept of transgender in its recent and broad meaning as designating anyone who challenges the gender binary. Understood in this sense, the term refers first of all to transsexuals, especially those who claim a transsexual identity and who may be at many points along a continuum of taking hormones and undergoing surgery or having no interest in medical intervention. But it also includes cross-dressers; drag queens and kings; bi-gendered people who are one gender by day and another by night; intersexuals who define themselves as such; the many gays, lesbians, and bisexuals who perceive themselves or are perceived by others as transgressively gendered; as well as straight masculine women and feminine men. It can potentially embrace the youth who adopts an androgynous look or who experiments with shifting gender presentations, the stay-at-home dad who has no interest in fulfilling the traditional male role, and, indeed, anyone who has rebelled against traditional gender stereotypes and refused to accommodate to them.[53]

I recognize that using the notion of transgender in this inclusive way is potentially problematic. It erases important inequalities in social power and location along different points on the continuum, downplays the very real physical dangers faced by only some of those who threaten gender dimorphism, and obscures the disagreements among groups with distinct and sometimes conflicting agendas. But the strength of a broad definition lies in making clear the great range of people who potentially have a

---

52. Halberstam reviews some of the large literature on this issue in *Female Masculinity.* See also Bornstein, *Gender Outlaw,* 134–35. Janice G. Raymond's *The Transsexual Empire: The Making of the She-Male* (Boston: Beacon Press, 1979) remains the strongest feminist critique of transsexualism.

53. Bornstein, *Gender Outlaw* and *My Gender Workbook.*

stake in dismantling the gender binary. As the rabbis recognized in their own inadequate way, our restricted gender categories do not work. They neither exhaust the spectrum of human gender variation nor create the foundations for a just society. They do not work because, as feminists have been arguing for several decades, they make a socially constructed, hierarchical relationship appear to be natural and divinely ordained, giving men economic, political, sexual, and religious power over women and constricting the possibilities of what it means to be human. They do not work because, as advocates of gay, lesbian, and bisexual liberation have recognized, they lock people into particular family structures and forms of desire, rewarding and punishing them based on the gender of their sexual-object choice. They do not work because, as transgender activists make clear, there are those who embody multiple and shifting gender possibilities for which we as yet have no names or generally available conceptual frameworks.

To admit the inadequacy of a binary concept of gender is to enlarge the boundaries of our conceptual and social universes by beginning the process of expanding notions of gender. To be sure, there is no easy way to dissolve or vault over the categories of male and female, both because they thoroughly shape the world in which we live and because they are inter-structured with profound inequalities in power and access to resources that cannot be wished away. Yet we can think concretely in the Jewish and larger contexts about what it might mean to move toward disman-tling gender dimorphism. In part, it involves reclaiming that part of the original feminist vision that called for a radical critique of gender dualism. As Jewish feminism has unfolded over the last thirty years, its enormous impact on Jewish life has been largely confined to women gaining access to formerly male modes of religious expression. Even in the liberal Jew-ish community, there has been little attempt seriously to shake up gender categories. Men have been reluctant to take on so-called women's com-mandments, such a candle lighting. Women have "feminized" male ritual garb in the process of adopting it, and feminists have as often celebrated gender differences (by creating new ceremonies for important biological events in women's lives, for example) as sought to overcome them.[54] Synagogue life is still organized around heterosexual couples; "singles' events" are organized with the purpose of getting people married; and gays and lesbians are accepted insofar as their relationships approximate heterosexual marriage. Meeting times and expectations of Jewish professionals still presuppose a traditional division of labor in which someone in the role of wife — generally a woman — attends to family obligations to free the other member of the couple for outside commitments. It is time to undertake a thorough, critical investigation of the persistence of gender roles, leading to a new phase in the feminist transformation of Judaism in which the liberal community takes a hard look at the ways its structures continue to assume and support the gender binary.

Transgender awareness and activism are crucial elements in moving to this next stage. Feminists must maintain a difficult tension among presupposing the existence of women, reconfiguring the meaning of that category, and seeking its demise. It is neither possible nor sensible to stop talking about men and women in a society in which gender inequality is a pervasive reality and in which "women" must band together to demand basic rights. But precisely for this reason, it is important to embrace transgenderism as a movement that gives concrete and embodied meaning to the notion of dismantling the gender binary by breaking the connection between body and gender and proliferating gender possibilities.

I do not know what the ultimate role of gender should be in a society that abandons gender dualism. But it seems to me that the most effective way to make clear the socially constructed nature of gender dimorphism is to begin by multiplying genders. Feminists have argued that we can experience the reality of a God who transcends maleness only by using a wide variety of gendered and non-gendered images.[55] Calling on God as Goddess, she, mother, queen, *Shekhinah*, birth-giver, wellspring, source, and so

---

54. Rebecca Alpert, "Challenging Male/Female Complementarity: Jewish Lesbians and the Jewish Tradition," in *People of the Body: Jews and Judaism from an Embodied Perspective*, ed. Howard Eilberg-Schwartz (Albany: State University of New York Press, 1992), 368.

55. See Judith Plaskow, *Standing Again at Sinai: Judaism from a Feminist Perspective* (San Francisco: HarperSanFrancisco, 1990), chap. 4, for one of many examples.

on breaks the hold of dominant male images of God in a way that cannot be achieved simply through theoretical discussion. Similarly, we can
fully understand the inadequacy of the gender binary only by beginning
to name the many ways of being in the world that fall outside the dual-
gender version of reality. The rabbis were our forerunners in this regard, in
that they were at least willing to think about the existence of persons who
threatened their gendered universe. Our awareness of gender and sexual
inequalities enables and requires us to go well beyond their tentative and
male-centered experiments with expanding gender categories.

The Jewish community must make synagogues and other Jewish communal institutions safe places both for people who consider themselves
transgendered and for all those who transgress gender norms. It must
engage in (another) round of basic consciousness-raising to explore the
ways in which gender norms fail almost everyone. Jewish organizations
should support the goals of the Intersex Society, which calls for ending
genital surgery for intersexed infants, surgery that has less to do with helping children than upholding society's two-gender system.[56] They should
support the elimination of gender categories from basic identification documents, such as licenses and passports, and, most important, cease using
such categories themselves on job and Jewish school applications and
other forms.[57]

Because gender dualism supports and is supported by compulsory
heterosexuality, moving beyond gender also entails rethinking the nature
of sexuality and family. The categories of man and woman presuppose the
heterosexual matrix to give them substance and make them meaningful.
Heterosexuality as an institution has persistently assumed the existence of
men and women linked in hierarchical social units that model and prepare
us for other forms of social hierarchy. If gender is no longer the defining
criterion of sexual normalcy, then we need to find new ways of imagining and structuring desire. If the family is no longer rooted in gender-role
differentiation, then we need to become aware of the many constellations

---

56. Kessler, "The Medical Construction of Gender," 25.
57. Fausto-Sterling, *Sexing the Body*, 111.

of intimacy that provide ongoing contexts for mutual support and child-rearing. When a married male-to-female transsexual continues living with and making love to her "wife," or two intersexuals enter into a long-term relationship, or a bisexual woman insists that she desires and seeks out people with dark, curly hair more than the "opposite" gender, the links between gender and an obligatory heterosexuality are disrupted.[58] These identities and family forms are not supposed to exist, and yet they do exist all around us. Like the *androgynus*, they invite us to imagine ways of living and loving outside the gender binary and summon us to create a world without the hierarchies of gender and sexual orientation.

In the context of the Jewish community, rethinking sexuality and family means ceasing to promote marriage as the universal norm for adult Jews. For some Jewish groups, especially those that have the strongest commitment to differentiated gender roles, this goal is still unthinkable.[59] In many Reform, Reconstructionist, and some Conservative congregations, on the other hand, lesbians and gay men are fully integrated members of the community. However, part of what has made this significant change possible is the assimilationist path taken by many gay and lesbian Jews whose relationships are like marriage except for the gender of their partners. While the choices of these Jews and the new openness of parts of the Jewish community should be welcomed and affirmed, their joint effect is to allow the umbrella of marriage to be enlarged a bit at its edges. Marriage remains the norm for Jewish life, and gender remains central to marriage, only now its definition includes committed relationships between two women or two men. This move continues to marginalize people who are obviously transgressively gendered. It is also does not yet take up the challenge of imagining sex and relational intimacy in a world of many, and possibly shifting, genders.

---

58. See Bornstein, *Gender Outlaw*, 31–40, and *My Gender Workbook*, 90–106, and Bolin, "Transcending and Transgendering," 460–82, for discussion of breaking the ties between gender and desire.

59. See Maurice Lamm, *The Jewish Way in Love and Marriage* (San Francisco: Harper and Row, 1980), 67, for a description and affirmation of the connection between gender differentiation and heterosexuality.

It is frightening to try to free ourselves from a two-gender system and to explore the new understandings of sexual desire that arise from such a change. Doing so entails living in that liminal period, as necessary as it is unsettling, that is part of any transition to new ways of organizing the world. Attempting to dismantle gender is an extraordinary challenge that signifies a new phase in both the feminist and glbt movements. But heterosexism and homophobia cannot finally be overcome without moving beyond the gender binary.

Chapter Two

Beyond Same-Sex Marriage
Continuing the Reformation of Protestant Christianity

MARVIN M. ELLISON

Protestant Christianity, born as a reform movement in the sixteenth century, is in need of further reformation, this time with respect to sex and sexual difference. This tradition has fostered injustice and caused serious harm because its ethic of relational intimacy has been constructed on the basis of heterosexual exclusivism, the assumption that the only acceptable sexuality is heterosexual, marital, and procreative. Heterosexism is in force whenever heterosexuality is both privileged and compelled and when other sexualities are devalued and discouraged, oftentimes violently, as deviant and immoral. To counter such sexual oppression, the prevailing heterosexist sex/gender paradigm must be critiqued and a revised ethical paradigm developed that respects a diversity of human sexualities and places the focus not on identity but on conduct and the character of relationships.

Within the last three decades, largely in response to the feminist and gay liberation movements within and beyond the church, a rethinking of sexuality and of Christian sexual ethics has been under way within white, North Atlantic Protestantism, the context within which I write as a Euro-American gay man in a long-term partnership with another man. As a Christian ethicist, I contend that seeking justice as rightly related community lies at the heart of all liberating spirituality. Justice-making means the ongoing project of setting wrongs right, strengthening fair and equitable connections among persons and groups, and making communities more inclusive and welcoming of difference, including sexual difference.

Renewal efforts within Protestant Christianity with respect to sexuality and sexual justice have been met with fierce resistance because the "heterosexual presumption" remains a major organizing principle for Protestant sensibilities and institutional life.[1] Peter Gomes, an African American Baptist, speaks of homosexuality as "the last prejudice" and surmises that because the social and religious divisions about sex have become so great, "the debate is almost undebatable."[2] Similarly, Episcopal priest and lesbian feminist theologian Carter Heyward conjectures that sexual justice may be "the most trivialized, feared, and postponed dimension of social justice in western society and, possibly, the world."[3]

Because Protestant Christianity has promoted marriage as the exclusive site for ethical sex, one strategy for challenging this tradition's heterosexist bias aims at enlarging its marriage paradigm to allow religious (and civil) marriage for same-sex couples.[4] Protestants are deeply divided about

---

1. Within the Protestant ecumenical movement, the battle over sexuality intensified when the Universal Fellowship of Metropolitan Community Churches, a denomination founded in 1968, applied for membership in the National Council of Churches of Christ. Although the UFMCC met the council's eligibility requirements, it was denied membership, not on the grounds of doctrine or polity, but because of the divide over sex: the UFMCC does not discriminate on the basis of sexual difference and has a significant number of lesbian, gay, bisexual, and transgender members and leaders. In reflecting on this ecumenical struggle, theologian Robin Gorsline observes: "Generally speaking, most of Christianity is not a safe haven for Christian-identified queers — or others — to discuss and explore questions of sexuality and spirituality" ("A Queer Church, Open to All," *Union Seminary Quarterly Review* 57, nos. 1–2 [2003]: 56).

2. Peter J. Gomes, *The Good Book: Reading the Bible with Mind and Heart* (New York: William Morrow and Company, 1996), 144, 145.

3. Carter Heyward, *Touching Our Strength: The Erotic as Power and the Love of God* (San Francisco: Harper and Row, 1989), 4.

4. As of July 2005, same-sex couples have gained the legal right to marry in the Netherlands, Belgium, Spain, Canada, and within the United States in the Commonwealth of Massachusetts. Various religious traditions, including Reform Judaism, the United Church of Christ, the Unitarian Universalist Association, the Universal Fellowship of Metropolitan Community Churches, and various Quaker groups, offer a rite for blessing same-sex unions. In addition, the Presbyterian Church (U.S.A.) and the Episcopal Church in the United States allow their clergy to bless same-sex unions so long as their clergy do not call

this prospect, in part because of divergent convictions about sexuality and marriage that exist across and within various denominations. More telling, the marriage debate is complicated and made more difficult because the dominant Christian tradition suffers from two major deficits when it comes to sexuality and relational intimacy: first, a noticeable ambivalence, if not outright hostility, toward sex, and second, a longstanding patriarchal bias.

The tradition of Christian marriage reflects and reinforces both deficits. On the one hand, marriage has been valued as a control on sexual passion and safeguard against sinful lust. When sex has been permitted at all, it has been allowed only within the context of heterosexual marriage, and even there it has been restricted, by and large, to procreative sex. On the other hand, marriage has been a patriarchal construct based on gendered roles of domination and submission, authority and dependence. Therefore, even when intimacy has been authorized, bonding takes place within a structure of injustice because of the sexist power dynamic that shapes heterosexual coupling — which only further diminishes the likelihood that genuine intimacy will occur.[5] My premise is that insofar as the Protestant Christian marriage tradition has been constructed on the basis of such sex-negative and patriarchal assumptions, it is not a noble tradition to defend and preserve, but rather one to interrogate and transform.

---

them marriages. On July 4, 2005, the United Church of Christ became the first mainline Christian denomination to support same-sex marriage when its General Synod passed a resolution affirming "equal marriage rights for couples regardless of gender." See Shaila Dewan, "United Church of Christ Backs Same-Sex Marriage," *New York Times*, July 5, 2005. The UCC "Resolution in Support of Equal Marriage Rights for All" may be found on the *www.ucc.org* website.

5. One of the casualties of a hierarchical gender order is the marital relationship itself. Patriarchal power structures do not foster intimacy. Christine Gudorf explains: "When one person has power over another — and the greater the power, the more profound the effect — trust becomes difficult. The powerless party is unlikely to fully trust the powerful party, and therefore avoids complete vulnerability" (Christine E. Gudorf, "Western Religion and the Patriarchal Family," in *Perspectives on Marriage: A Reader*, ed. Kieran Scott and Michael Warren [New York: Oxford University Press, 2001], 296). See also Karen Lebacqz, "Love Your Enemy: Sex, Power and Christian Ethics," in *Moral Issues and Christian Responses*, ed. Patricia Beattie Jung and Shannon Jung (Belmont, CA: Wadsworth, 2003), 65–74.

As the battle rages within Protestant Christianity about granting the freedom to marry to same-sex couples, it is certainly necessary to make a compelling religious case for marriage equality.[6] At the same time, it is important to recognize that extending marriage to same-sex couples would be, at best, a mixed blessing. On the positive side, marriage equality would affirm gay and lesbian intimate partnerships as morally principled, loving relationships. On the negative side, it would mean reinforcing compulsory coupling, a dynamic that Protestant Christianity has encouraged by expecting all (at least able-bodied, nominally heterosexual) adults to marry. As ethicist Beverly W. Harrison observes, "The Reformers, none more passionately than Calvin, embraced marriage almost as a duty." In fact, marriage had to be compelled within a patriarchal religious system because "if men must marry women, whom they view as deficient in humanity, the external role of 'duty' necessarily must be invoked."[7] Furthermore, by focusing exclusively on the duty of marriage, Protestant Christianity has consistently failed to celebrate other ways in which people make families and engage in meaningful intimate association.

This point cannot be overemphasized: although the exclusion of same-sex couples from marriage is an injustice that needs correction, the trouble with marriage does not lie primarily in this exclusion. The problem lies in marriage itself or, more precisely, in the institutionalizing of compulsory heterosexuality. Therefore, the larger problematic is how a religious tradition has fostered fear of sexuality, legitimated male control of women's lives, and promulgated compulsory (patriarchal) marriage in response,

---

6. For a progressive interfaith statement in support of marriage equality, see the 2004 "Open Letter to Religious Leaders on Marriage Equality" on the website of the Religious Institute for Sexual Morality, Justice, and Healing. For suggestions on how religious leaders can promote marriage equality, see the Action Kit prepared by the Freedom to Marry Project. For progressive yet divergent perspectives, see Marvin M. Ellison, *Same-Sex Marriage? A Christian Ethical Analysis* (Cleveland: Pilgrim Press, 2004); Mark D. Jordan, *Blessing Same-Sex Unions: The Perils of Queer Romance and the Confusions of Christian Marriage* (Chicago: University of Chicago Press, 2005); and David G. Myers and Letha Dawson Scanzoni, *What God Has Joined Together? A Christian Case for Gay Marriage* (New York: HarperCollins Publishers, 2005).

7. Beverly Wildung Harrison, *Justice in the Making: Feminist Social Ethics*, ed. Elizabeth M. Bounds et al. (Louisville: Westminster John Knox Press, 2004), 55.

thereby causing great damage, first, by reinforcing gender oppression and placing women tightly under male authority and control; second, by making alternatives to sexist and heterosexist relationships seem unimaginable; and third, by demonizing sexual nonconformists as moral deviants and "enemies of God," whose bodies and lives could, therefore, be excoriated with impunity.[8]

In contrast, a liberating Christianity, in promoting sexual justice as an indispensable component of a more comprehensive social justice, must advance a larger change agenda than extending the freedom to marry to gay men and lesbian women or even restructuring marriage on egalitarian terms, as necessary and important as these changes most certainly are. Relational justice, if it is to take firm root in this religious tradition, requires more: a positive revaluation of sexuality, including appreciation for the goodness of gay (and non-gay) sex; the dismantling of the prevailing sex/gender paradigm that privileges heterosexuality; and conscientious efforts to provide the social, economic, and cultural/religious conditions so that all persons, whether partnered or not and whether heterosexual or not, may flourish and be honored within their communities, including their faith communities.

To make this case, I begin by highlighting certain aspects of the Protestant legacy with respect to sexuality and marriage that are highly problematic while also pointing out other insights that may be useful for framing a contemporary Christian ethic. After analyzing how marriage traditionalists draw on the more problematic legacy to oppose same-sex marriage, I offer a critique of the traditional Christian marriage paradigm and then outline an alternative, justice-centered ethic of relational intimacy that is explicitly sex positive, as well as respectful of sexual difference. In conclusion, in dialogue with Protestant reformer John Calvin, I caution

---

8. Kelly Brown Douglas, using the term "platonized Christianity" to describe the dualistic distortions that have plagued Western Christianity, analyzes how an oppressive Christian tradition, in demonizing sexuality, has entered into alliance with state power to punish non-normative people as "sexual deviants" and, therefore, enemies of God. See her *What's Faith Got to Do With It? Black Bodies/Christian Souls* (Maryknoll, NY: Orbis Books, 2005), esp. part 1.

against making marriage the "new orthodoxy" for gay (or non-gay) people and, as a counterproposal, lift up resistance to compulsory marriage as a Christian virtue for both the married and non-married, the heterosexual and non-heterosexual.

Protestant Commonalities about Sexuality and Marriage

There is no unified Protestant perspective on a contentious topic like sexuality and marriage, given the denominational and cultural diversity among Protestants, the absence of a centralized teaching authority, and the conflicting ways in which Protestants interpret and give weight to contemporary and traditional sources, including the Bible.[9] Furthermore, because Christians within each Protestant denomination are deeply divided about these matters, it is far more accurate to speak of divergent Protestantisms. For example, United Methodist theologian John Cobb observes that in a post-Freudian era, "most Christians acknowledge that humans are sexual beings and that the desire for sexual contact with others is natural and inevitable," but he carefully qualifies his statement by saying most, not all.[10] Moreover, it is important to appreciate how even moderately affirmative responses to sexuality, such as Cobb's, stand in stark contrast to the deep suspicion about sexuality that Christian theologians have exhibited from the earliest centuries of the church and which has only begun to be critiqued in recent decades.

Under the influence of a prevailing body-spirit dualism, Christianity, including its Protestant streams, has fostered a fear of sex as dangerous and polluting, something to restrict and keep under tight control.

---

9. The biblical ground has been well covered, but without resolving the debates about sexual difference, in part because interpreters approach the textual traditions with such differing presuppositions, including whether the issue to address is the "problem of homosexuality" or sexual oppression, that is, heterosexism. For two opposing views, see Dan O. Via and Robert A. J. Gagnon, *Homosexuality and the Bible: Two Views* (Minneapolis: Fortress Press, 2003). See also Craig L. Nessan, *Many Members, Yet One Body: Committed Same-Gender Relationships and the Mission of the Church* (Minneapolis: Fortress Press, 2004).

10. John B. Cobb, Jr., *Matters of Life and Death* (Louisville: Westminster John Knox Press, 1991), 94.

A contemporary sexologist sums matters up this way: "The Christian Church brought an overlay of sinfulness to almost every aspect of human sexuality.... Though there were modifications of the basic teachings by various Protestant writers, and a general weakening of religious influence in the nineteenth and twentieth centuries, the guilt feelings remain."[11] This anti-sex residue remains so pervasive that many Christians equate sin with sexual activity and conflate morals with sexual prohibitions. As the editors of a textbook on religion and sexuality report matter-of-factly, "Many scholars have characterized Christianity as the world religion most antagonistic to sexual pleasure."[12] For this reason, it is not surprising that in a culture heavily influenced by Christian sensibilities, sex is "presumed guilty until proven innocent," cast perennially as a problem, and burdened with an excess of significance.[13]

Although Protestant theologians often lift up companionate marriage as a distinctive Protestant contribution to the enhancement of cultural mores, the earliest Protestant Reformers did not dissent from their tradition's overall sex-negativity.[14] They held to the conviction that marriage is the only proper site for sexual activity and, further, that the only sanctioned marital sex is procreative. They viewed marriage as a necessary safeguard against sinful lust and valuable because it served to restrain erotic desire if not extinguish it altogether. In keeping with the traditional

---

11. Vern L. Bullough, "Christianity and Sexuality," in *Religion and Sexual Health: Ethical, Theological, and Clinical Perspectives*, ed. Ronald M. Green (Boston: Kluwer Academic Publishers, 1992), 15.

12. Phil Zuckerman and Christel Manning, "Sex and Religion: An Introduction," in *Sex and Religion*, ed. Christel Manning and Phil Zuckerman (Belmont, CA: Thomson Wadsworth, 2005), 4.

13. Gayle S. Rubin, "Thinking Sex: Notes for a Radical Theory of the Politics of Sexuality," in *The Lesbian and Gay Studies Reader*, ed. Henry Abelove, Michele Aina Barale, and David M. Halperin (New York: Routledge, 1993), 11.

14. Beverly Harrison writes: "We Protestants, not least we Reformed Christians, continue to believe that we have largely overcome these [spiritualistic and gender] dualisms. Far too readily we wrap ourselves in self-congratulation that the Reformation broke the hold of these baleful dynamics of sexual asceticism.... The truth is that nothing in the Reformation can be read as a genuine reversal of this negative antisexual, antifemale, antisensuality heritage" ("Human Sexuality and Mutuality," in Harrison, *Justice in the Making*, 55).

understanding that for Christians the best sex is "no sex," Protestants
encouraged Christian husband and wife to move as quickly as possible
beyond youthful passions so that they might live together, faithfully, as
Christian — and celibate — brother and sister.[15] Granted, the Reformers
departed from Roman Catholicism's elevation of virginity and celibacy as
superior to the married life and placed greater emphasis on the Christian
duty to marry. However, their revaluation of marriage occurred not because marriage was regarded as spiritually or morally superior, but because
the Reformers were acutely alert to the power of sinful lust and had such
deep doubts that a consistent lifestyle of celibacy was attainable.

In addition to this ongoing sex-negativity, Protestant Christianity has
exhibited a second deficit that has shaped its marriage tradition: a patriarchal pattern that has legitimated male control of women, as well as
some men's control of less powerful, lower-status men. Although husband
and wife might be regarded as spiritually equal, the husband has been
expected to stay in charge of the family, as well as to serve as its public representative. "All *should* marry," the Reformers' logic went, "because
God's intention from the beginning had been to unite men and women in
marital union and bid them to procreate. Almost all *must* marry because
the lustful urges that had arisen from the Fall could be contained without
sin only within marriage."[16] Patriarchal marriage as obligatory only further facilitated male control of women's sexuality, their labor, and their
lives even though husbands and fathers were, for the most part, officially
encouraged to be benevolent in the use of their power.[17]

---

15. Mark D. Jordan, *The Ethics of Sex* (Malden, MA: Blackwell Publishers, 2002), esp.
chaps. 3–5.

16. Rosemary Radford Ruether, *Christianity and the Making of the Modern Family* (Boston:
Beacon Press, 2000), 74.

17. On the complicity of patriarchal Christianity in legitimating male control of women,
along with contemporary challenges to religious sanctions for male entitlement and efforts
to put an end to abuse among intimate partners, see Joy M. K. Bussert, *Battered Women:
From a Theology of Suffering to an Ethic of Empowerment* (New York: Division for Mission
in North America, Lutheran Church in America, 1986); Marie M. Fortune, *Sexual Violence: The Unmentionable Sin* (Cleveland: Pilgrim Press, 1983); Carolyn Holderread Heggen,
Sexual Abuse in Christian Homes and Churches (Scottdale, PA: Herald Press, 1993), and
Traci C. West, *Wounds of the Spirit: Black Women, Violence, and Resistance Ethics* (New

Importantly, the Protestant marriage paradigm gives permission for at least heterosexual intimacy. However, it does so only within a structure of unequal social status and power. The gendered hierarchy of "two becoming one flesh" brings together a husband-provider with a dependent wife as a next-of-kin unit, but the two are united in such a way that the husband remains in charge and the wife is subsumed under his authority.[18] In addition to promoting marriage as a Christian duty, the Reformers also closed down women's religious communities, further restricting women's options for living independently of male control. In Protestant cultures, the submissive wife became the operative definition of the good Christian woman.

In contrast to the Catholic tradition, Protestantism early on abandoned the notion of marriage as a sacrament and instead identified the institution as an "order of creation," instituted by God for the good of the human community and properly administered by civil authorities. Another significant innovation was the identification of companionship as the chief purpose of marriage. While marriage was also prized because it served the purposes of restraining lust and encouraging procreation, Protestants beginning with John Calvin increasingly emphasized its unitive purpose and celebrated Christian marriage as the faithful expression of committed love between spouses. Wilson Yates speaks of this shift in thinking as "a watershed in [the Protestant] theory of marriage: before Calvin the primary purpose of marriage was considered to be procreation; with Calvin, procreation was reinterpreted to be a blessing flowing from companionship; after Calvin the idea of companionship emerged as the central theological focus in all the major Protestant traditions."[19] Drawing on biblical motifs regarding covenantal relationships, Protestants began to highlight

York: New York University Press, 1998). On same-sex domestic abuse, see Marvin M. Ellison, "Setting the Captives Free: Same-Sex Domestic Violence and the Justice-Loving Church," in *Body and Soul: Rethinking Sexuality as Justice-Love*, ed. Marvin M. Ellison and Sylvia Thorson-Smith (Cleveland: Pilgrim Press, 2003), 284–99.

18. On Christian family ideology, see Kathy Rudy, *Sex and the Church: Gender, Homosexuality, and the Transformation of Christian Ethics* (Boston: Beacon Press, 1997), and Ruether, *Christianity and the Making of the Modern Family*.

19. Wilson Yates, "The Protestant View of Marriage," in *Perspectives on Marriage: A Reader*, 2nd ed., ed. Kieran Scott and Michael Warren (New York: Oxford University Press, 2001), 446.

the values of fidelity, commitment, and loyalty in marital unions, but also to underscore the virtues of mutual affection and compatibility between partners, themes further developed by the Puritans, Congregationalists, and Quakers. Eventually, Protestants would make greater allowance for divorce, precisely on the grounds that incompatibility marks the absence of true companionship and, therefore, signals an often irreparable rupture of the marriage bond.[20]

Significant changes in attitude and practice have occurred within mainstream Protestant denominations during the past century, including more positive understandings of sexual love and the bonding power of intimacy, greater acceptance of divorce and remarriage, widespread acceptance (and use) of contraception and abortion as means of family planning, and increasing support for women's empowerment in church and society, including women's leadership in ordained ministries. At the same time, resistance to these developments, especially changes in women's power and status, has become more visibly organized within conservative evangelical and fundamentalist Protestantism. As heterosexual family and social relations have shifted in more egalitarian directions, and as Protestant Christians have begun more assertively to critique the patriarchal and anti-sex biases of their religious tradition, a counter movement has gained momentum to reassert a male-dominant paradigm for family, church, and society. This movement insists on male headship and female submission and pushes a campaign for sexual purity that condemns teenage sex, restricts access to reproductive health services, and promotes abstinence-only sexuality education. As Rosemary Ruether points out, "At this moment all the Christian churches, Catholic and Protestant, are in deep internal schism," and there is little prospect of reconciling fundamentalists and progressives because "their outlooks are based on irreconcilably

---

20. Feminist religionists have also emphasized that it is the introduction of violence into a marriage or intimate partnership that breaks the covenant, not the decision of the battered partner to leave the relationship. See Mitzi Eilts, "Saving the Family: When Is the Covenant Broken?" in *Abuse and Religion: When Praying Isn't Enough*, ed. Anne L. Horton and Judith A. Williamson (Lexington, MA: Lexington Books, 1988), 207–14; and also Marie M. Fortune, *Keeping the Faith: Guidance for Christian Women Facing Abuse* (San Francisco: HarperSanFrancisco, 1987).

different presuppositions," including those about women, sexuality, and the marital family.[21]

The conservative backlash, especially against women's empowerment, is the proper context in which to make sense of current denominational struggles over "the problem of homosexuality." Homosexuality is presumed in the popular imagination to result from willful "gender inversion" or role reversals in which persons refuse, or at least fail, to conform to gender roles and power dynamics that are presumably prescribed by God and nature. Although conservatives try to legitimate their anti-gay sentiments by claiming ancient roots for them, historian George Chauncey argues that gay-bashing is "a unique and relatively short-lived product of the twentieth century," precipitated by the social anxiety that many men, in particular, have felt in response to the dramatic shifts in gender roles and to their diminished social and economic power, first during the Depression of the 1930s and subsequently because of the social upheavals during and following the Second World War.[22] The effort to inhibit the social visibility of gay men and lesbians (bisexual and transgender people are, by and large, ignored), as well as to deny their full social and ecclesiastical standing, aims at enforcing "the closet" with its "don't ask, don't tell" strategy that maintains the public pretense that the world is, indeed, exclusively heterosexual.[23] At the same time, the backlash against gay rights seeks to block any gender nonconformity and especially women's enhanced freedom and empowerment. Equally important, it aims at intimidating "normal" heterosexuals and discouraging them from violating conventional gender norms and power dynamics.

Animosity in the West toward gay men and lesbians has been constructed on a foundation built on Christian condemnation of sodomy. Among Christian authorities sodomy has been an expansive category of prohibited sexual activities that at various times has included not only male-male anal sex, but also every kind of non-procreative sex between

---

21. Ruether, *Christianity and the Making of the Modern Family*, 223–24.

22. George Chauncey, *Why Marriage? The History Shaping Today's Debate Over Gay Equality* (New York: Basic Books, 2004), 14.

23. Steven Seidman, *Beyond the Closet: The Transformation of Gay and Lesbian Life* (New York: Routledge, 2002).

heterosexual partners. The early Protestant Reformers did not challenge the prevailing negative judgment in their tradition against non-marital, non-procreative sex. Martin Luther rejected same-sex sexual activity as an "idolatrous distortion instilled by the devil."[24] Similarly, John Calvin condemned such behavior as a sin against nature. By the end of the sixteenth century, all of Christian Europe had enacted legislation making sodomy a capital offense. Between 1555 and 1680, some thirty "sodomites," the label attached to violators of the law, were put to death in Geneva, the center of John Calvin's theocratic experiment in shaping civic life.

Contemporary Calvinists are struggling with this legacy in differing ways. On the one hand, a 1978 Presbyterian study concluded that "unrepentant homosexual practice does not accord with the requirements for ordination" of church leaders, but examining committees were advised not to question candidates directly about their sexuality.[25] At the same time, the church reaffirmed its 1970 position to work for the decriminalization of same-sex relations between consenting adults. On the other hand, a 1980 study document from the United Church of Canada took a different stance, arguing that "there is no reason in principle why mature, self-accepting homosexuals, any more than mature, self-accepting heterosexuals, should not be ordained or commissioned."[26] A 1977 United Church of Christ study argues similarly that "the only general difference between heterosexuals and homosexuals is sexual preference," and that there should be a single ethical standard — love intertwined with justice — for both heterosexual and same-sex relations.[27] A 1991 Presbyterian study document of human sexuality failed to gain official endorsement

---

24. *Luther's Works*, vol. 3, 255, cited in Evangelical Lutheran Church in America, *Human Sexuality and the Christian Faith: A Study for the Church's Reflection and Deliberation* (Minneapolis: Evangelical Lutheran Church in America, 1991), 28.

25. See Marvin M. Ellison, "Homosexuality and Protestantism," in *Homosexuality and World Religions*, ed. Arlene Swidler (Valley Forge, PA: Trinity Press International, 1993), 149–79.

26. Cited in "A Compilation of Protestant Denominational Statements on Families and Sexuality," 3rd ed., ed. G. William Sheek (New York: National Council of Churches of Christ, 1982), 87.

27. United Church of Christ, *Human Sexuality: A Preliminary Study* (New York: United Church Press, 1977), 137, 103.

by the church, in large part because it called the church to "repent of the sins of sexism and heterosexism" and because it voiced the conviction that "homosexual love, no less and no more than heterosexual love, is right and good."[28]

Today, all mainstream Protestant denominations publicly support civil rights protections for gay people and denounce anti-gay violence. Some have adopted what might be termed a rejecting, non-punitive stance that declares homosexuality wrong and unacceptable for Christians but insists that homosexual persons should be treated fairly. In popular language, one is encouraged to "hate the sin, not the sinner." Rather than punish, the church should encourage gay men and lesbians to repent and convert to a heterosexual life.[29]

Other Protestants have moved to a position of qualified acceptance in light of their reading of contemporary medical and psychological research that indicates a minority of persons are constitutionally homosexual in orientation and unable to reorient their sexuality toward heterosexual eroticism. Because change in sexual orientation is not likely for these persons, abstinence is recommended. If that is not possible, gay men and lesbians are encouraged to live in an ethically responsible manner and "make the best of their painful situations without idealizing them or pretending that they are normal."[30]

This position of qualified acceptance does not question heteronormativity or the basic assumption that heterosexuality alone is normal, natural,

---

28. Presbyterian Church (U.S.A.), *Presbyterians and Human Sexuality 1991* (Louisville: Office of the General Assembly, 1991), 18.

29. On limits of tolerance as a response to sexual and other forms of social difference, see Janet R. Jakobsen and Ann Pellegrini, *Love the Sin: Sexual Regulation and the Limits of Religious Tolerance* (New York: New York University Press, 2003). Their challenge is to consider how it might be possible "to resist and challenge exclusion and at the same time change the terms of inclusion" (149). Because attitudes and practices with respect to sexuality and intimacy have been shaped so profoundly by the dominant cultural form of Protestant Christianity in the United States, they also make this suggestion: "Because sex is so peculiarly linked to religion in America, to think about sex differently mandates thinking about religion differently" (150).

30. James B. Nelson, *Embodiment: An Approach to Sexuality and Christian Theology* (Minneapolis: Augsburg, 1978), 196.

and capable of expressing the full meaning and divinely intended purpose of human sexuality. A theological and moral division is emphasized between heterosexuality and homosexuality. However, it is precisely this dividing line that has become subject to questioning and critique, as well as the adequacy of the prevailing categories for understanding human sexuality and evaluating intimate relations. If sexual diversity, not uniformity, is characteristic of the human landscape, and if identity is no predictor of conduct or moral choices, then a recasting of the Christian paradigm about sexuality and intimate life is in order. The debate now under way about same-sex marriage provides the most recent occasion for addressing these concerns.

Traditionalists Defend the Normativity of Marital Heterosexuality

Discourse about sexuality is always about more than sexual intimacy and interpersonal relationships. It is also rife with assumptions about the social order, moral boundaries, and power. On this score, early on in *Heterosexism: An Ethical Challenge,* Patricia Jung and Ralph Smith offer two helpful suggestions. First, moral debate about sexuality and sexual expression should address human sexuality comprehensively and not become fixated on homoeroticism or same-sex relationships. "We can expect little progress in overcoming the barriers erected by heterosexism," they point out, "if we continue to talk only about homosexuality."[31] When talk is "only about homosexuality" and devalues homoeroticism, such discourse reinforces heteronormativity. Second, while the topic of homosexuality elicits strong feelings, heterosexual dominance is not reducible to individual prejudice or the fear and hatred of some individuals toward others. Rather, heterosexism is better viewed as "a reasoned system of bias" that is enforced throughout a social system, favors heterosexual persons, and disfavors bisexual and homosexual persons. By "reasoned" Jung and Smith do not mean that sexual oppression is rationally defensible, but rather that heterosexism is "rooted

---

31. Patricia Beattie Jung and Ralph F. Smith, *Heterosexism: An Ethical Challenge* (Albany: State University of New York Press, 1993), 5.

in a largely cognitive constellation of beliefs about human sexuality"[32] and that it is these foundational beliefs that must be critiqued.

These insights are helpful in analyzing the debates about same-sex marriage because opponents of marriage equality construct their arguments on the basis of certain deeply held, but also deeply flawed, convictions about sexuality and marriage. Their central presumption is that marriage requires gender difference and that, therefore, only a union of a man and a woman constitutes real marriage. While marriage is certainly also about commitment and fidelity, marriage, the argument goes, requires more than sharing intimacy with another person or even entering into a lifelong partnership. As Robert Gagnon writes, "The vision of marriage found in the Jewish and Christian Scriptures is one of reuniting male and female into an integrated sexual whole."[33] What makes that integration possible, traditionalists assert, is the proper joining of two sexually differentiated persons, each expressing appropriate gender identity as masculine or feminine, each conforming to expected gender role and behavior, and each expressing the appropriate sexual desire for his or her gendered "opposite."

Gagnon and other traditionalists argue that heterosexuality alone is God's intended design for creation, a design they contend is evident in a binary sex/gender schema in which biological or anatomical sex first gives rise to "proper" masculine or feminine gender identity and then, in lock-step fashion, to "normal" heterosexual sexual desire and finally to procreation in the context of marriage. This paradigm reflects what sociologist Leonore Tiefer calls the sexological model of sexuality, an ideological framework that "pervades our thinking and rationalizes and justifies our choices so completely that it is only with extreme difficulty that we can even contemplate alternatives."[34] This model privileges biological factors, makes universal claims about sexuality as naturally determined and

---

32. Ibid., 13.

33. Robert A. J. Gagnon, "Why 'Gay Marriage' Is Wrong," p. 1, available on Robert Gagnon's website.

34. Leonore Tiefer, "The Social Construction and Social Effects of Sex Research: The Sexological Model of Sexuality," in *Sexuality, Society, and Feminism*, ed. Cheryl Brown Travis and Jacquelyn W. White (Washington, DC: American Psychological Association, 2000), 100.

immutable, and "has promulgated that old cliché, 'anatomy is destiny.'"[35] The major shortcomings of this paradigm are twofold. First, it views sexuality in a biologically reductionistic and ahistorical fashion. Second, it fails to critique power and sexuality, particularly the socio-political impact of sexism, racism, and other structures of injustice on gendered/racialized lives and gendered/racialized sexualities. Moreover, it does not reckon with the negative consequences of granting exclusive normativity to (white/male) heterosexuality.

In keeping with the naturalistic or sexological paradigm, traditionalists insist that marriage occurs only where there is the "right fit," meaning the "right" (penis-in-vagina) anatomy plus procreative possibility, sexual compatibility, and what Gagnon calls the "other gender differences that we today characterize with the slogan 'men are from Mars and women are from Venus.'"[36] According to the logic of gender dualism, only heterosexual marital unions may be complete and, therefore, holy. Gender complementarity is essential to marriage, so the argument goes, because males and females are fundamentally different and yet attracted — supposedly by their gendered differences — to form complementary unions of two people who on their own are judged incomplete. "The marriage bond," ethicist Max Stackhouse contends, "is a community of love between those who are 'other.' This means not simply 'an-other' person, but one who is truly 'other,' even, and especially including, the body, its characteristics, and the social roles and expectations to which males and females are differently exposed."[37] From this perspective, the normatively human is heterosexual and exclusively so.

In addition, traditionalists portray all gay sex as immoral because even if the sex occurs within a stable, loving relationship, it takes place within an improper context. The only authorized context for sex is marriage, and they define marriage, of course, as exclusively heterosexual and open to

---

35. Ibid., 97.

36. Robert A. J. Gagnon, "The Bible and Homosexual Practice: Key Issues," in Dan O. Via and Robert A. J. Gagnon, *Homosexuality and the Bible: Two Views* (Minneapolis: Fortress Press, 2003), 65.

37. Max L. Stackhouse, "The Heterosexual Norm," in *Homosexuality and Christian Community,* ed. Choon-Leong Seow (Louisville: Westminster John Knox Press, 1996), 141.

procreation. The lack of procreative possibility, however, is not the final reason that same-sex bonds are seen as morally problematic. The assertion is made, without taking into account the actual life-experience or moral wisdom of non-heterosexual persons, that same-sex couples are incapable of morally principled sexual relations because presumptively they lack a biological mandate for procreation and, therefore, have no natural basis for monogamy and fidelity. Ironically, this kind of natural determinism is endorsed by Protestants claiming to represent a religious tradition that celebrates moral freedom!

In particular, gay men are stereotyped as promiscuous, first of all because they are men, and second because by choice they are men without wives. Lacking wives, they purportedly have no reason for not entering into limitless sexual liaisons. Being male and unmarried means living apart from the civilizing context of marriage and, therefore, being at risk of misconduct and moral turpitude. It is only through marriage that men are placed securely under the moral influence of women and required to become responsible adults, both socially and sexually. According to traditionalists (and despite all the evidence to the contrary from statistics about heterosexual marital infidelities and abuse), heterosexual marriage alone can restrain otherwise rapacious male sexuality and channel it toward the constructive end of creating new families. Because gay men are unmarried, they are demonized as "out of control" sexually and also, paradoxically, envied because they purportedly "flaunt" their independence from marriage, the social control that Protestant Christianity has insisted must be placed securely on top of and surrounding sexuality.

Critique of the Heterosexist Marriage Paradigm

Marriage traditionalists posit gender difference as the core structure of marriage in keeping with a bipolar gender paradigm that assumes men and women are more dissimilar than similar in their humanity and that sexual desire is sparked only when "opposites attract." Marriage is regarded as a natural, pre-political institution that reflects a divinely willed order of creation. In contrast, a social constructionist approach regards

sexuality as subject to change and, therefore, amenable to greater human-
ization or dehumanization, depending on prevailing social conditions and
sex/gender politics. In particular, as Tiefer explains, this alternative model
"directs our attention explicitly toward identifying forces of regulation and
how they establish sexual expectations and norms."[38] Accordingly, advocates for the freedom of same-sex couples to marry approach marriage as
a historically variable institution that not only changes but *should* change
to be in alignment with the best of civic and moral values. Even with
respect to gender, for example, the institution of marriage has been significantly altered. Elements once considered essential have been critiqued
and judged unjust, such as the legal doctrine of coverture or "one-flesh
union" that granted a husband ownership of his wife (and her property)
and made it legally impossible for a husband to be prosecuted for marital
rape. Such notions have been widely discredited, largely because of the
feminist movement and its push for moral and legal recognition of the full
personhood of women.

Traditionalists and progressives also have contrasting reading strategies
when they read the Bible and, therefore, draw vastly different conclu-
sions of what the Bible authorizes in terms of sexual difference. For the
most part, traditionalists focus their attention on developing scriptural
"proof" that homosexuality is incompatible with biblical mandates. For
them, the question of whether normative humanity is exclusively heterosexual is a settled matter. In contrast, advocates for opening marriage to
same-sex couples who employ a justice hermeneutic when they read scripture operate with quite different assumptions and discover quite different
insights, in keeping with Protestant theologian Robert McAfee Brown's
keen observation that "what we bring to scripture often determines what
we draw from scripture."[39] Their contrasting reading of "what the Bible
says" derives less from how they interpret any particular text and more
from fact that they approach the Bible with a different moral interest —

---

38. Tiefer, "The Social Construction and Social Effects of Sex Research," 82.
39. Robert McAfee Brown, *Theology in a New Key: Responding to Liberation Themes* (Philadelphia: Westminster, 1978), 81.

to name and correct heterosexism as an injustice, rather than to defend heterosexual supremacy — and, therefore, they come to scripture with a different question. In particular, they define the religious/moral problem not as the "problem of homosexuality" but rather as anti-gay oppression and the ongoing social and religious hostility shown to sexual minorities. Accordingly, in contrast to traditionalists, other Protestants do not focus their attention on asking whether homosexuality is biblically warranted, but rather on whether the devaluing, disrespect, and mistreatment of gay, lesbian, bisexual, and transgender persons are, in any way, in alignment with the core biblical mandate to seek justice, honor the stranger, and protect the vulnerable and marginalized. The Bible says very little about homosexuality, and what is said is obscure, mistaken, or irrelevant to the contemporary debates about same-sex love. However, the Bible says much about injustice and how faithfulness to God is demonstrated by the community's commitment to challenge oppression and rebuild a more inclusive, welcoming social order.

Advocates for marriage equality also draw on certain other Protestant emphases to develop their case: first, by focusing on the unitive rather than procreative purpose of marriage; second, by redefining marriage as a covenantal relationship between coequals; and, third, by underscoring the fundamental moral obligation to deepen respect for women and lgbt persons. George Chauncey notes that three historical changes have paved the way for same-sex civil marriage: first, the freedom to choose one's intimate life-partner has become a basic human right; second, civil marriage has become a central means for distributing a wide range of social and economic benefits; and third, marriage laws have become more gender-neutral and egalitarian.[40] This last point is particularly significant because, as philosopher Richard Mohr observes, "Now that gender distinctions have all but vanished from the legal *content* of marriage, there is no basis for the requirement that the legal *form* of marriage unite members of different sexes." For many, given their commitment to gender

---

40. Chauncey, *Why Marriage?* 59–86.

equality, the conventional one-man, one-woman definition of marriage has become "a dead husk that has been cast off by marriage as a living institution."[41]

This shift toward gender equality and a de-gendered notion of marriage is deeply troubling to marriage traditionalists, who fear that church and society may be moving in the direction of rejecting gender difference as the basic organizing principle for marriage and other social institutions. If good order requires not only gender difference but also gender hierarchy, then men must be placed in charge and women must be subordinate to male authority throughout the social order as the natural and divinely intended way. This male supremacist cultural paradigm perpetuates power differentials and maintains "man's world, woman's place"[42] as the normative social order in which women's lives are considered secondary and derivative in relation to men's. On this score, many contemporary evangelical Protestants follow Karl Barth by insisting that male dominance was ordered by God at creation and cannot be altered. As Barth writes, "The essential point is that woman must always and in all circumstances be woman; that the command of the Lord, which is for all eternity, directs both man and woman to their proper sacred place and forbids all attempts to violate this order."[43] Importantly, this hierarchical gender order requires seeing men and women as fundamentally different, a difference captured most pivotally in the institutionalizing of heterosexuality as a "union of opposites." In phrasing that echoes the conservative slogan that "God created Adam and Eve, not Adam and Steve," Barth writes, "Man and woman are not an A and a second A.... [They] are an A and a B, and cannot, therefore, be equated."[44] By this logic, defining marriage as exclusively

---

41. Richard D. Mohr, "The Case for Gay Marriage," in *Morals, Marriage, and Parenthood: An Introduction to Family Ethics*, ed. Laurence D. Houlgate (Belmont, CA: Wadsworth, 1999), 83.

42. Elizabeth Janeway, *Man's World, Women's Place: A Study in Social Mythology* (New York: Morrow, 1971).

43. Karl Barth, *Church Dogmatics*, III, 156, quoted in Adrian Thatcher, *Marriage after Modernity: Christian Marriage in Postmodern Times* (Sheffield, England: Sheffield Academic Press, 1999), 88n30.

44. Barth, 169, quoted in Thatcher, *Marriage after Modernity*, 88n30.

heterosexual reinforces marriage as a patriarchal institution, a gendered hierarchy between two unequal parties.

Because it is no longer acceptable to speak, at least publicly, of women's inferiority, marriage traditionalists speak instead of gender complementarity, which has become code language for male control and female subordination. Given how important women's leadership is even in the Christian Right, language that might connote female inferiority has been supplanted by softer language that emphasizes male and female role differences, a variation on the separate-but-equal theme. However, as religious feminists point out, there is little doubt that the "overarching issue is the defense of traditional gender hierarchy in patriarchal marriage."[45] Even though men and women may be spiritually equal, "in the flesh" a good woman is admonished to keep her place and be compliant toward male authority. Female goodness depends upon her being feminine, that is, socially dependent and sexually available to her husband. Similarly, a good man, defined as overtly heterosexual and masculine, demonstrates his virtue by his reliability as a worker and husband-provider.

In a globalizing capitalist market economy with ever-widening economic inequalities and a highly disruptive restructuring of work and family life, increasing numbers of heterosexual men are struggling with a crisis in masculinity as they confront unemployment, underemployment, and the necessity of having a wage-earning wife to subsidize the family's income. One strategy some men use to compensate for their heightened economic and social dependency is to reassert their male and heterosexual privilege, a strategy the Christian Right reinforces in its "traditional family values" campaign and anti-gay rhetoric by emphasizing that "normality" for men means participating in, and being head of, a heterosexual marital family. According to this heterosexist worldview, heterosexuality represents compliance not only to conventional patterns of male-female exchange, but also to an entire cultural paradigm of work, family, and community life. For beleaguered men, heterosexual identity becomes a badge of personal virtue (read superiority). Even though a man may not be the successful

---

45. Ruether, *Christianity and the Making of the Modern Family*, 168.

economic provider for his family that he might wish to be, he can, never-theless, claim his manliness and hold on to his self-worth by reassuring himself, and perhaps others, that he has at least not shirked his family re-sponsibilities by "turning queer." Repudiating gayness and asserting male authority in the family are twin components of a heterosexist cultural paradigm securely fastened by eroticizing male control of women. "Real men" are presumed to desire dominance over women and socially subor-dinate men, just as "real women" supposedly desire being placed under a powerful man's direction.

To stem the tide against further erosion of male power and to block additional gender changes in and beyond marriage, traditionalists insist on drawing a line to prevent queers, those most publicly identifiable as sex/gender nonconformists, from gaining state sanctioning or religious blessing for their families and intimate associations. Denying human rights, especially the right of civil (and religious) marriage, to gay people is the immediate objective, but the Christian Right has a much larger target audi-ence for its restrictive and highly punitive "family values" project. Its major preoccupation is to monitor and help police the heterosexual cultural ma-jority, significant numbers of which are already in noncompliance, or at risk of noncompliance, with respect to conventional patriarchal norms.

Many heterosexually identified women and men, insofar as they have adopted patterns of sexual and gender freedom explored first by lgbt people, are living *as if* they themselves are queer whether they explic-itly identify "that way" or not. Consider, first, how contracepted rather than procreative sex has become the normative sexual practice for a ma-jority of heterosexual couples. Sex is engaged in largely for the purpose of sharing pleasure and enhancing intimate bonding, a practice that is quite queer. Second, many heterosexuals are experimenting with greater flexi-bility in gender roles and sharing power more equitably in their intimate relationships, again something quite queer. Third, many have developed nonconventional family forms, including both younger and older cou-ples living together openly without either ecclesial or state legitimation, again something quite queer. "Contrary to popular belief, and even some gay rights rhetoric," cultural critic Michael Bronski argues, "gay people have not been patterning their lives on the structures of heterosexuality; rather the opposite has occurred. Heterosexuals who have increasingly been rejecting traditional structures of sexuality and gender have been reorganizing in ways pioneered by gay men and lesbians." Furthermore, Bronski proposes, "Only when those in the dominant culture realize that *they* are better off acting like gay people will the world change and be a better, safer, and more pleasurable place for everyone."[46]

Toward a Justice-Centered Christian Ethic of Relational Intimacy

In contrast to a traditionalist paradigm that views sex as a dangerous power and equates good order with male (and heterosexual) dominance, a progressive Christian ethic honors eroticism as a source of embodied energy that suffuses not only sexual activity but also life pursuits more broadly. Humans, in their sexual and social diversity, share a desire for intimate connection with others, with the earth, and with God. They also have a shared capacity for psychological wholeness and moral self-direction. Moreover, an egalitarian framework encourages resistance to moral evil and, accordingly, supports and celebrates those who resist sexual injustice, including those who refuse to comply with heterosexist sex/gender norms. As a consequence, once the assumptions of gender complementarity and "opposites attracting" are questioned and no longer hold the human imagination captive to a rigidly dualistic sex/gender paradigm, it becomes possible to affirm the goodness of all sexual and social relating based on mutual respect and care, regardless of gender, race, and so forth. This affirmation resonates with an insight feminist theologian Mary Daly named long ago, that "the categories of heterosexuality and homosexuality are patriarchal classifications" that mystify rather than identify in any helpful way the qualities of authentic relationship. "In a non-sexist society,"

---

46. Michael Bronski, *The Pleasure Principle Sex, Backlash, and the Struggle for Gay Freedom* (New York: St. Martin's Press, 1998), 242–43, 249.

Daly observed, "the categories of homosexuality and heterosexuality would be unimportant."[47]

Although neither sex nor marriage is necessary for personal fulfillment, it is wrong to exclude an entire class of persons from these routes to plea-sure and intimacy. "The desire for a significant other with whom we are uniquely conjoined," Daniel Maguire rightly insists, "is not a heterosexual but a basic human desire. The programmatic exclusion of gay persons from the multiple benefits of erotic attraction, which often opens the way to such a union, is arbitrary, harmful, cruel, and therefore sinful."[48] Unfortunately, there is ample historical evidence to demonstrate how sexual oppression has managed to dehumanize persons and keep the human community fractured along multiple axes. Whether by refusing to sanction marriage between slaves, or by prohibiting interracial unions in the United States until the last quarter of the twentieth century, or more recently by opposing same-sex partnerships, religious and other social conservatives have discovered that manipulating people's pain and fear around sexuality and restricting intimate bonding are exceedingly effective means of social control.[49]

If the twin problems with respect to Christian marriage reside, first, in positing gender difference (and, in actuality, gender inequality) as the core structure of marriage and, second, in defining marriage's purpose as the containment of erotic desire (and solidifying male control of women), then re-visioning marriage as right-related mutuality between sexually attracted coequals would not be a threat to marriage but rather to *pa-triarchal* marriage and, by extension, the legitimacy of other unjust social relations. In fact, affirming same-sex partnerships could well serve as an impetus for the ethical and spiritual revitalization of marriage and other

47. Mary Daly, *Beyond God the Father: Toward a Philosophy of Women's Liberation* (Boston: Beacon Press, 1963), 125–26.

48. Daniel Maguire, "The Morality of Homosexual Marriage," in *Same-Sex Marriage: The Moral and Legal Debate,* ed. Robert M. Baird and Stuart E. Rosenbaum (Amherst, NY: Prometheus Books, 1997), 59.

49. Suzanne Pharr, *In the Time of the Right: Reflections on Liberation* (Berkeley, CA: Chardon Press, 1996). Also, Susan Brooks Thistlethwaite, "Enemy Mine: Why the Reli-gious Right Needs Homophobia," *Chicago Theological Seminary Register* 91, no. 3 (2001) (The Castaneda Addresses 1998–2001: Confronting Homophobia in Bible and Theology): 33–40.

relations by placing the doing of justice at the heart of all social relating, beginning with the most intimate. If mutual respect, caring, and an equitable sharing of power and resources were expected in marriage and other relationships, then extending the freedom to marry to same-sex couples might prod faith communities to acknowledge that gender difference, and therefore gender itself, is irrelevant to the moral quality of marriage and other relationships. It might mark, as well, a shift toward honoring as ethically good and, therefore, as genuinely holy only those intimate connections that have the character of friendship and are freely entered into — and mutually desired — by consenting adults of equal legal and moral standing.

The traditional Christian sex ethic — celibacy for singles, sex only in marriage — is no longer adequate, if it ever was, for at least two reasons. First, the Christian marriage ethic has not been sufficiently discerning of the variety of human sexualities, including differing orientations, among them bisexual, heterosexual, homosexual, and even asexual.[50] It has also not paid adequate attention to the range of responsible sexual expression, including that of sexually active singles and those in committed partnership with more than one person.[51] Second, it has not been sufficiently discriminating in naming the ethical violations of persons even within marriage. A reframing of Christian ethics is, therefore, needed that avoids pandering to people's fears and refuses to sensationalize "the sin of sex," but instead realistically addresses the complex realities of diverse human sexualities, equips people throughout their lifetime to use their erotic power responsibly, names the violation of person's bodies and spirits as sinful and wrong,[52] and seeks to enhance both the dignity of persons and the quality of justice in our communities. In sum, the central expectation — and single standard — for intimate (and other) relationships should be

---

50. See Ellison and Thorson-Smith, *Body and Soul*, part 2: "Sexualities," 99–197.

51. Karen Lebacqz, "Appropriate Vulnerability: A Sexual Ethic for Singles," in *Sexual Ethics and the Church: After the Revolution* (Chicago: Christian Century Foundation, 1989), 18–23; Robert E. Goss, "Proleptic Sexual Love: God's Promiscuity Reflected in Christian Polyamory," *Theology & Sexuality* 11, no. 1 (September 2004): 52–63.

52. See Marie M. Fortune, *Sexual Violence: The Sin Revisited* (Cleveland: Pilgrim Press, 2005).

justice-love, understood as mutual respect and care, a fair sharing of power, and ongoing accountability to those who suffer oppression and exploitation. This ethic, it should be noted, resonates deeply with the best of Calvinist and Reformed Protestant insights about the virtues of companionate partnerships even as it moves to critique, as Calvin never did, the patriarchal and anti-sex assumptions that have prevented many Protestant Christians from paying sufficient attention to how justice within intimate bonds enriches the possibilities for truly joyous loving.

The development of a justice-centered Christian moral discourse about sexuality and intimacy involves making a wager similar to the one that Lutheran ethicist Larry Rasmussen makes in another context, namely, that "Christianity can help, but not without reformation."[53] Although the dominant Christian tradition conveys a strong sex-negativity with a moralistic bent toward control, the good news is that this tradition is neither monolithic nor unalterable. On a broad range of concerns from family values to divorce and from abortion to human rights, there are voices of critique and dissent in addition to those of fear and compliance. As a living faith tradition, Christianity either must be open to fresh insights about the human condition and adapt to altered conditions or else risk becoming irrelevant, reactionary, and increasingly decadent.[54]

Dramatic shifts in Christian teaching have occurred (or are occurring) about women's status within family, church, and society; about contraception and abortion; and about the status and rights of lgbt people. Theologian John Cobb cites the dramatic shifts in attitude toward divorce and remarriage to illustrate how transformations have previously occurred within the tradition. "Protestants are becoming so accustomed to this acceptance of divorce and remarriage as the best response in many circumstances," Cobb points out, "that they might forget how drastic a change this is from past Christian teaching." Since Protestants often rely on biblical guidance on moral issues, the change regarding divorce is "particularly

53. Larry Rasmussen and Daniel C. Maguire, *Ethics for a Small Planet: New Horizons on Population, Consumption, and Ecology* (Albany: State University of New York Press, 1988).

54. This is the thesis of Daniel C. Maguire's *The Moral Core of Judaism and Christianity: Reclaiming the Revolution* (Minneapolis: Fortress Press, 1993).

noteworthy since it is the acceptance of a practice that is rejected explicitly in the Bible." In fact, Cobb underscores, "it is Jesus himself who opposed divorce!"[55] The fact that a reversal on divorce has taken place is strong proof of how this religious tradition has remained dynamic by staying open to revision.[56] A historian's take on this ongoing process of critiquing and revising Christian moral insight is helpful on this score. "One benefit of remembering old church controversies," Mark Jordan points out, "is to be reminded how many of them have been surpassed."[57]

The purpose of a justice-centered Christian ethic is not to control or inhibit sexual desire, but rather to *empower* people to live more freely in their bodies; to deepen their capacity for and enjoyment of tender, erotically charged lovemaking; and to help them make more life-giving decisions about giving and receiving intimate touch. Its goal is relational justice and well-being for all.[58] Therefore, it seeks to *raise, not lower,* moral standards. Living ethically means acting in ways that enhance self-respect and respect for others and that encourage community to flourish in all its messiness and conflict. Toward this end, the Christian faith community should teach people to demand *more, not less,* in terms of what they deserve in their intimate (and other) relations, as well as what they owe to others.

The Danger That Same-Sex Marriage Poses

The current debate regarding same-sex marriage offers an opportunity, welcomed by many but feared by others, for re-envisioning both sexuality and marriage. Breaking decisively with patriarchal Christianity's

---

55. Cobb, *Matters of Life and Death*, 97.

56. Ibid. Cobb stresses that reversal on divorce is singularly noteworthy because the prohibition was not only commanded by the central authority of the Christian tradition but it also "appears at a far more central place than is the case with other doctrines on which many Protestants continue to appeal to Scripture as authoritative," including the scattered "texts of terror" used to discredit same-sex love (97).

57. Jordan, *The Ethics of Sex*, 174.

58. See Mary E. Hunt, "Same-Sex Marriage and Relational Justice," *Journal of Feminist Studies in Religion* 20, no. 2 (Fall 2004): 83–92; see also the roundtable discussion that follows with responses by Marvin M. Ellison, Emilie M. Townes, Patrick S. Cheng, Martha Ackelsberg, Judith Plaskow, and Angela Bauer-Levesque (93–117).

sex-negative legacy would make it possible, at long last, to give sexuality its due as a treasured moral resource for intimate connection and also to define mature intimate sociality not in terms of gender but in terms of covenantal commitments freely entered into, and lived out, by the parties involved. It is tantalizing to note that same-sex marriage has the potential, as legal scholar Nan Hunter suggests, "to disrupt both the gendered definition of marriage and the assumption that marriage is a form of socially, if not legally [and, I would add, religiously] prescribed hierarchy."[59] All this would enhance the well-being of persons and the common good.

At the same time, I am troubled that expanding the reach of marriage to include same-sex couples may pose a danger, although it would not be the danger against which most traditionalists warn, namely, the dissolution of marriage as a pivotal cultural institution and practice. My fear is not that marriage will disappear, but that it will become further inscribed as morally and religiously obligatory for yet another segment of the population, this time same-sex couples. From a justice-centered Christian perspective, the same-sex marriage debate raises the question of what solidarity and integrity require for living in community with those who are neither pair-bonded nor interested in marriage. Insofar as marriage becomes, ironically, the "new orthodoxy" for those once castigated as "sexual deviants," marriage will only become more staunchly privileged as the signifier of "normality," all to the detriment of single persons and those in plural and communal partnerships, such as men and women religious.[60] Because civil marriage has the backing of the state, it is true that extending marriage eligibility to same-sex couples will give at least some disenfranchised persons greater access to a range of (state and federal) economic

---

59. Nan D. Hunter, "Marriage, Law and Gender: A Feminist Inquiry," in *Sex Wars: Sexual Dissent and Political Culture*, ed. Lisa Duggan and Nan D. Hunter (New York: Routledge, 1995), 112.

60. Mary Hunt, in inviting gay men and lesbians "to take leadership in breaking the two-by-two pattern that is alleged to have begun with Noah and his nameless wife," contends that "friendship, not coupledness, ought to be the relational norm, *especially within the Christian tradition*" (Mary E. Hunt, "You Do, I Don't," in *Reframing Sexual Ethics: A Sourcebook of Essays, Stories, and Poems*, ed. Susan E. Davies and Eleanor H. Haney [Cleveland: Pilgrim Press, 1991], 254), my emphasis.

and social benefits, including spousal health insurance, Social Security survivor benefits, and the right of automatic inheritance. However, making marital status the exclusive conduit for these benefits does little to correct the entrenched patterns of social and economic inequities that are rapidly expanding within the global capitalist social order. Moreover, by focusing so intensely on acquiring the (legal) right to marry, social justice advocates may inadvertently help reinforce conservative efforts to privatize social welfare and "promote marriage" as the primary governmental strategy for alleviating poverty.[61]

Moving society toward greater distributive justice requires a multidimensional approach, but one strategy might be to *decouple* state-conferred benefits from marital status and distribute these communal resources on the basis of resident or citizen status or, better yet, human need. Another corrective measure would be to offer state support for a variety of arrangements, both marital and non-marital, including domestic partnerships, cohabitation agreements, civil unions, and an assortment of caregiving-dependency relations. Some legal scholars and public policy advocates are exploring, for example, what it would mean to *decenter* the marital family, defined by sexual (and reproductive) affiliation, and emphasize instead the caretaking family, which has at its core diverse relationships of care and dependency, such as parents' care of children, adult children's care of aging parents, and non-familial associations in which people respond to one another's needs.[62]

---

61. The Bush administration has pushed Congress to dedicate upward of $1.6 billion to fund programs to promote marriage, especially among the urban young and poor, as an alternative to liberal welfare programs, in the hopes that "single moms" will become attached to gainfully employed husbands who will manage to lift the family out of poverty and, therefore, off the public dole. On the myth of upward mobility and the difficulty of supporting a family on minimum-wage employment, see Barbara Ehrenreich, *Nickle and Dimed: On (Not) Getting By in America* (New York: Henry Holt, 2002); Elizabeth M. Bounds, Pamela K. Brubaker, and Mary E. Hobgood, eds., *Welfare Policy: Feminist Critiques* (Cleveland: Pilgrim Press, 1999); and Chuck Collins and Felice Yeskel, *Economic Apartheid in America: A Primer on Economic Inequality and Insecurity* (New York: New Press, 2000).

62. Martha A. Fineman, *The Autonomy Myth: A Theory of Dependency* (New York: Free Press, 2003). See also Lisa Duggan and Richard Kim, "Beyond Gay Marriage," *The Nation* 281, no. 3 (July 18/25, 2005): 24–27.

We should not fear that ending the monopoly of state-sanctioned marriage would end marriage as a valued cultural practice, which for many
people continues to be shaped in accordance with their religious tradition.
After all, as many as 85 percent of all weddings in the United States are
performed by a priest, minister, rabbi, or imam.[63] However, disentangling
the state from marriage and family would help clarify that the state's business is not that of regulating adult, consensual sexual relationships, other
than guaranteeing the safety of persons. Rather, the state's proper and necessary role is to assure that all persons, whether single, partnered, or living
in (religious and other kinds of) community, have fair access to the social
and economic resources necessary to flourish. Moreover, such disentangle-
ment would go a long way toward clarifying the church's proper business,
which is not to be the "moral police" or to impose one relational model
on a pluralistic society, but rather to help educate and support people
for living in justice-loving ways in an increasingly complex multicultural
global society.

These proposals about revising public policy with respect to the marital
family reflect the wisdom, though not the actual directives, offered by
Protestant reformer John Calvin, who similarly described the role of the
government as providing stability and justice for its members. Although
Calvin did not make the connections many contemporary Christians are
making with regard to sexuality and social justice, those standing in the
Protestant Reformed tradition are well advised not to seal off the so-called
private from the public, but rather to recognize that oppression and abuse
of power also take place among intimates. The mandate to pursue justice
must be extended explicitly to family life and intimate association, as well
as to political and economic power relations.

At the same time, Calvin's notions of divine sovereignty and human
vocation are resources that could well be tapped for a contemporary Christian social ethic of justice-love. As theologian Nancy Duff argues, "The
affirmation of the freedom of God is essential to the doctrine of vocation,"

---

63. Gretchen A. Stiers, *From This Day Forward: Commitment, Marriage, and Family in
Lesbian and Gay Relationships* (New York: St. Martin's Griffin, 1999), 5.

especially in honoring that God "calls each of us into the world for a purpose." While some, perhaps most, are called to live and act and love in the world as heterosexually identified, others are called to live as celibate and yet others as gay, lesbian, bisexual, and so forth. "The doctrine of vocation," Duff contends, "challenges arguments which deny the freedom of God to call people to different identities and tasks."[64]

If sexual difference rather than uniformity is characteristic of God's good creation, then it is past time for Christians to repent of their sinful confusing of heterosexism with God's will or of trying to make complicity in sexual injustice appear virtuous. The fact that some Christians "in good conscience" show shameless disrespect for gay people's lives, partnerships, and families is evidence of the fact that sin abounds in a faith tradition that has not yet managed to cast off its patriarchal and anti-sex distortions. However, unless evil is named, it cannot be recognized, and if evil is not recognized, it cannot be resisted. The gift offered by gay, lesbian, bisexual, and transgender Christians is to name properly the problem that is dividing church and society, causing enormous suffering, and sowing doubt about God's sovereign graciousness. The sin is not, and never has been, homosexuality or same-sex love. Rather, the sin is compulsory heterosexuality.

God's Spirit is at work, stirring the waters and empowering those harmed by injustice to rise up, protest, and claim their full humanity as persons created in the image of God. God's Spirit is also at work, stirring the waters and empowering those who have, consciously or unconsciously, participated in oppressing others (and perhaps even themselves), so that they, too, may awaken in order to repent and to enter into solidarity with those they have previously refused to see as fully human. It is by resisting evil, including sexual injustice, that Christians, alongside others, may gain fresh insight into justice-love as the central meaning of human life, regardless of the sexual identities or marital status at play.

---

64. Nancy J. Duff, "Christian Vocation, Freedom of God, and Homosexuality," in *Homosexuality, Science, and the "Plain Sense" of Scripture*, ed. David L. Balch (Grand Rapids, MI: William B. Eerdmans Publishing, 2000), 262.

For too long, wanton indulgence in the sin of heterosexual self-aggrandizement and social dominance has prevented many Christians from unmasking the big lie, namely, the perverse notion that holy love is somehow possible only between persons of the "right" gender, race, and so forth. When the big lie is exposed and injustice resisted, it becomes possible to grasp — and be grasped by — the good news about godly love: no qualitative moral difference exists between same-sex love and heterosexual love. At the same time, a longstanding theological insight might gain ever deeper resonance among us: where there is justice-love, there is God — not god as a heterosexual idol, but rather the Holy One who extends mercy without limit and never ceases to be wildly passionate about justice, including relational justice, for all creation.

Chapter Three

Elements of a Ṣamadiyyah Shariah

GHAZALA ANWAR

Islam, Iman, and Iḥsan (Submission, Faith, and Creative Aesthetics)

Umar ibn al-Khattab said: One day when we were with God's messenger, a man with very white clothing and very black hair came up to us. No mark of travel was visible on him, and none of us recognized him. Sitting down before the Prophet, leaning his knees against the Prophet's knees, and placing his hands on his thighs, he said, "Tell me, O' Muhammad about Islam."

He replied, "Islam means that you should bear witness that there is no god but God and that Muhammad is God's messenger, that you should perform the ritual prayer, pay the alms tax, fast during Ramadan, and make the pilgrimage to the House if you are able to go there."

That man said, "You have spoken the truth." We were surprised at his questioning the Prophet and then declaring that the Prophet had spoken the truth. He said, "Now tell me about Iman (faith)."

He replied, "Faith means that you have faith in God, His angels, His Books, His messengers, and the Last Day, and that you have faith in the measuring out, both its good and its evil."

Remarking that the Prophet had spoken the truth, he then said, "Now tell me about doing what is beautiful (Iḥsan)."

The Prophet replied, "Doing what is beautiful means that you should worship God as if you see Him, for even if you don't see Him, he sees you." . . .

Then the man went away. After I had waited for a long time, the Prophet said to me, "Do you know who the questioner was, Umar?" I said, "God and His messenger know best." He said, "He was Gabriel. He came to teach you your religion."[1]

The above hadith (report) is a description of what Muslims have understood their religion to be. Within this basic agreement among the majority of Muslims exists a diversity of opinion regarding the finer points of *Islam, iman,* and *iḥsan.* A well-established precept (expressed in another hadith) that has guided enlightened discussions and debates is that "diversity of opinion within [the scholars of] the Muslim community is a mercy from God" because it gives options and brings ease into the lives of the diverse members of the *ummah* (the Muslim community). The distinction between (a) a sincere difference of opinion that is a sign of God's mercy and (b) opposition and hostility generated due to the lack of integrity and a concern for personal gain (on the part of its leaders and scholars) needs to be maintained. Another precept (also expressed in a well-known hadith) is that *actions are judged [by God] according to their intentions* and that only God can know the motivations behind an action. Purity of intention, *ikhlas* (sincerity), depends on thinking every thought and doing every act to please God.

The following essay expresses the view that, first, on the broad points of *Islam* — *iman, iḥsan,* and *ikhlas* (as expressed in the hadith above) — there is no point of disagreement between heterosexual and homosexual Muslims. Within the homosexual Muslim community the same range of beliefs, attitudes, and practices with respect to Islam is represented as exists in the rest of the Muslim *ummah.*[2] Second, differences in sexual orientation, like differences in language, skin tone, and gender, are all expressions of God's creative genius and point back to God. The intention of this essay is to bring ease into the lives of Muslim sexual minorities and to create a space for them to become full members of the community, sharing its responsibilities and enjoying its spiritual protection and support.

---

1. Muslim: Iman 1; Bukhari: Iman 37.
2. The entire Muslim community over space and time.

as-Ṣamad: God the Unique, Incomparable, and Unmatched

Say Allah is One. Allah is Incomparable (as-Ṣamad). He was not born and from Him none was born. And none is a match (kufu) for Him. (*Ikhlas Quran 112*)

One of the many descriptive names used for God in the Quran is Ṣamad, the Unique, Incomparable, and Unmatched. Like Allah the Ṣamad, same-sex couples do not procreate, but they love, they create, and they nurture relationships that are tied together not by an earthly womb but by Divine Compassion. The culminating moments of same-sex lovemaking do not coincide with the natural processes of human reproduction. It may be an appropriate proposition, then, for a Muslim individual or a Muslim community that does not participate in the reproductive assumptions of heterosexuality to associate with the Ṣamadiyyah quality of God and name itself Ṣamadiyyah.

This theological reflection is inspired by the Ṣamadiyyah and scholars of Jakarta. It is dedicated to those Muslims who affirm their love of Allah and experience their love for their same-sex partners as a reflection of their Love for Allah as Ṣamad. It is undertaken with the hope of reforming and extending Muslim family ethics and law to include Ṣamadiyyah relations and to honor same-sex love.

A Glimpse of Ṣamadiyyah Life

In 2002, Madia, an organization that promotes interfaith harmony and cooperation, made possible my interview with Ratna and Saima, a Ṣamadiyyah couple, in Jakarta. Ratna taught at a major university at the time, and Saima was a student of theology.[3] For her master's thesis Ratna had "smuggled" herself into a women's prison as an inmate for three months. The head of that prison lost his job as a consequence of her findings regarding the administration of the prison. After that she proceeded

---

3. For the sake of privacy names of the interviewees have been changed.

to the Netherlands for further studies. But before the completion of her studies, she was recalled by her superiors in Jakarta, who disapproved of the communist leanings of her supervisor of studies in the Netherlands. It was during her stay overseas that Ratna came into her lesbian identity.

Upon her return Ratna boarded in a large house in an elite neighborhood of Jakarta. It was owned by an Iranian woman and was a haven for Ṣamadiyyah of various ethnic and national backgrounds. Generally, when a Ṣamadiyyah revealed her sexual orientation to her family, her family erroneously concluded that she had lost her faith and this caused an estrangement from the family often lasting for several years. Ṣamadiyyah consider this period of estrangement the most difficult aspect of their lives. Their families' opinion that they have gone astray, however, does not change their relationship with the religion that they were brought up in; they continue to observe Islam as before. Eventually the relations mended, and these women were able to regain an unspoken acceptance from their families. Due to the continuing affiliation with Islam, and despite the rejection of their families, the residents (of the house that Ratna lived in as a young woman) prayed and fasted and observed certain rules. No alcohol, drugs, gambling, or lovers other than the partners of the residents were allowed in the house. This, however, did not prevent them from participating in the wider lesbian culture of Jakarta.

Within the circle of friends of the Ṣamadiyyah house was a Chinese lesbian house where the rules were quite relaxed. Residents and visitors could drink alcohol and play cards. The rule about monogamy was not strictly imposed, although residents were encouraged to be discreet about their secondary lovers. The very different cultures in the two contemporary lesbian group homes indicate that a tacit Shariah informed the culture of the Ṣamadiyyah house. Even though the formal Shariah criminalized its residents and the wider Muslim community shunned them, the women had not lost their sense of self-worth and had not abandoned the Shariah. The unspoken theology that informed these women's practice is what I hope to express in the following paragraphs.

The owner of the Ṣamadiyyah house was butch. Her partner was a refined femme with long painted nails who had a black belt in martial arts.

On occasion she used her martial skills against her butch partner when she had evidence that her partner was seeing other women. The rest of the residents sympathized entirely with the femme, and the house eventually disintegrated because the partners could not resolve their differences.

Unlike the residents of the Ṣamadiyyah house of Ratna's youth, where religious sentiment found limited communal expression, Ratna's partner Saima, a younger woman, participated actively in the progressive Muslim theological circles of Jakarta. Of the four Muslim women present at the interview (Saima; Ratna; the director of Madia, who graciously acted as a translator; and myself), Saima was the only one who wore an "Islamic" headscarf. The interview took place on the doorstep of Saima's tiny and very modest student accommodation. During the interview Saima spoke much less than Ratna while ensuring that we felt welcomed by offering us tea and fruit. While Ratna was influenced by Marxist ideas and did not focus much on religion, for Saima religion was of central importance and she was accepted as a Ṣamadiyyah by her Islamic theological circles. She mentioned that she had recently returned from an Islamic conference in Malaysia where there was a debate as to whether covering of the hair was required by the Quran and that her mentor, a noted Muslim male scholar, was encouraging her to reconsider her decision to wear a headscarf. The two women seemed to be in a happy and stable relationship.

The interview with Ratna and Saima indicated that Ṣamadiyyah of Jakarta participate in the wider women's movement. In the year prior to the interview a women's conference was organized in Aceh, where women had suffered a great deal under conditions of civil war. Two hundred and fifty women's organizations participated in this conference. In response to the separatists' demand for an Islamist state in Aceh that would implement the Shariah, the women at the conference asked, "Shariah according to whom? If women are going to be ruled by the Shariah, then women have the right to interpret and formulate the Shariah." The women with whom I spoke stressed that Indonesia is not Islamic but Muslim and that they are Muslims within a religiously pluralistic society.

Even though Ṣamadiyyah participated in the women's movement, they were invisible as Ṣamadiyyah. An informal underground network was coordinated by a Ṣamadiyyah who sold water on commuter trains and did not carry a mobile phone (so it was not possible for me to contact her during my short visit). The "underground" Ṣamadiyyah community in Jakarta was not interested in any activism that would focus on its rights. In fact, its members were very suspicious of the wider women's community reaching out to them on the issue of Ṣamadiyyah rights and needs. So far they had preferred to remain aloof and isolated. The persecution of feminists by an earlier political regime (conducted with the help of Islamist women according to my interviewees) may have influenced this wish to remain hidden. Yet Saima's participation in theological circles that encouraged feminist readings of the Quran and accepted Ṣamadiyyah women indicates the opening of a public space for Ṣamadiyyah life.

Conversations within the *Ummah* Regarding Ṣamadiyyah

During the same trip to Jakarta, I gave a talk entitled "Lesbian Shariah" to a group of (male) theologians from Muslim and Christian seminaries. Among those who attended the talk was a former minister of religious affairs. I was relieved and surprised at the seriousness and attention given to my talk and the openness of the discussion afterward. None of the theologians put forth the argument that homosexuality was forbidden in Islam or Christianity. Instead, they asked me questions like, for example, "In case of divorce, would a lesbian couple be required to observe *iddah* (period of waiting) as the wife in a heterosexual couple is required to under Shariah?"[4] The *adab* (respect) with which a group of eminent theologians from the largest Muslim country listened to what I had to say encouraged me to imagine a respected place for Ṣamadiyyah relationships within the Shariah and within Muslim societies.

Adab (etiquette) is central in traditional Islamic culture. *Adab* is ritualized respect. *Adab* is the *ẓahir* (outer form) of respect which is an inner attitude. *Adab* is harmony. Through observance of *adab* among people

---

4. In order to confirm possible conception.

unfamiliar to one another or engaged in unfamiliar and difficult conversations, the possibility of a harmonious resolution is maintained. *Adab* cautions participants engaged in a difficult conversation that what is at stake is a shared and mutually upheld tradition — a source of beauty and solace in one's life — that is the sum total of all our interactions with one another. An important part of *adab* is *ghad-e basr*, that is, averting our gaze to avoid exposing the other. The physical or mental gaze of the subject taking responsibility for respecting the privacy of the object ensures a mutually respectful inter-subjectivity. *Satr*, covering over the faults and shortcomings of another, or even of a debate or dispute, is an extension of and aid to *ghad-e basr*.

Much is lost in a conversation in which *adab* is not observed, regardless of what else may have been achieved. Efforts at winning an argument within the *ummah* — that cause us to disregard *adab* — are self-defeating. Presenting our case with meticulous etiquette, without any attachment to whether we will win our case, bears fruit that appears in its time after the conversations have ended. Muslim etiquette and ethics are the *zahir* (outer) and *batin* (inner) of our good actions (*'aml salih*). Etiquette that does not embody and establish an ethic and an ethic expressed without etiquette both miss the balance that Muslims are called to strive for. *Ghad-e basr* and *satr* should not be confused with the façade of inclusion created by "don't ask, don't tell." Questions are asked without exposing the other. The eminent Jakarta theologians did ask questions, and the questions assumed the inclusion of lesbians within the *Shariah* family law. In that conversation a major point of contention was conceded without any direct reference to it.

A Ṣamadiyyah Quranic Ethics

Human language and discourse inevitably suffer from limitations, but discourse that is aware of its limitations is superior to one that lacks this awareness. The Arabic Quran assumes a male God, but all assumptions and presumptions about God are deconstructed in general disclaimers like

Praise be to Allah who is above and beyond what is predicated of Him.[5] The Arabic Quran assumes the linguistic convention of addressing its audience in the male pronouns, but the implication that the guidance or welfare of men takes priority over that of women is countered by Quranic statements like the following: *"So their Lord responded to their prayers that 'verily I shall not waste the good deed of any among you whether male or female, you are of each other. . . .'"*[6] and *"And whosoever does good whether **male or female** and **he** has faith they shall enter paradise and they shall not be wronged in the least. . . ."*[7] The male singular pronoun *he* is used to refer to both male and female, establishing the principle of inclusion despite exclusive linguistic usage. The Arabic Quran mentions no female prophets, yet it vindicates the position of an unnamed woman who argued with the Prophet regarding a point of family law and thus validates the protest of an individual who differed from the Prophet: *"God heard the woman who argued with you, O Prophet, regarding her spouse (zauj) and complained to God. . . ."*[8] The Quran is both the word of God and the word of the Prophet Muhammad (praise be upon him).[9] It is also the composite faith profile of the *ummah*.

The Quran, at any given time, is the aggregate of the faith, understanding, and actions of the Muslim *ummah*. The most important context for understanding and extrapolating from the Quran is our (1) *iman bil ghaib* (faith in the unseen realm), (2) *the quality and depth of our prayers* (3), and *our generosity in sharing what we have been given*.[10] These are the conditions set forth by the Book for deriving guidance from it. This is the *shanu nuzul* (the context of revelation), which will determine a guided (rather than a misguided) reading of the Book that is living, dynamic, and interactive.

---

5. al-An'am (The Cattle) 6:100.

6. Aal Imraan (House of Imran) 3:195.

7. an-Nisa (Women) 4:124, also an-Nahl (The Honey Bee) 19:97, and Ghafir (Forgiver) 40:40.

8. al Mujadila (The woman who disputes) 58:1.

9. "The Quran is entirely the word of God and, in an ordinary sense, also entirely the word of Muhammad" (Fazlur Rahman, *Islam* [Chicago: University of Chicago Press, 1979], 31).

10. al-Baqara (The Cow) 2:3.

Gender in the Quran

> Glory to the One who created all pairs from what grows from the earth and from among themselves and from what they know not. (Yasin, 36:36)

Gender may be socially constructed, yet there is a biological basis for it that is undeniable. While in certain contexts maleness and femaleness may be mapped along the same continuum, there is also a complementarity or even polarity of male and female within each human and between humans. Pairs may exist in a variety of combinations of maleness and femaleness in ways that we may just be discovering or may not yet have discovered. Yasin 36:36 cautions the reader against understanding Quranic reference to couples in heterosexist terms, for the bipolarity of male and female gives rise both to homosexuality and to heterosexuality.[11]

The purview of male/female complementarity that the Quran cites as a sign of God's creative genius is much wider than heterosexuality. It encompasses complementarities within a person and within partnerships that do not include sexual expression. The maleness or femaleness of one's partner, regardless of whether one is heterosexual or homosexual, is equally an object of awe and attraction. In the case of a heterosexual person, the initial difference of gender with one's object of love and desire gives way to a discovery of myriad similarities and differences. In the case of a homosexual person, the initial similarity of gender with one's object of love and desire gives way to a discovery of myriad differences and similarities. This discovery is equally significant to self-knowledge in the two cases. Unlike human genitalia, sexual attraction and desire are not apparent to the eyes. Nonetheless, no one would argue that the genitalia are more real or more important than the desire that drives humans to *cohabit* (to become each other's garment). No one would argue that two humans ought to cohabit without the desire to do so. The desire to cohabit expresses mutual intimacy between the partners. This intimacy does not interfere with the intimacy that a Muslim desires to experience with God

---

11. al-Hujaraat (The Apartments) 49:13; an-Najm (The Star) 53:45; al-Qiyama (The Resurrection) 75:39; al-Lail (Night) 92:3.

(during Ramadhan). Although abstention from sexual relations by the seeker unto Allah during the time of the *i'tikaf* retreat (during Ramadhan) and while donning the pilgrim's attire, the *iḥram*, in the precincts of the Ka'aba, signifies that there are times once a year and once in a lifetime when a Muslim is to focus exclusively on his or her own spiritual life.

> And when My servants ask you concerning Me, then surely I am very near; I answer the call of the caller when he calls on Me, so they should answer My call and believe in Me that they may walk in the right way. Permitted to you, on the night of the fasts, is the approach to your women. *They are your garments and you are their garments.* Allah knows what you used to do secretly among yourselves; but He turned to you and forgave you; so now associate with them, and seek what Allah has ordained for you, and eat and drink, until the white thread of dawn appears to you distinct from its black thread; then complete your fast till the night appears; but do not associate with your wives while you are in retreat in the mosques. Those are limits (set by) Allah: Allah makes clear His Signs to people: that they may learn self-restraint.[12]

The modesty regarding sexual desire that hides the genitalia expresses itself in an exuberance of gender-differentiated and non-differentiated attires, gestures, and attitudes creating a semiology of courtship. To the extent that societal and legal structures interfere with and violate the heterosexual and homosexual courtship dances that must follow their own inner knowing, degeneration, decay, and misery set in. When reproduction, a side effect of (and at times the reason for) heterosexual courtship, is made the primary reason for it, it implies that the goal of the society is to maintain the rule of the father and the subjugation of women rather than to worship and submit to God. Acknowledging more than just the heterosexual courtship dance indicates a humility and acceptance of the creative genius of the Creator. The free and creative interplay of the various courtship dances leads to a culture that is complex, flexible,

---

12. al-Baqara (The Cow) 2:186–87.

life affirming, and pleased with itself in pleasing God. It is a culture that continuously reminds itself that it should not make a god out of hetero-sexuality, no matter how common it might be, and that God is beyond gender.

Gender roles are constructed around the bipolarity of a male/female reproductive couple. Most individuals would probably adopt the gender roles assigned to them and would even be grateful because of the convenience. What saves gender roles from being an agent of oppression is that the key to success in the eyes of Allah is not conformity to assigned gender roles but *taqwa*, mindfulness of the Will of God in our interaction with the creatures of God.

> O people! We have created you male and female and have made you nations and tribes that you may know one another. The noblest among you, in the sight of Allah, is the best in conduct (the highest in *taqwa*). Allah is Knower, Aware.[13]

Taqwa is a precondition for community. What cannot be shared does not generate community. This is true of gender roles, as well. If Muslim men and women are to become one community, then they must be flexible about gender roles and gender assignments. There can be no choice about the adoption or rejection of culturally transmitted gender roles without there also being a choice about sexual orientation.

Natural Inclination, Desire, and Procreation

> And among His signs is that He created you (plural) from earth and now you are humans spread everywhere. And among His signs is that He created for you mates from among yourselves so that you may find repose (*sukun*) in them and instilled love (*muwaddah*) and mercy (*rahma*) between you. Verily in this are signs for those who reflect.[14]

---

13. al-Hujaraat (The Inner Apartments) 49:13.
14. ar-Room (The Romans) 30:20–21.

Verse 30:20 goes beyond Adam and Eve in tracing human origin in dust. Verse 30:21 does not specify the gender composition of the mates but simply states that humans are created as mates for each other. This includes all couples, regardless of gender composition. The nature of this mateship rests in the repose, love, and mercy that transpire between the mates and not in their gender identity. Neither is this verse concerned with reproduction.

> So remain steadfast in the Just Way (*deen*), the natural constitution (*fitra*) by which Allah created people; there is no altering of Allah's creation. This is the established Way (*deen*) but most people do not know.[15]

In this verse natural inclination or the human norm (*fitra*) is to be treated fairly and with compassion (*deen*) regardless of gender identity or sexual orientation. The foundation of the *deen* that must inform all our actions and deliberations and our *Shariah* are 'adl (equity, fairness) and *ihsan* (kindness, compassion).[16] Moreover, the principles concerning mateship (*zawaj*) are *muwaddah* (love), *rahma* (mercy), *sukun* (comfort, repose), and *libas* (garment, commitment). This is the *fitra* or natural ethics of sexual relations. For an observant Muslim, pursuit of sexual desire must be guided by these principles.

Shahwa (desire) is a longing or yearning for a thing that involves both body and soul. Ethically, *shahwa* is of two kinds: *sadiqa* (true) or *kaziba* (false). *Shahwa sadiqa* (true desire) arises out of a person's inborn/natural needs.[17] Without its fulfillment, the person tends toward an unsound state, for example, the *shahwa* for food in a state of hunger. *Shahwa kaziba* (false desire) is again of two kinds: (1) that without which the person does not tend toward an unsound state,[18] and (2) *shahwa kaziba zalima* (false and oppressive desire), that with which one's own or another's body or

---

15. ar-Room (The Romans) 30:30.
16. an-Nahl (The Honeybee) 16:90.
17. Quran 21:102; 41:31; 43:71; 52:22; 56:21; 77:42.
18. Quran 3:14; 4:27; 16:57; 19:59.

soul tends toward an unsound state, for example, *sifah* (lust) or the desire to rape.[19]

Ṣalat (ritual prayer) and *shahwa* (desire) both involve bodily activities. The former offers up the body in submission; the latter submits to the needs of the body. There is a dynamic and mutually supportive balance between *ṣalat* and *shahwa sadiqa*. This insight is expressed in the well-known saying attributed to the Prophet (peace be upon him) that *nikah* (marriage) constitutes half of *iman* (faith). There is an antagonistic relation among *ṣalat* and *shahwa kaziba* and *shahwa kaziba zalima*. Indulgence will veer the individual away from *ṣalat* and from God.[20]

If paradise stands for ultimate spiritual success, then erotic depictions of paradise indicate that spirituality and sexuality are inextricably related. References to the provision of seductive mates and the satisfaction of *shahwa* of the righteous in paradise leave no doubt that human sexual desire is integral to being human. The mention of both male and female companions or the gender non-specificity of the companions allows the descriptions to be read as referring to both heterosexual and homosexual partnerships. There is no evidence to suggest that there will be procreation in paradise or that heterosexual sex is superior to homosexual sex because it leads to procreation. Paradise will be inhabited by those who on this earth overcome their base desires (*shahwa kaziba*) through self-discipline and live according to their ethical nature.

Ṣamadiyyah and Liwat (the Sin of the People of Lot)

When we experience limitation and darkness instead of freedom and light due to our reading of a Quranic *ayah*[21] (verse), we ask Allah for guidance. His signs, whether in the Quran or writ large in the universe, are merely an occasion or locus for God's Guidance. The Quran is not God. It is a complex, nonlinear system of signs and symbols that points to or leads to God. The signs do not lend any meaning without faithful eyes, righteous hands, and a sincere heart that strives to please God. Our intention in

---

19. Quran 7:81; 27:55.
20. Quran 19:59.
21. Literally "sign."

reading God's signs, whether in the Quran or outside of the Quran, must be to please God. And God is much easier to please than humans. The Quranic injunction *wa la tashtaru bi ayaati samanan qaleelan: and do not sell My signs/verses for a small price*[22] applies to the case of justifying injustice and inhumanity based on divine signs/verses of the Quran. It applies to justifying the oppression, persecution, and even murder of Muslim sexual minorities based on a certain reading of the verses referring to the People of Lot.

The Jakarta theologians did not mention the Quranic references to the People of Lot during my presentation on lesbian Shariah. Perhaps they, like me, felt that these verses were not relevant to the case of sexual minorities within the *ummah*; obviously they were not relevant to the case of female homosexuality.

> And Lot when he said to his people, "Surely you commit an ob-scenity; a sin that none has outstripped you in, in the world / you approach (*tatuna*) men and rob the traveller and do evil in your meetings." And his people had no answer except to say, "Bring God's torment upon us if you are one of the truthful."[23]

The People of Lot are depicted as being wayward transgressors. They satisfied their lust with men instead of women, they robbed travelers instead of assisting them, and they did evil in their meetings instead of promoting good. They were generally inclined to oppressive and sinful behavior, but the sin that is most often mentioned and thus can be considered to be the most oppressive was that they satisfied their lust with men instead of women. Lot's exasperated and rhetorical question to them — *a ta'atunar rijala dounan nisa shawatan? Do you approach men instead of women with lustful desire (shawa)? —* has been read for centuries to mean that Lot was categorically condemning homosexuality.[24]

---

22. al-Baqara (The Cow) 2:41; al-Maidah (The Table Spread) 5:44.
23. al-'Ankabut (The Spider) 29:28–29.
24. And Lot as he said to his people, "Do you commit an obscenity no other has outstripped you in. You satisfy your lust (*shawa*) with men (*rijal*) instead of women (*nisa*). You are a people who have transgressed the limit." His people had no answer except to say:

And when our messengers came to Lot, he was unhappy and felt straitened on account of them. He said, "This is a distressful day." And his people came rushing towards him. And they used to commit crimes from before. He said, "O my people, these my daughters are purer for you. So fear God and do not disgrace me with regard to my guests. Is there not among you a single right-minded man?" They said, "You know that we do not need your daughters and indeed you know well what we want." He said, "Would that I could overpower you or that I could take to a powerful refuge." They said, "O Lot, we are messengers from your Lord; they shall not reach you. So travel with your family in the night and let not any of you look back; except your wife, verily that which afflicts them will afflict her. Indeed their appointed time is the morning. Is not the morning near?" So when our decree came, we turned it upside down and rained on it stones of baked clay one after another. Marked from your Lord and they are never far from you.[25]

When Lot asks, "Do you approach men instead of women with lustful desire (*shahwa*)?" is he addressing only the men of his village? If so, why did the women, half the population of any human society, incur the wrath of God? I have heard Ṣamadiyyah men make the argument that the verses referring to *liwat* apply to the case of heterosexual men engaging in homosexual acts involving anal intercourse. According to this interpretation, it is unnatural and thus prohibited for heterosexual men to engage in homosexual acts and it is unnatural and thus prohibited for all to engage in anal sex. The fact that Lot's wife, a heterosexual childbearing woman, is also included in the punishment clearly indicates that the crime of the People of Lot cannot be simplistically equated with male homosexuality or with anal sex. Lot's wife could not have been implicated in either. We

---

"Expel them from your city, they profess to be pure." So we saved him and his family except for his wife who was among those who remained behind (7:80–83). And Lot when he said to his people, "Do you commit obscenity while you see? Do you approach (*tatuna*) men to satisfy your lust instead of women? Nay, but you are a people who behave senselessly" (an-Naml 27:54–55).

25. Hud 11:77–83.

may never know the exact nature of the (sexual) crime of the People of Lot except that it represented a major lapse in faith and good deeds.

When Lot asks, "Do you approach men instead of women with lustful desire (*shahwa*)?" he means *shahwa zalima kaziba*, that is, a false unjust desire. In principle, a false sexual desire can be pursued by any person, regardless of gender or sexual orientation, and is equally reprehensible. Lot's question, then, is posed to all those who engage in the satisfaction of their false sexual desires. To read it to refer to all homosexual men is to misread it, and to read it to apply only to homosexual acts between heterosexual men is seriously to limit its ethical import.

The People of Lot were condemned not because they relentlessly pursued their false desires (*shahwa kaziba zalima*). Their sexuality was unnatural because it was oppressive and not because it involved anal penetration. They were (heterosexual or homosexual) sexually approaching other men in the absence of feelings of love, mercy, comfort, and commitment. They were satisfying a false desire at the expense of their own soul and the expense of the person whom they were exploiting or raping.

The verb *ta'tuna* (you approach, come to), used in Lot's question, is also used in Mary 19:92, 94:

> And it does not befit the Most Compassionate One to betake a son. Verily all in the heavens and the earth *come to* (*aati*) the Most Compassionate as His worshipers/ servants. He surrounds them all and keeps a count of them all. And all of them will come to (*aati*) Him on the Day of Resurrection as individuals. Verily those who have faith and do good deeds the Most Compassionate One will make love for them.[26]

The Most Compassionate One stands in the same relationship with all creatures in the heavens and the earth. Since all come to worship the Creator, all must come to or approach each other as co-worshipers. This primary relationship is the overarching one under which all other human

---

26. Mary 19:92–96.

relationships are subsumed, including the one between spouses. As co-worshipers, having faith and doing good is the overarching injunction under which all our intentions and actions are subsumed, including those related to making love. What matters is not biology but ethics.

If vaginal heterosexual intercourse were permissible only because it led to impregnation, then it would eliminate the need for vaginal intercourse ninety-nine out of a hundred times that it is engaged in. Vaginal intercourse may lead to conception, but the intention must always be mutual pleasure as insemination can be achieved without penetration. It is not vaginal or anal intercourse but mutual consent, desire, gentleness, and permitting one's body to express one's love, to please and be pleased, that fulfill what the Quran ordains between lovers. It is entirely unnatural and counter-intuitive to reduce sexual expression between lovers to vaginal heterosexual intercourse. Intercourse is merely one moment in a stream of moments of intimacy — born out of the indwelling of souls together (*li tuskunu ilaiha*), which expresses itself in various ways during the day and the night. The essence is the indwelling of the souls together; it is a sign of God's creative genius. That one derives spiritual pleasure and emotional solace through physical contact indicates that the body and soul are coterminous as long as the breath circulates through the nostrils.

In Islamic jurisprudence, the critical distinction between approaching a spouse with or without the feelings of love (*muwaddah*) and compassion (*rahma*) that would make intercourse permissible or prohibited is replaced by a distinction between heterosexual and homosexual intercourse to the great defeat of love and mercy in heterosexual marriages and the oppression of sexual minorities. By making all heterosexual (vaginal) intercourse within marriage lawful and all homosexual (anal) intercourse unlawful, the issue has been displaced from how one approaches one's spouse to the gender of one's spouse or an anatomical location. The obsession with the prohibition of anal intercourse on the part of those who presumably have no experiential context for it belies a refusal to take responsibility for the quality of the heterosexual intercourse that is engaged in. Water flows from a higher to a lower surface, but love flows between equals. In a male-dominated and gender-stratified world where the common experience of women in heterosexual relations is one of discrimination, exploitation, humiliation, abuse, and violence, love finds it much easier to flow between two women than between a woman and a man. In such a world love between two women may more closely approximate the Quranic sexual ethics than heterosexual relations. And heterosexual relations might be more vulnerable to the sin of *liwat* than Ṣamadiyyah relations. This becomes clear to us when we attend to the content of a relationship.

The Exterior (ẓahir) and Interior (batin) of a Relationship

He is the First and the Last, and the Outward (*az-Ẓahir*) and the Inward (*al-Batin*); and He is Knower of all things.[27]

Like *ṣamad*, *batin* and *ẓahir* (inner or hidden, and outer or apparent) are among the beautiful names or qualities of Allah. All entities, including relationships, participate in both these attributes. The inner qualities (*batin*) that inform an erotic relationship, according to the natural ethics (*fitra*) of sexual relations, include love, mercy, comfort, emotional safety, and commitment (*muwaddah, rahmah, sukun, libas*). The consent of both parties in the form of a *nikah* (a written or verbal contract in front of at least two witnesses) and its continuous public acknowledgment is the *ẓahir* (manifest or outer form) of an erotic relationship. The *ẓahir* of a relationship is as important as its *batin*. One without the other is unsatisfactory and unsustainable, even when lovers living in the moment of the truth of their love may not find the *ẓahir* necessary. The *ẓahir*, a public commitment, provides an organic and supportive form for the *batin*, the content of their love. It provides the social and communal support without which a relationship cannot develop or last. *Nikah* is as much a public commitment on the part of the couple toward each other as it is a commitment of the community toward the couple. It is an acknowledgment that the uniqueness of their love for each other is woven together with infinite other unique loving and committed relationships to form the fabric of the community. *Nikah* is "public ownership" of the relationship; that is, the couple acknowledges the relationship publicly, and the community owns it and supports it. The

---

27. al-Hadeed (The Iron) 57:3.

bodies of the lovers, their *ẓahir*, make it possible for their *batin* to merge. Their *nikah*, the *ẓahir* of their relationship, makes it possible for the *batin* of their relationship to fold into the *batin* of the *ummah*.

The relationship of Ratna and Saima had a *batin* and a *ẓahir*. They cared for each other, and their relationship was acknowledged and supported by their friends. They provided a *hisn*, a protected, safe, and loving space for each other, that is the intention of *nikah*. However, Shariah law and thus the wider Muslim community did not recognize or support their relation-ship. The love engendered in their relationship could not pour into the solidarity that nurtures the roots of the *ummah* and gives it life. Neither could the *ummah* support their relationship.

A Ṣamadiyyah Shariah

Shariah is the Divine Will for our actions. *Fiqh* is the human understanding of the Divine Will, that is, human understanding of Shariah. However, in general the distinction between Shariah and *fiqh* is collapsed, and the term *Shariah* is used for both. *Fiqh* is a product of Muslim juristic thinking that does not transcend its times. It is only divine in its intention to understand and do the Will of God to please God. Shariah stands for Muslim com-munities' commitment, based in faith, to govern individual and collective lives by ethical principles and laws. Islamic law provides guidelines for our inborn ethical nature (*fitra*). It represents the best thinking and under-standing of the *ummah* at a given point and must change with changing circumstances and with our individual and communal ethical evolution. For Muslims interested in integrating their theology, ethics, and practice, it is imperative to develop a framework for Islamic law (*usul ul fiqh*) that is based in the ethical principles of the Quran. The above discussion was such an attempt at extrapolating the Quranic ethics of sexual relations.

Historically, laws governing the early Muslim empire preceded legal theory (*usul ul fiqh*). Early Islamic legal theorists (*fuqaha*) focused on super-imposing a legal framework on existing legislation, which would provide a theological justification for legal practice and limit further legislative activity by providing a framework based on (1) authoritative sources (the

Quran and hadith) and (2) methodological principles (*qiyas, ijma', ijtihad,* and *maslaha,* and other secondary principles). The lack of foundational ethical principles in the classical framework remains a fatal deficiency in Islamic legal theory. It has led to legislation completely at odds with the overall theological vision and ethical imperative of the Quran. Foundational principles of *rahma* (compassion), *'adl* (justice, equity), and *ihsan* (benevolence, kindness), of central importance in the Quran, must inform and complete the Islamic jurisprudential framework of sources and methodology:

> He wrote compassion upon Himself.[28]

God bound himself by the law of compassion (*rahma*) and bound humans by the laws of justice (*'adl*) and kindness (*ihsan*):

> Surely Allah commands *'adl* (justice) and *ihsan* (kindness) and giving to the kinsfolk, and He forbids indecency and evil and rebellion; He admonishes you that you may be mindful.[29]

These guiding principles, which are called upon several times a day to negotiate the small and large challenges that life presents us with, determine how the Quran and the Sunnah of the Prophet may be interpreted to arrive at law. No Shariah laws may be proposed that are seen to be contrary to these principles. Following the example of the *mujadila,* the one who argued with the Prophet and was vindicated, when observant and informed Muslims raise a concern regarding lack of *'adl, ihsan,* or *rahma* in a law, then such a law must be reviewed and reformed. In the case of laws governing sexual ethics, in addition to the observance of the general conditions of *'adl, ihsan,* and *rahma,* the Quranic values of *muwaddah* (love), *sukun* (repose, tranquility), and *libas* (intimacy, commitment, complementarity) must be served.

The metaphor used in the Quran to describe the relationship that ties humanity and especially the *ummah* together is a filial one.[30] All members

---

28. al-An'am (The Cattle) 6:12, 6:54.
29. an-Nahl (The Honey Bee) 16:90.
30. Quran 4:1.

are brothers and sisters expected to share filial love and responsibility, including the incest taboo. I have heard traditional Muslim men say that a woman of an older generation is a mother, one of the same generation is a sister, and one of the younger generation is a daughter. This is also expressed in how people, especially strangers whose names are unknown to one, are addressed. The incest taboo among close blood relatives, the primary incest taboo, can never be lifted, but the incest taboo among members of the *ummah*, the secondary incest taboo, may be lifted through a *nikah* agreement. The strict modesty code of dress, gaze, and gait ensures that this incest taboo is respected. The modesty code is more relaxed among blood relatives and among members of the same sex between whom *nikah* is not permitted. Thus, it is commonly observed by outsiders that Muslim cultures are homosocial cultures where same-sex friendships enjoy longevity, depth, commitment, and passion. The hesitation of the *ummah* to allow for same-sex *nikah* must also arise from having to rethink gender segregation (which remains an important pillar of Muslim social life). Marriage (*zawaj*), divorce (*talaq*), and adultery and fornication (*zina*) are distinctions that attempt to assist members of the *ummah* in their efforts to fulfill their true desires, to abstain from pursuing false desires, and to establish right sexual relations.

Sexual Relations on the Scale of Values

A Muslim is held accountable for his or her action by the awareness of God, by *taqwa*. Each action must be deliberated upon and its ethical value assessed before it is undertaken. For the determination of the ethical value of an action or thought, a fivefold scale was developed by classical jurists. The scale ranges from (a) obligatory (*fard*) to (b) recommended (*mustaḥsan*) to (c) permissible (*mubah*) to (d) frowned upon (*makruh*) to (e) prohibited (*haram*). Any action or thought can be placed within one of the five categories. In placing an action or thought on this scale of value, the following operative principles are observed: (1) the value of an action depends on the intention behind the action, and (2) the value of an action changes depending upon the context. Thus, eating pork, generally prohibited, becomes permissible when no other food is

available for survival. The use of alcohol, generally prohibited because
it tampers with the rationality and mindfulness necessary for holding a
person responsible for his or her actions, is permissible as an ingredient in
medicines.

The Quranic term *zauj* (spouse, partner, group) is general, not specific
to gender. Marriage (*zawaj*), a committed relationship, is the opposite of
sifah, lust or lechery. While both have in common the urge to satisfy a
sexual desire, they are set apart by the presence or absence of commitment to the welfare of self and other based in the natural ethics of sexual
relations. Marriage is entered upon formally through a *nikah,* an agreement that provides a safe and protected space (*hisn*)[31] for our desire to
love and be loved[32] and within which the inborn yearning for relatedness
(love, mercy, consolation, and security) is nurtured and protected. *Hisn* is
an evolved form of *libas*, as a tent is an evolved form of a cloak. Lovers
who come under one cloak or become each other's cloak then build a
tent of commitment around their relationship. This is *hisn.* According to
the tradition, *nikah* can only be contracted between a man and a woman.
It assumes that all homosexual relations are unnatural, that is, against *fitra* and thus prohibited. However, the above discussion of Quranic verses
presents an inclusive vision of mateship (*zawaj*) and an understanding of
fitra that relate them to ethical living and not gender identity or sexual
orientation. Therefore the conditions governing the *nikah* agreement must
now be revised to make it inclusive of all couples, regardless of their gender
composition and sexual orientation. The conditions for *nikah* agreements
must be revised to include Ṣamadiyyah couples.

In Shariah discussions of *nikah*, a good match (*kifaa*) between the
spouses is generally measured in terms of social status, family reputation,
and lineage. While markers of social status may be relevant to an extent,
the determination of a good match ought to refer primarily to parity in the
ability to love, to show mercy, to comfort another, and to complement his

---

31. Literally, "fortress."
32. Quran 4:24–25; 5:5.

or her shortcomings that comes with the depth of humanity that a person is able to achieve. This parity is difficult to gauge by external means, but the history of relationships in the families of origin of the prospective spouses may provide an indicator. It is in this context that family histories and the involvement of the respective families in the *nikah* process may be useful. *Kifaa* (a good match) requires monogamy. When the two spouses are well matched, a sense of equilibrium prevails and a naturally monogamous relationship ensues. Monogamy is a precondition for *kifaa*, as one man cannot by definition be a good match to more than one woman at the same time. The Prophet's Meccan marriage initiated by the older widow Khadija exemplifies this well-matched, naturally monogamous marriage, which lasted till her death and remained the ideal for the Prophet. It spanned at least twenty-five years of a harmonious partnership. None of his later marriages could ever approximate his marriage with Khadija.

Temporary marriage, *muta'*, is considered permissible in the Ja'afiri school (followed by the majority sect among the Shi'a), but it is prohibited by all the Sunni schools.[33] Temporary marriage does not express the intention of *hisn* (protecting the fortress of a committed relationship) and the values of love, mercy, and solace that *hisn* intends to protect. It is mutual consent without any emotional or social commitment. It is a safety valve that saves one from *zina* (violation of the incest taboo) when one is in the grip of a strong sexual desire. A middle ground between the two positions would be to argue that *muta'* between two consenting unmarried adults, like abortion in the first trimester only, is not *haram* (prohibited) but *makruh* (discouraged, inadvisable). Under certain circumstances it is preferable to the other alternatives that an individual may be inclined to follow.

Polygyny is serial *muta'* (temporary marriage). Each time the husband of a woman in a polygynous marriage visits his other wife (or wives), the intimacy and the emotional and spiritual commitment of her marriage is severed. The *hisn* (protecting fortress) for her soul dissolves. Then another

---

33. Each side supports its argument for or against *muta'* by citing an-Nisa (The Women) 4:24.

temporary agreement of the soul is contracted when the husband revisits her. Polygyny, considered permissible (*mubah*) under all schools of Islamic law, ought to be reevaluated as *haram*. It does not measure up either to *'adl* or to *ihsan*, let alone to *muwaddah* or *rahma*. In certain unusual or extenuating contexts it may not be prohibited but *makruh* (discouraged). Under such circumstances the permission of the existing spouse(s) must be made a precondition to contracting another *nikah*. The crucial factor that saves multiple marriages from becoming *zulm* (oppressive) is the consent of all spouses.[34] Every party involved in a non-monogamous *nikah* has the complete freedom to refuse to enter such a situation, the complete freedom to leave it if it is not satisfactory, and the assurance that all relations are equal in terms of commitment, social recognition, and the distribution of time and resources. These conditions keep this problematic conglomerate from becoming oppressive or entirely unjust and lend it a degree of coherence and integrity. These three conditions also distinguish it from patriarchy, which imposes the rule of the father and the possession of women against their will. When there is a circumstance that overrules the prohibition on polygamy, the question arises as to whether only one or both spouses can have multiple partners simultaneously. In the case when both partners take multiple spouses, the complexity of the situation increases exponentially, and there seems very little hope that such a situation would be satisfactory for any party or last for very long. But as long as the conditions of integrity, consent, public ownership, and commitment are maintained equally for each of the relationships and all the relationships, such marriages may be admissible under exceptional circumstances.

One such exceptional circumstance is when Ṣamadiyyah in a monogamous marriage wish to reproduce. In such a case they may enter into a second (nonsexual) *nikah* and parenting agreement with a person of

---

34. Under Islamic law a wife cannot prevent her husband from marrying a second time, but she can choose to dissolve her own marriage. However, in Pakistan a man is required by law to obtain the permission of his first wife before he is allowed to take a second wife. Islamists have protested that this law curbs the God-given right of a man.

the other sex (solely) for the sake of procreation (through artificial insemination). Both parties would share the joys and responsibilities that parenthood entails. Their respective same-sex partners would have the option of entering into a parenting agreement if they chose to do so. This would safeguard the right of the child to know and be raised by both of his or her biological parents.

One can argue that the last ten years of our Prophet's life, his Medinan years, were exceptionally challenging and showed extenuating circumstances. The Prophet's Medinan marriages exemplify a state that is non-monogamous, unstable, and conflict ridden, as is documented in the Quran itself. Our Prophet's cousin Zaynnab preferred to be a co-wife of the Prophet rather than the only wife of his adopted son.[35] His other wives refused to accept an offer of a simultaneous divorce when he was not able to meet their joint demand for a materially comfortable life.[36] That the Prophet deterred his son-in-law Ali from marrying more wives while he was married to his daughter Fatima indicates that he considered monogamy the norm and polygyny inadvisable.[37] The ethical awareness of the *ummah* has reached a level at which, like slavery and sexual access to slave women, polygyny too ought to become a chapter of the past.

Zina (fornication and adultery) has been understood to refer to entering into sexual relations outside of *nikah*. Rape is subsumed under *zina* and is

---

35. And when you said to him to whom Allah had shown favor and to whom you had shown a favor: Keep your wife to yourself and be careful of (your duty to) Allah; and you concealed in your soul what Allah would bring to light, and you feared men, and Allah had a greater right that you should fear Him. So when Zeyd had performed that necessary formality (of divorce) from her, We gave her to you as a wife, so that there should be no difficulty for the believers in respect of the wives of their adopted sons, when the latter have performed the necessary formality (of divorce); and Allah's command shall be performed (al-Ahzab [The Allied Clans] 33:37).

36. O Prophet! say to your wives: If you desire this world's life and its adornment, then come, I will give you a provision and release you in a fair manner (al-Ahzab [The Allied Clans] 33:28).

37. "I heard the Messenger of God May Allah's blessings be upon him say, and he was standing in the pulpit, 'The Bani Hisham ibn Mughirah have asked my permission to marry their daughter to Ali ibn Talib. I do not give permission, again I do not give permission, again I do not give permission except if Ibn Abi Talib wants to divorce my daughter and marry their daughter. For she is a part of me, what hurts her hurts me'" (*Book of Nikah*, Sahih al-Bukhari, Darus Salaam, Riyadh, no. 5230 [1999], p. 934).

considered *zina bil jabr* (zina by force). One may speculate that the term *zina* is derived from or related to the Hebrew word *zonah* (prostitute). Hind's remark at the time of the conquest of Mecca when women took an oath that included abstention from *zina,* "Does a free woman commit *zina?*" implies that what *zina* may have meant to the first generation of Muslims might be quite different from what it has come to mean to later generations.[38] *Zina* may have referred to forms of "marriages" that were outlawed by Islam.[39] Given that women today are at least as free as in pre-Islamic Mecca of the sixth and seventh centuries and that they have made significant gains toward a gender-equitable society, there is a need to rethink the category of *zina* so that it may resonate with our contemporary sense of unethical (sexual) behavior and remain a plausible interpretation of the Quranic concept of *zina:*

And come not near *zina.* Surely it is shameful and an evil way.[40]

The woman and the man guilty of *zina* — flog each of them with a hundred stripes: Let not compassion move you in their case, in a matter prescribed by Allah, if you believe in Allah and the Last Day: and let a party of the Believers witness their punishment. A

---

38. Leila Ahmed, *Women and Gender in Islam* (New Haven, CT: Yale University Press, 1992), 58.

39. "What zina meant before the advent of Islam — in a society in which several types of union were legitimate — is not clear, nor apparently was it always clear to the converts to Islam. After being conquered by Muhammad, the men of Taif complained in taking the oath that zina was necessary to them because they were merchants — in other words they attached no stigma to the practice. One woman taking the oath said, 'Does a free woman commit zina?' a response construed to mean that she felt that any union that a free woman entered into could not be termed zina. When first used in Islam, therefore the term may have referred to other types of marriage, including polyandrous ones, and to forms of 'temporary' marriage, also practiced in the Jahilia, which Islam would outlaw.... If, in prohibiting zina, Islam was to some degree outlawing previously accepted practices, this perhaps would account in part for the otherwise surely extraordinary Quranic ruling (Sura 4:19) that four witnesses are required to convict anyone of zina. The ruling suggests both that those engaging in such sexual mis-conduct were doing so with some openness — the openness appropriate to relatively accepted rather than immoral or prohibited practices — and that Muhammad realized such practices could not be instantly eradicated" (ibid., 44–45).

40. al-Isra (The Night Journey) 17:32.

man guilty of *zina* [a *zani*] shall not marry save a woman similarly guilty of *zina* [a *zania*] or an unbeliever: and a *zania* shall only be married to a *zani* or an unbeliever. To the Believers such a thing is forbidden.[41]

Zina is sexual misconduct. One who engages in sexual misconduct to the extent that he or she earns the description of a *zani* or a *zania* is to be punished publicly. The prohibition for a *zani* or a *zania* to marry anyone except another *zani* or *zania* indicates that persistent sexual misconduct destroys the faith and character of a person. However, for those who fall into it briefly and without intention and repent soon after the transgression, their repentance is accepted, and they are not accorded the title of *zani* or *zania,* as can be understood from the following verses:

And the servants of the Most Merciful are they who walk on the earth in humility, and when the ignorant address them, they say: Peace. And they spend the night prostrating themselves before their Lord and standing. They say, "Our Lord! Avert from us the Wrath of Hell, for its Wrath is indeed a grievous-affliction. And when they spend, they are not extravagant and not niggardly, but hold a balance between the two. They invoke not, with Allah, any other god, nor slay life which Allah has made sacred except in the requirement of justice, *nor commit zina;* — and any that does this meets his punishment. (But) the Penalty on the Day of Judgment will be doubled to him, and he shall dwell therein in abasement, — *Unless he repents, believes, and does good, for Allah will change the evil of such persons into good, and Allah is Oft-Forgiving, Most Merciful, and whoever repents and does good has truly turned to Allah with an (acceptable) repentance.* And they do not bear false witness, and if they pass by futility, they pass by it with dignity. When they are admonished with the Signs of their Lord, they do not turn away as if they were deaf or blind.

---

41. an-Nur (The Light) 24:2–3.

And they say, *"Our Lord! Grant us spouses and offspring who will be the comfort of our eyes, and give us (the grace) to lead the righteous."*[42]

In the most general sense *zina* stands for the breaking of the universal incest taboo (that binds together the human family) without the ritual of *nikah*. The incest taboo is a meta-symbol for the prohibition against all forms of sexual violation. The incest taboo seeks to provide a safe and loving space for children to grow up in. It prohibits parents and siblings from sexual access to the most vulnerable and completely dependent (minors) in the family. It implies that sexual violations cut deeper into our self than a violation of our property or other kinds of injuries to our body. The requirement of witnesses to *nikah* and the mention of the names of the parents of the two parties safeguard against the unintentional breaking of the incest taboo.

Zina refers to sexual relations not accompanied by love, mercy, public ownership, and commitment. Such sexual encounters do not lead to relationships that are a solace in an individual's life and are a serious breach of Quranic sexual ethics. Sexual relations not initiated by *nikah* may be divided into two kinds of *zina*: *zina bil ikhtiyar* between two consenting adults and *zina zalima*, exploitative, oppressive, or unfair sexual conduct. *Zina bil ikhtiyar* between two consenting adults, when kept hidden to the extent that no third person knows of it as a good aspect of the two individuals' lives, is *haram* (prohibited). However, when a few persons of good character know of the couple's relationship as one based on care and companionship, it is no longer *haram*, as the partners have included witnesses to their liaison. An ethical sexual relationship to which some individuals of good character are witness is not *zina* even when no formal written or public commitment has been made between the couple. Such a relationship must be evaluated on the basis of the general Quranic ethics of *'adl* and *ihsan* and the particular ethics of *muwaddah*, *rahma*, and *sukun*. It may then be evaluated to be similar to *muta'*, polygamy, or *nikah* and be considered under the appropriate category. If a sexual liaison is given no public acknowledgment and is entirely secret, then it would seem that it is

---

42. al-Furqan (The Criterion) 25:68.

motivated not merely by a hesitation to make a (long-term) commitment, but by the desire to keep secret an abusive or exploitative aspect of the relationship, one which violates *'adl* and *ihsan* either with regard to one of the parties or a third party affected by the liaison. It would be *zina zalima*, a liaison that satisfies a *shahwa kaziba zalima* (false, oppressive desire) and would be considered *haram* (prohibited). Obviously all non-consensual sexual activity, including assault and rape, would be evaluated as *zina bil jabr*, thus *haram* and punishable under law.

In the light of Quranic (sexual) ethics, the *zina* mentioned in the Quran must be read as *zina zalima*, one motivated by *shahwa kaziba zalima*. *Zina zalima* is a violation of the incest taboo and is essentially different from *zina bil ikhtiyar*. Classical Islamic law distinguishes between *zina* (adultery or fornication) and *zina bil jabr* (rape). However, it subsumes *zina bil jabr* as a subcategory under *zina*. This grave error in judgment and the requirement of four male witnesses in establishing *zina* has had the consequence that the perpetuators of *zina bil jabr* are never brought to justice and the women victims of *zina bil jabr* are victimized a second time by having to prove themselves innocent of *zina*. *Zina zalima*, especially *zina bil jabr*, must be considered a punishable crime as indicated by the hundred lashes prescribed by the Quran for it. *Zina bil jabr*, a grave transgression, cannot be punished by *rajam* (stoning to death). Capital punishment for *zina* is not prescribed by the Quran. Nor does the Quran prescribe *rajam* as a punishment. In the Quran *rajam* is mentioned as a threat given to prophets by those who opposed and persecuted them.[43] Just like eating human flesh, stoning a human or even an animal to death is an extremely cruel and unacceptable behavior and has grave repercussions for the spiritual health of a community that even in theory supports such behavior. It is unimaginable that a God who binds Himself to Compassion and His creatures

---

43. Prophet Shuaib is threatened with *rajam* (Hud 11:91). Abraham is threatened with *rajam* (Mary 19:46). Three unnamed prophets are threatened with *rajam* (YaSin 36:18). Moses seeks refuge in God from being stoned to death by Pharaoh (ad-Dukhan [The Smoke] 44:20). The companions who hid in a cave because they were being persecuted for their faith caution each other that if the truth about their faith is disclosed they will be stoned to death (al-Kahaf [The Cave] 18:20).

to ʿ*adl* and *iḥsan* would enjoin the practice of *rajam*. Like polygyny and sexual access to slave women, *rajam* must also be stricken off Muslim law books.[44]

When two people tied together in the knot of *nikah* realize that the *batin* (the emotive and spiritual qualities of their relationship) have irretrievably disappeared, then it is best that they acknowledge this publicly by obtaining a *talaq* divorce. *Talaq*, after which a chapter of the Quran is named, is as permissible as is *nikah*. What is not permissible is to remain in *nikah* when one is not able to love and comfort one's spouse. *Talaq* is a return from the erotic to the wider filial bond where the secondary incest taboo is restored between former spouses.

With Difficulty There Is Ease (inna ma'al usri yusra)[45]

As stated at the beginning, the intention of this essay is to bring ease in the lives of the Muslim sexual minorities that suffer from self-alienation or alienation from the *ummah* due to their sexual orientation. The sincerity (*ikhlas*) that Ṣamadiyyah bring to their faith creates an inner ease in their lives despite the social challenges that their sexual orientation presents. This in itself is a manifestation of Divine Grace.

---

44. The hadith that is quoted to justify the inclusion of this punishment in the books of Shariah is questionable on many counts. This subject deserves a detailed examination that is not possible here. John Burton traces the legal fiction that there was a Quranic verse that prescribed *rajam* for *zina* which was eaten by the Prophet's favorite and youngest Medinan wife's (Ayesha's) goat and was thus lost. Since Ayesha was accused of adultery and then exonerated by the Quran itself, there may be some symbolic significance here worthy of further reflection (see John Burton, *The Collection of the Quran* [Cambridge: Cambridge University Press, 1977]).

45. Quran 94:5–6.

Chapter Four

Gender and Same-Sex Relations in Confucianism and Taoism

ANN-MARIE HSIUNG

Heterosexism, the oppression of people who do not conform to the dominant norm, prevails in the modern world, but one can question whether it holds true universally. This chapter examines the notions of gender, sexuality, and family in Confucianism and Taoism, as well as practices in traditional Chinese society. While a heterosexist reading of Confucian and Taoist texts may seem to support homophobia, there is no real evidence of homophobia in Confucian and Taoist traditions. In fact, they take no offense toward and at times even encourage same-sex relations.

It is true that contemporary Chinese *tongzhi* or comrades, referring to gay men, lesbians, and bisexuals,[1] experience discrimination as a result of the devaluing of same-sex eroticism. What's more, many assume that traditional Chinese culture is anti-gay, and they regard homosexuality and bisexuality as unwelcome Western imports.[2] However, I argue that there is a cultural break between modernity and a more tolerant past.[3]

---

1. *Tong* literally means "same/homo," while *zhi* means "will, aspiration, or ideal." *Tongzhi* is most commonly used in contemporary China, Taiwan, and Hong Kong. Chou Wah-shan has argued for the usage of *tongzhi* and the need "to build up indigenous *tongzhi* politics that need not reproduce the Anglo-American experiences and strategies of lesbigay liberation." See Chou Wah-shan, *Tongzhi: Politics of Same-Sex Eroticism in Chinese Societies* (New York: The Haworth Press, 2000), 1–4.

2. Ibid., 42.

3. Ibid. See also Bret Hinsch, *Passions of the Cut Sleeve: The Male Homosexual Tradition in China* (Berkeley and Los Angeles: University of California Press, 1990), 167; Stephen Likosky, *Coming Out* (New York: Pantheon, 1994), 24.

Only in the twentieth century did Western hegemony penetrate East Asia and Southeast Asia. Ironically, the so-called Western countries exported homophobia but now claim to be a haven for homo/bisexuality. Contemporary *tongzhi* turn to Western models for resources without realizing the rich insights that can be drawn from their own traditions. In order to bridge the gap between Chinese traditions and the modern world and, more importantly, to offer resources to *tongzhi* for their struggles for safety and well-being, we need to examine critically the gender system in Confucianism and Taoism that appears to support homophobia and consider how these traditions may offer resources to counter sexual oppression.

Chinese Gender System

Contrary to the dualisms of man/woman, masculinity/femininity, and homosexuality/heterosexuality familiar in Western gender culture, Chinese gender culture is marked by yin/yang polarity and androgyny. While yin is responsive or feminine and yang is activating or masculine, the interdependent and correlative interaction of yin and yang forms the foundation of Chinese cosmology in which Confucianism and Taoism are based. Androgyny is shown in the well-known circle of the yin-yang symbol in which the dark half of yin has a yang embryo and the white half of yang has yin. This symbol can also be seen as a double-fish circle[4] with the shapes of two fish (yin and yang) embracing each other. Yin and yang, now figured as two curved fish in which the yin fish has a yang eye and the yang fish a yin eye, swim toward each other and penetrate each other without fixed boundaries. This yin-yang configuration represents the Chinese gender system in terms of a dynamic equilibrium.

Because of this fluidity, the Chinese gender system defies exclusiveness or essentialism. A woman is predominantly yin while a man is predominantly yang, but every person is a combination of both yin and yang.

---

4. For the usage of the double-fish circle and its diagram, see Liu Xiaogan, "A Taoist Perspective: Appreciating and Applying the Principle of Femininity," in *What Men Owe to Women: Men's Voices from World Religions*, ed. John C. Raines and Daniel C. Maguire (Albany: State University of New York Press, 2001), 246.

Yin and yang, while considered to underlie all the events and phenomena in the universe, do not "produce" anatomical women and men; rather, they produce "relational subjectivities named mother and father, husband and wife, brother and sister, and so on."[5] Accordingly, the principal relations among the five cardinal human relationships[6] in the Confucian world display a cosmic order in which yin is placed below yang: yin/wife and yang/husband, yin/son and yang/father, yin/subject and yang/ruler. Yin and yang, though interdependent, are also without doubt ordered hierarchically in the Confucian social-familial system. Yang subordinates yin as it encloses the lesser force in itself.

Confucius regards men and women more in terms of their familial and social roles than their anatomical sex. In premodern China, one's identity was based on a family kinship system rather than on the gender of one's erotic object of choice.[7] People were not classified by sexual orientation, and the terms *homosexual, heterosexual,* and *bisexual* were not known even though I use them in this chapter as adjectives to differentiate practices.[8] Similarly, since everyone has, first and foremost, a familial-societal role to play in Confucian society, there is no evidence of an independent or autonomous gay, lesbian, or bi-sexual identity as in modern Western cultures. As Chou Wah-shan argues, "Gender is seen through the lens of class and social roles rather than any essential abstract traits such as appearance or the body."[9]

The late-sixteenth-century Chinese physician Li Shichen recognized the instability of the bodies he recorded as non-male (*feinan*) and non-

5. Tani E. Barlow, "Theorizing Woman: Funü, Guojia, Jiating (Chinese Woman, Chinese State, Chinese Family)," in *Body, Subject and Power in China*, ed. Angela Zito and Tani E. Barlow (Chicago: University of Chicago Press, 1994), 258.

6. The five basic human relations in Confucian world are father-son, husband-wife, ruler-subject, elder brother–younger brother, and friend-friend.

7. For more detailed elaboration, see Chou Wah-Shan, "Homosexuality and the Cultural Politics of *Tongzhi* in Chinese Societies," in *Gay and Lesbian Asia: Culture, Identity, Community*, ed. Gerard Sullivan and Peter A. Jackson (New York: Harrington Park Press, 2001), 29.

8. I try to use *homosexual* and *heterosexual* with caution in premodern context, for, as Sommer puts it, "their literal meanings of 'same-sex' and 'different-sex,' and to characterize practices of relationships only." See Mathew Sommer, *Sex, Law and Society in Late Imperial China* (Stanford, CA: Stanford University Press, 2000), 353–54n.6.

9. Chou, *Tongzhi*, 20.

female (*feinu*) who could not become biological fathers or mothers because of bodily defects.[10] It seems clear to this physician that there is no stable gender, nor does gender come automatically. Gender is culturally made, not naturally formed. Tani E. Barlow thus states, "What appear as 'gender' are yin/yang differentiated positions: not two anatomical 'sexes,' but a profusion of relational, bound, unequal dyads, each signifying difference and positioning difference analogically.... A *xiaozi*, or filial son, is differentially unequal to mother and father, yin to their yang."[11]

Gender relations in Confucian discourse are not structured in a fixed male-female binary, but rather are interwoven in hierarchical kinship, generation, class, and age patterns. A subject is yin to his emperor while yang to his wife. Similarly, a wife is yin to her husband while yang to her son or her husband's concubine. Yin and yang are relative. Sexual differentiation is subject to the momentary balance of the two forces.[12] Chinese medical discourse supports Confucian discourse on this, as Charlotte Furth points out: "In Chinese biological thinking, based as it was on yin-yang cosmological views, there was nothing fixed and immutable about male and female as aspects of yin and yang.... In medicine yin and yang permeate the body and pattern its functions, and here as elsewhere they are interdependent, mutually reinforcing and capable of turning into their opposites."[13] Such a natural philosophy could well lead to tolerance toward a wide range of sexual and gendered behavior.

Confucianism, though it is largely viewed as yang within Chinese philosophy because of its uplifting spirit, manifests its own yin-yang harmony and appreciation for androgyny. The ideal person (*junzi*) for Confucius is one who demonstrates qualities of being as stable and steady as a mountain and as fluid and flexible as water,[14] incorporating the masculine and the

---

10. Barlow, "Theorizing Woman," 258–59.
11. Ibid., 259.
12. See Charlotte Furth, "Androgynous Males and Deficient Females: Biology and Gender Boundaries in Sixteenth and Seventeenth Century China," *Late Imperial China* 9, no. 2 (1988): 3.
13. Ibid.
14. See *Lunyu* (*The Analects*) 6.21, in *Xinyi sishu duben* (*New Four Books Reader*), ed. Xie Bingyin, et al. (Taipei: Sanmin, 1987), 129.

feminine. Confucius terms his ideal ruler and ideal state as "father-mother official" (*fumu guan*) and "father-mother state" (*fumuzhibang*) respectively, combining masculine strength and feminine gentleness.[15]

Taoism, on the other hand, in representing yin in Chinese philosophy with its abundance of feminine principles, reveals unyielding strength in major passages. For instance, Lao Zi highly extols water: "Nothing in the world is as soft and weak as water, yet in corroding the firm and strong, there is nothing which can surpass it."[16] Such water imagery — the obstinate power (yang) is embedded in the soft and weak water (yin) — is androgynous.[17] In both Taoism and Confucianism, yin and yang are like the double-fish circle mentioned earlier, embracing each other and flowing toward each other. By and large, Chinese scholars aspire to embody both Confucian and Taoist traits, though they tend to be more Confucian at a younger age and Taoist at an older age. One may also note that the macho-masculinity so popular in Western culture is not prevalent in Chinese culture. Chinese men, especially scholars and literati in the premodern era, were characterized largely and favorably by femininity. Again, no fixed yin/yang pattern exists, at least theoretically, in Confucianism and Taoism. This fluidity opens up multiple possibilities for gender relations.

Heterosexual Relations Upheld in Confucianism and Taoism

There is broad tolerance for a variety of sexual relations in Chinese culture, and the modern homosexual/heterosexual binary cannot be found in

---

15. Ann-Marie Hsiung, "The Construction of Women in Traditional Chinese Culture: A Review of the Early Classics and Historical Conduct Books," *Nantah Journal of Chinese Language and Culture* 2, no. 1 (1997): 170–71.

16. *Laozi* 78, trans. Rhett Y. W. Yong and Roger T. Ames, *Lao Tzu: Text, Notes, and Comments* (San Francisco: Chinese Materials, 1977), 303.

17. Roger T. Ames is perhaps the first scholar who challenges Joseph Needham's view of Taoism as "feminine" in orientation. For detailed discussion and more examples regarding the androgynous qualities in *Laozi*, see his "Taoism and the Androgynous Ideal," in *Women in China: Current Directions in Historical Scholarship*, ed. Richard W. Guisso and Stanley Johannesen (New York: Edwin Mellen Press, 1981), 21–45.

traditional China. At the same time, heterosexual relations have special status in Confucianism and Taoism within a favored framework of family and reproduction, particularly in Confucianism. Family is upheld as the vital foundation of society and country in Confucian discourse. The first chapter of *The Great Learning* (*Daxue*), one of the crucial Confucian texts, highlights a gradual progression to world peace: "Cultivation of self results in an orderly family; an orderly family contributes to a well-managed state/country, which subsequently leads to the peace of the whole world."[18] Family is the cornerstone of the state, and family (*jiaqi*) is constituted by heterosexual marriage: harmonious/congenial relations between husband and wife, parents and children, the elders and the younger (the young respect the elders who, in turn, care for the young). This notion is further elaborated in *The Means* (*Zhongyong*), considered the essence of Confucianism, which quotes *The Book of Songs* (*Shijing*) to illustrate how the ideal of personhood (*junzi*) can be realized:

> Happy union with wife and children is like the music of lutes and harps. When brothers live in concord and at peace, the harmony is sweet and delightful. "Let your family live in concord, and enjoy your wife and children," Confucius says, "your parents will then be pleased!"[19]

A harmonious family is considered ideal and is celebrated as the desired outcome of heterosexual marriage. Confucianism thus supports heterosexual marital relations insofar as reproduction and the continuation of the family line are highly valued in the tradition. Moreover, among all the Confucian virtues, filial piety is deemed the highest. In *The Analects* (*Lunyu*), Confucius talks about filial piety in a number of passages, such as being respectful to one's parents and not traveling far without one's

---

18. *Daxue* (*The Great Learning*) 1, in *Xinyi sishu duben*, 1 (author's translation).

19. *Zhongyong* (*The Means*) 15, *Xinyi sishu duben*, 34. English translation is by Tu Wei-Ming except the last line (by author). See Tu Wei-Ming, *Centrality and Commonality: An Essay on Confucian Religiousness* (Albany: State University of New York Press, 1989), 30–31.

parents' knowledge. Those who please their parents are regarded most highly.[20]

To raise sons and daughters and make sure they marry and establish their own families is the greatest satisfaction of parents in traditional China. Mencius elaborates Confucius's notion of filial piety in this regard: "When a man is born his parents wish that he may one day find a wife, and when a woman is born they wish that she may find a husband. Every parent feels like this."[21] To fulfill parental expectations is the primary requirement of filial piety. Mencius goes a step further to illustrate the role of father and mother in terms of their guidance of their son and daughter:

> When a man comes of age his father gives him advice. When a girl marries, her mother gives her advice, and accompanies her to the door with these cautionary words, "when you go to your new home you must be respectful and circumspect. Do not disobey your husband." It is the way of a wife or concubine to consider obedience and docility the norm.[22]

The passage shows the expected gender roles assigned to men and women. Heterosexual marriage is clearly the embedded message here, with male authority in the Confucian tradition very much in evidence.

The strong endorsement of heterosexual relations might be viewed as homophobic, as reflected in two of Mencius's passages. Mencius remarks, "There are three ways of being unfilial, the worst among all is to be without heir (*buxiao yousan, wuhou weida*)." He mentions the wise king Shun, who marries without telling his parents, for fear of failing to produce an heir.[23] Chinese parents, in general, not only expect their adult children to marry, but they also anticipate their children having offspring in order to continue the family line. Confucianism has a strong sense of continuation in the context of a patrilineal family. To have male descendants to carry on

---

20. See, for instance, *Lunyu* (*The Analects*) 2.5–2.8 and 4.18–4.21, *Xinyi sishu duben*, 75–77 and 103–4.

21. *Mengzi* (*Mencius*) 3.2.3, *Xinyi sishu duben*, 440. This passage is translated by D. C. Lau, *Mencius* (Suffolk, UK: Penguin Books, 1970), 108.

22. Ibid., 3.2.2, *Xinyi sishu duben*, 437, Lau 107.

23. Ibid., 4.1.26, *Xinyi sishu duben*, 487. Adapted from Lau's translation; see Lau, 127.

the family name and to honor one's ancestors is considered primordially important in the Confucian tradition. Heterosexual marital relationships are, therefore, intertwined with the duty of filial piety and reproduction. Chinese typically cannot bear to be labeled unfilial, and this stigma places great emphasis on complying with the norm of heterosexual marriage. Mencius, in explaining why the sage king Shun married without informing his parents, openly supports the heterosexual marital relationship as the most important human relationship:

> He would not have been allowed to marry if he had told them. A man and woman living together is the most important of human relationships. If he had told his parents, he would have to put aside the most important of human relationships and this would result in bitterness against his parents. This is why he did not tell them.[24]

Informing one's parents before marriage is normally required as a gesture of filial piety in Confucian discourse, yet it can be skipped, knowing that "the most important human relationship" would thus be hindered and that would subsequently lead to tension with one's parents. Mencius's most quoted line — "*buxiao yousan, wuhou weida*" (among three unfilial deeds, without offspring is the worst) — has become a popular catchphrase within Chinese culture and may reinforce a bias against non-reproductive sexuality, including same-sex relationships.

Unlike Confucianism, Taoism does not have concrete or extensive writings about heterosexual human relations. Imagery in some passages, however, does indicate the importance of heterosexuality, as in the following Laozi statement: "Tao gives birth to One, One gives birth to Two, Two gives birth to Three, Three gives birth to all the myriad things. All the myriad things carry yin on their back and embrace yang in their front; through the blending/union of the two *qi* (yin and yang), the harmony is achieved."[25] This passage is subject to multiple interpretations. The

---

24. Ibid., 5.1.2, *Xinyi sishu duben*, 524. Lau, 139.
25. *Laozi* 42. The English translation is adapted from John C. H. Wu, trans., *Tao Teh Ching: Lao Tzu* (Boston: Shambhala, 1989), 87.

first half of the passage appears to be Taoist creation theory while the second half lays the foundation for the yin-yang theory in Taoism and other Chinese schools of thought, including Confucianism. The yin-yang notion displayed here corresponds to the yin-yang symbol and androgyny discussed earlier. The imagery presented by the whole passage could reinforce the imperative to reproduce and, therefore, the importance of heterosexual relations (yin and yang) for achieving harmony. Zhuangzi, like Laozi, does not talk much about concrete human relations or society in general, and yet in one of his less known passages, he highlights authenticity (*zhen*) and, in line with Confucianism, offers at least an implicit affirmation of heterosexual relations and reproduction: "When a man has the authenticity within himself, his spirit may move among external things.... It could be applied to human relationships: In the service of parents, it is love and filial piety.... What matters in serving parents is that you do please them."[26] The pattern of filial children serving their parents is clearly founded on heterosexual marriage. However, this affirmation does not require a heterosexist interpretation. To affirm heterosexual relations does not obligate one to disparage or devalue non-heterosexual relations.

The Taoist case most likely to spark homophobia can be found in one trend of religious Taoism, developed later from philosophical Taoism. It traces back to Laozi's ideal of yin-yang balance and interprets it as the need to balance the yin and yang energy through sexual intercourse between a man and a woman. Homosexual activity is disapproved of here because it could hinder one's health (physical harmony). A weakened yang is thought to lead to unhealthy offspring. R. H. Van Gulik explains the logic this way: "A man's semen is his most precious possession, the source not only of his health but of his very life; every emission of semen will diminish this vital force, unless compensated by the acquiring of an equivalent amount of

---

26. *Zhuangzi* 31 "*yufu*" (the old fish man). The English translation is mainly by the author and partly adapted from A. C. Graham, *Chuang-Tzu: The Inner Chapter* (London: Mandala, 1981, 1991), 252.

yin from the woman."[27] Obviously, this passage could give credence to a heterosexist bias.

Cultural Forces Working against Homophobia in Confucian and Taoist Discourse

Even though some texts could encourage homophobia, no concrete evidence of homophobia exists in traditional China. As Sandra A. Wawrytko notes: "Throughout Chinese history, Confucian morality tended toward austerity, representing the conservative forces of society. Yet in the various Confucian-tinged moral codes that developed throughout the centuries, homosexual activity is not singled out for special rebuke."[28] What, then, are the cultural forces that may counter or dissolve the development of homophobia? How do Confucianism and Taoism display tolerance toward relations deviating from the heterosexual norm? The earlier discussion of the Chinese gender system provides one answer. Others can be found in some of the social practices laid out by Confucianism and Taoism, as well as in the classical dictums of early Confucian and Taoist texts that have had a fundamental influence on Chinese culture.

First, the strict practice of sexual segregation in Confucian society opens space for same-sex relations. Men active in the public sphere tend to bond with other men while women confined to the private domain are likely to bond with other women. They often form "brotherhoods" or "sisterhoods," and references to homosexual or homoerotic relations are frequently found in reports of such bonding.[29] Moreover, because of the absence of a homosexual/heterosexual dichotomy in premodern China,

---

27. R. H. Van Gulik, *Sexual Life in Ancient China: A Preliminary Survey of Chinese Sex and Society from ca. 1500 B.C. till 1644 A.D.* (Leiden: E. J. Brill, 1974), 47.

28. Sandra A. Wawrytko, "Homosexuality and Chinese and Japanese Religions," in *Homosexuality and World Religions*, ed. Arlene Swidler (Valley Forge, PA: Trinity Press International, 1993), 205.

29. See, for instance, ibid., 202–3; Pan Guangdan, "Zhongguo wenxian zhong tongxing lian juli" (Examples of Homosexuality in Chinese Documents), in *Xing xinli xue (The Psychology of Sex)* (Beijing: Sanlian, 1987), 538; Song Geng, *The Fragile Scholar: Power and Masculinity in Chinese Culture* (Hong Kong: Hong Kong University Press, 2004), 139.

the affirmation of heterosexual relations would not lead logically, and did not lead historically, to the repression/oppression of the other. It is no offense to be homosexual as long as the primacy of family obligation and reproduction is not compromised. Marriage was based much more on societal and familial duty than on personal affection.

In the institution of marriage, husband and wife play assigned roles: the husband deals with the outside world in meeting other men or forming liaisons with courtesans. The wife manages household matters concerning her husband's concubines, if any, and maids and female relatives. It is rather common for married men, especially scholars, to form emotional and even sexual or erotic bonds with other men, as they also do with courtesans or good-looking young men of whom they are fond. As for married women, the private domain could be a haven for engaging in same-sex relations since Confucian society represented by men does not bother much about women's affairs as long as they dutifully perform their wifely roles in filial service to the in-laws and reproduction. Simply put, same-sex relations in traditional society were not viewed as sin. The sexual crimes subject to sanction were incest and adultery committed by married women,[30] because these acts threatened to damage the family structure and could result in unidentifiable offspring.

Furthermore, although Confucianism heavily stresses social order, hierarchical family relations, and heterosexual marriage to ensure the continuation of the family line, at the core of Confucianism is concern for human dignity and integrity, which could provide antidotes to the possible development of homophobia within traditional China. The key word that runs through all the early Confucian classics is *ren*,[31] a central concept

---

30. Wawrytko, "Homosexuality," 205–6; Brian E. McKnight, *The Quality of Mercy: Amnesties and Traditional Chinese Justice* (Honolulu: University of Hawaii Press, 1981), 60.

31. *Ren* occurs some 105 times in 58 of the 499 passages in *The Analects*. The Chinese character *ren* is formed by the characters of "two" and "person" signifying relation. Roger Ames argues this *ren* is the same term as "person," yet with graphic addition of the numeral "two" it has many implications, such as "qualitative achievement" and "the transformation of self." See David L. Hall and Roger T. Ames, *Thinking through Confucius* (Albany: State University of New York Press, 1987), 111, 115.

in Confucian philosophy often rendered as benevolence, kindness, love, compassion, human-heartedness, and humanity. Unlike the Christian emphasis on correct worship, the classic Confucian focus is on achieving humanity (*ren*), the core characteristic of Confucius's religiosity.[32] *Ren* denotes the qualitative transformation of the self and constant effort to become a better human being. The components of "two" and "person" in the Chinese character for *ren* do not signify a relationship between two identical persons; rather, they evoke a harmony between persons.[33] Confucius frequently remarks about *ren* in *The Analects*, including this well-known dictum: "Do not impose on others what you yourself do not desire." The relational self is marked by consideration and inclusiveness of others into one's self. Confucius views *ren* as a vital force behind all ritual action or laws, and it qualifies one for ritual performance: "What does one who has no *ren* have to do with ritual action or with music?" The human being has an active, participatory role in life, and it is not enough to follow the prescribed laws. The laws themselves have to be reviewed regularly based on *ren*. The teaching on *ren* shows that the persons are self-defining: "It is the human being who is able to extend the Way."[34] The self-transforming person can enlarge the existing order insofar as the historical past can be reshaped in light of new conditions. As Roger Ames argues, "For each unique person the way of achieving humanity is necessarily going to be different."[35]

Another unifying theme in Confucius's thinking, usually defined in terms of *ren*, is *shu*, rendered as consideration, reciprocity, or "placing oneself in another's place."[36] *Shu* is personal and is often paired with *zhong*, "doing one's best as one's authentic self."[37] They connect to *Zhongyong's* elaboration of *cheng* (sincerity), which entails *ren* as self-completing and

---

32. Ibid., 245.
33. Ibid., 287.
34. The above three quotes about *ren* are from *Lunyu* 12.2, 3.3, and 15.29. The English versions are adapted from Ames, *Thinking through Confucius*, 123, 245, and 115.
35. Ames, *Thinking through Confucius*, 115.
36. D. C. Lau's translation. Ibid., 50.
37. Ibid., 287.

zhi (to realize) as completing things/others.[38] Mencius's lines below provide the most comprehensive vision:

> All the ten thousand things are there in me. There is no greater joy for me than to find, on self-examination, that I am true to myself. Try your best to treat others as you would wish to be treated yourself, and you will find that this is the shortest way to [ren].[39]

If we extend Confucius's concern for personal dignity and well-being to a modern discourse of sexuality, it could be read in this way: one should be true to one's sexual orientation, which is part of one's authentic self, and if the existing laws appear oppressive, one should have a hand in changing them. In Confucian context, one's self-realization entails respect for others. One must therefore respect others' differences, including their sexual orientation. Confucius's *junzi*, a self-realized person who embodies *ren*, is at harmony with others and does not require others to be the same as oneself.[40] The insistence on sameness is oppressive and proceeds from an unhealthy insecurity.

I argue that if Confucius had had a modern understanding of sexual difference, he would have had compassion toward same-sex couples and may have even revised the norm of heterosexual marriage. The following lines from *The Analects* support my view: "I so detest inflexibility." "When faced with the opportunity to practice *ren*, do not give precedence even to your teacher." "*Junzi* is devoted to principle but not inflexible in small matters."[41] Confucius is not as immovable as many think. Instead, he dislikes inflexibility and is ready to disregard petty moral rules in order to honor higher principles. As "a sage of the time," Confucius also is one who appropriates the past in the context of the present. In other words, he makes constant efforts to improve and "renew" himself. Moreover, the

---

38. *Zhongyong* 25; see *Xinyi sishu duben*, 50.
39. *Mengzi* 7.1.3; English version, see Lau, 182.
40. *Lunyu* 13.23, *Xinyi sishu duben*, 218.
41. *Lunyu* 14.34 (32), 15.35 (36), 15.36 (37). The English versions are adapted from D. C. Lau, *Confucius: The Analects* (London: Penguin Books, 1979), 129, 137.

magnanimity of the Confucian vision, as expressed below, further upholds my argument and counters any tendency toward homophobia:

> Confucius transmits the ancient sage king Yao and Shun. . . . Just like heaven and earth, there is nothing they would not carry. . . . The myriad of things grow together without harming one another; the various Tao go together without violating each other. The lesser virtues flow continuously like river currents, and the grand virtues go silently and deeply in their mighty transformations. This is why the heaven and earth are great.[42]

Taoism is concerned with longevity or, as we may call it in modern terms, healthy living. The relation between sexuality and health is a primary concern of religious Taoism. For the dominant Taoist discourse, appropriate heterosexual intercourse may be the ideal way for men and women to achieve ultimate health due to the harmony attained by yin-yang balance. Therefore, homosexual relations seem to be discouraged. However, under the correlative Chinese gender system, same-sex couples may not be excluded from obtaining a similar health benefit of balance, even if not as effectively, as long as one of them increases his or her inner resource of yin or yang through nutritional adjustment or physical/mental cultivation. Master Mantak has summed up the situation this way:

> The Taoists are too wise to condemn anything outright, as everything leads back to Tao. So the question really is how can it be against nature, or the Tao, if the Tao created it? Homosexuality is not against the Tao, but it is also not the highest experience of the Tao possible. It's impossible to experience the full balance of male-female polarity with homosexual love. . . . The problem is greater for two men than for two women, because their double yang energy is too expansive and more easily leads to conflict. A double yin energy can be harmonious, as yin is yielding. . . . Both cases can lead to

---

42. *Zongyong* 30, *Xinyi sishu duben*, 57–58. The English translation is mainly by the author and partly adapted from Tu Wei-Ming, 86.

subtle organ imbalances that require attention if best health is to be maintained.[43]

Classic Taoism's recurrent theme of non-coercive acts (*wuwei*) appears to be a counterforce to possible homophobia, as well. Laozi states:

> When the universe recognizes beauty as beauty, then the ugliness has just appeared; when all recognize goodness as good, then the not-good has just appeared.... The sage king thus works without interfering, and teaches without talking; the myriad of things arise and are active — and he rejects none of them.[44]

Laozi stresses in more than one passage that the ruler's attitude should be "non-acting" (*wuwei*): he should not interfere in people's affairs, but rather let people develop themselves, complete themselves, and become self-transformed. Furthermore, Taoism treasures what is natural. Zhuangzi elaborates further the notion of relativity that defies logic and any fixed conceptualization:

> What is It (*shi*) is also Other (*bi*), what is Other is also It. There they say "That's it, that's not" from one point of view, here we say "That's it, that's not" from another point of view.... Where neither It nor Other finds its opposite is called the axis of Tao.... The concept regarding "that's it" is endless, and so is "that's not." One should thus behold clarity.... The lighting up of "That's it, that's not" is the reason why Tao is flawed.... Tao contains no divide, and speech contains no certainty.[45]

---

43. Mantak Ghia and Michael Winn, *Taoist Secrets of Love: Cultivating Male Sexual Energy* (Santa Fe, NM: Aurora Press, 1984), 206.

44. *Laozi* 2. English version is partly by Lafargue and partly by the author. See Michael Lafargue, *The Tao of the Tao Te Ching: A Translation and Commentary* (Albany: State University of New York Press, 1992), 92.

45. *Zhuangzi* 2 "*qiwu lun*" (the sorting which evens things out). This is a lengthy chapter in which Zhuangzi gives many examples/stories that defy dichotomy. The English version is mainly based on A. C. Graham's translation, with some modification by the author. See Graham, *Chuang-Tzu*, 53–54. For the Chinese text, see *Xinyi Zhuangzi duben* (*New Zhuangzi Reader*), ed. Huang Jinhong (Taipei: Sanmin, 1997), 62–64.

Such Taoist theory corresponds to and supports the earlier discussed absence of dualisms in Chinese vocabulary. Zhuangzi clearly rejects false dichotomizing. For Zhuangzi, division could lead to self-contradiction insofar as "neither side of a dichotomy is wholly true."[46] With the dissolution of rigid categories, one can "respond anew to the totality of every new situation."[47] Tao is holistic and undivided. Since there is no clear-cut demarcation between heterosexual and homosexual relations, there is no notion of affirming one while condemning the other. The Taoist ideal overlaps with the Confucian ideal. They both recognize every human being's uniqueness and encourage each to develop fully.[48] This ideal serves as a cultural counterforce to homophobia and likely accounts for the historical tolerance of sexual difference.

Same-Sex Eroticism in Late Imperial China

There are ample examples of male homosexual or same-sex erotic relations in traditional China. References to homoerotic relations run throughout Chinese history, but the peak periods are considered to be from the later Han to the Six Dynasties period (221–590 C.E.) and the late-Ming to the Qing period (the seventeenth to nineteenth centuries).[49] Official historic records from the Han dynasty (206 B.C.E.) onward almost always devote a special section to the emperor's male favorites (*xingchen*). It is perhaps only natural to assume that the ruling class's interest would influence people in general, especially the officials and literati. Late imperial China, in particular, witnesses the popularity of male homoeroticism, which developed

---

46. Graham, *Chuang-Tzu*, 12.

47. Ibid., 8.

48. For more discussion and examples of the shared values between Confucianism and Taoism, see Ann-Marie Hsiung, "Reconsidering the Shared Ground between Confucianism and Taoism," *Asian Culture* 23, no. 4 (1995): 63–69.

49. Though scholars in general view the second highlight in Chinese homosexual history to be the seventeenth-century late-Ming period (see, for instance, Song Geng, *The Fragile Scholar*, 138), the most recent study has extended it to the nineteenth century. Wu has focused her study from the seventeenth century onward and shows the continued proliferation of male homoerotic discourse up to nineteenth century. Wu Cuncun, *Homoerotic Sensibilities in Late Imperial China* (New York: Routledge, 2004), esp. 2–5, 22, 37.

into a social fashion that affected many individuals' taste and style. Certain clarification of terminology is needed to provide an accurate picture of homosexual relations in premodern China. It is worth noting again that there are no equivalent terms for *homosexual* and *heterosexual* in traditional China. Chinese terms used to describe homosexual activity are allusive rhetoric and devoid of sexual aspects, as Hinsch observes:

> It was usually discussed using poetic metaphors referring to earlier men or incidents famed for association with homosexuality. Chinese terminology therefore did not emphasize an innate sexual essence, but concentrated rather on actions, tendencies, and preferences. In other words, instead of saying what someone "is," Chinese authors would usually say whom he "resembles" or what he "does" or "enjoys." Another popular way of describing homosexual was in terms of social roles. Hence early records mentioning men who had sexual relationships with the emperors call them "favorites," a description of their political status, not of an innate sexual essence.[50]

This approach runs counter to the Western tendency to isolate sexual orientation as the "truth" of one's being, thereby neglecting all the myriad other aspects of life and personality. In the Chinese tradition homosexual activities are described in social rather than sexual terms. The well-known allusions referring to male homosexual relations, such as "the cut sleeve" (*duanxiu*) and "sharing the peach" (*fentao*), as well as Lord of Longyang and Anling, are from the anecdotes involving the emperor and his favorites.[51] These allusions dated from Han (206 B.C.E. to 220 C.E.) and

---

50. Hinsch, *Passions of the Cut Sleeve*, 7.

51. Both *duanxiu* and *fentao* are actions of tenderness. The incident of *duanxiu* was first recorded in Ban Gu, *Hanshu* (*History of the Han*), vol. 93. The emperor Aidi of Han (r. 6 B.C.E.–1 C.E.) once took a nap with his male lover Dong Xian, and he woke up to find the long sleeve of his gown trapped under the soundly sleeping Dong. In order not to disturb Dong's sleep, he had his sleeve cut off from the gown. The story of *fentao* was recorded in "*shuona pian*" ("the difficulties of persuasion") in *Han Fei Zi*, the works of the well-known Legalist thinker Han Fei who died in 233 B.C.E. It was about Duke Ling of Wei's (534–493 B.C.E.) handsome courtier Mizi Xia, who once picked a peach from the duke's garden, ate half, found it unusually delicious, and saved the remaining half for the duke; the duke publicly praised Mizi's love for him. Longyang and Anling are the names

pre-Han, mainly the Warring States period (403–221 B.C.E.), and served as synonyms for homosexuality throughout premodern Chinese history even as new terms, such as *nanfeng* (male custom, male fashion, or male practice),[52] *waichong* (outer favorite),[53] and *qi xiongdi* (adopted brothers) were added and widely used in late imperial China. A man who engages in homosexual activity may be described as one who has passion for "the cut sleeve" or as a man "sharing the peach." He could also be referred to as one who enjoys male beauty (*nanse*) or male custom. Perhaps these sensibilities explain why Chinese same-sex intimacy is not as emotionally fraught as it is in the West. As Chou rightly states, "Relations between people of the same gender can be very physical and intimate without suspicion of abnormality and perversity."[54]

The florescence of homoeroticism in late imperial China can be traced to the revision of Confucianism through the school of mind (*xinxue*), which emerged around mid-Ming period (fifteenth and sixteenth centuries) as a reaction against the strict orthodoxy of Cheng Zhu Neo-Confucianism (*lixue*), which was dominant in the early Ming.[55] Late-Ming thought, which was characterized by the infusion of Taoism and Buddhism into Confucianism, witnessed a transformation from *lixue* to *xinxue*. The school of mind, founded by Wang Yangming (1472–1592), extended Mencius's view about human beings as endowed with innate good nature and stressed

---

of good-looking courtiers whose love stories with the kings are from pre-Han records as well. See Liu Xiang, *Zhan'guo ce* (*Intrigues of the Warring States*), vols. 25 and 14.

52. *Nanfeng* first appears in *Jin Pin Mei* (*Golden Lotus*), the famous fiction in late Ming China, known by its pornographic aspect of opposite-sex and same-sex relations.

53. For instance, Feng Menglong, the late Ming literatus, writes about *waichong* (outer favorite) and *neichong* (inner favorite) to refer to one's (sexual) interest in men and women, respectively. The use of *wai* (outer) and *nei* (inner) to indicate male and female, however, has been prevalent since ancient times. See Wu, *Homoerotic Sensibilities*, 44.

54. Chou, *Tongzhi*, 22.

55. Neo-Confucianism (*lixue*), founded by Zhu Xi and the Cheng brothers in the thirteenth century, advocates "preserving heavenly principle and getting rid of human desire" (*cun tianli, qu renyu*); it generates anti-sex conservatism that deviates from early Confucian teaching about the naturalness of human sexuality. The School of Wang or *xinxue* revives the early Confucian teaching by affirming the Mencius text that views human nature as good and treats sex as part of human nature, posits the potential sagehood of every person, and goes a step further to embrace human emotions and desires.

the human heart as a valid source of experience and realization. This development had a profound influence on literati and opened up liberating attitudes in the late-Ming era. The later exponents of Wang Yangming took an interest in the body and its passions (*qing*), thus transforming the social ethos, as de Bary puts it, from "desirelessness to desirefulness"[56] and giving rise to homoeroticism in the cult of *qing* (love, passion, emotion, sentiment, feeling, and sensibility).

Qing is commonly rendered as love between man and woman, yet it covers a much wider range of human relations and emotions, such as those among friends or siblings and with nature. In Confucian discourse, *qing* reflects propriety (*li*) and reveals one's inner humanity. Unlike the Christian notion of love usually reserved exclusively for marriage, *qing* is a deep, affectionate sentiment permeating any intimate relationship. Notably, it does not necessarily require a sexual encounter and often occurs outside the marital context.[57] The cult of *qing*, popular in the late-Ming literary scene, was well noted in Tang Xianzu's (1550–1616) famous play *The Peony Pavilion* (*mudan ting*), which treats *qing* as a vital force transcending life and death. It is also explicitly expressed in Feng Menglong's (1574–1646) preface to his *History of Qing* (*Qing shi*), a collection of over eight hundred short stories about love:

> Had heaven and earth had no *qing* they would not have produced the myriad of things. Had the myriad of things had no *qing* they would not have eternally given each other life. . . . I intend to establish a school of *qing* to teach all who are living, so that a son will face his father with *qing* and a minister will face his lord with *qing*. One can, then, deduce the relations of all the various phenomena from this single point of view. The myriad things are like scattered coins; *qing* is the string that binds them together.[58]

---

56. See Wu, *Homoerotic Sensibilities*, 35.
57. For an elaborate exploration of *qing*, see Chou, *Tongzhi*, 16–17.
58. Feng Menglong, *Qing shi* (*History of love*), in *Feng Menglong quan ji* (*Collective Works of Feng Menglong*) (Shanghai: Shanghai guji, 1993, reprint), 7–9. The English version is by Huayuan Li Mowry in *Chinese Love Stories from "Ch'ing-shih"* (Hamden, CT: Archon Books, 1983), 13.

Feng attempts to recast Confucian morality and ethic relations in the new light of *qing,* which appears to be a blend of Confucian *ren* and Taoist *zhen* (authenticity). However, his vision challenges conventional social norms associated with Confucian moral codes by extolling *qing* as the highest virtue in a wide range of human relations, including male homoerotic relations. In *Qing shi* he collects love stories from throughout Chinese history. A chapter entitled *"qingwai lei"* (love-exterior-category), contains thirty-nine stories devoted exclusively to male-male love relations dating from antiquity to the Ming dynasty, each centering on *qing.* One story suggests that male-male relations are health enhancing, contrary to the conventional Taoist view regarding intercourse between two yang as harmful to health. Any such negativity is countered by *qing:*

> Mr. Boqi was also fond of male-love (*hao wai*). . . . Even after he had turned eighty, he was in fine health. Someone asked him how, after so many affairs with men (*wai shi*), his health had not suffered. Amused, he answered: "in this matter I have consumed more heart [associated with *qing*] and less kidney [associated with sexual vitality], and so I have been spared illness [from overindulgence]."[59]

Feng Menglong even argues at the end of his *"qingwai lei"* chapter that love (*qing*) should not be confined to heterosexual relations:

> I have heard Grand Master Yu say, "Women are for bearing children, men are for providing enjoyment. When it comes to beauty in this world, it is men who win over women. Among bird species like the phoenix, peacock, fowl and pheasant, pattern and colour belong to the males; and the sheen of dogs and horses is the same. . . ." Well, the world certainly contains those who have this kind of inclination (*pi*), [so] how can love (*qing*) [be thought to] exist only in a man's relationships with women (*nei*)?[60]

---

59. Feng Menglong, *Qing shi,* 836. The English version is mainly from Wu, *Homoerotic Sensibilities,* 43–44.

60. Feng, *Qing shi,* 860. For English translation, see Wu, *Homoerotic Sensibilities,* 44.

According to Feng, since *qing* is the string that binds myriad things together, *qing* may be viewed as a sensibility toward everything in the world, including human beings and natural entities, such as rocks, trees, birds, mountains, and rivers. Such sensibility or *qing* enhances personal expressiveness. Feng viewed himself as *qingchi* (obsessed with *qing*), and he even grouped people into those with *qing* (*youqing ren*) and those without *qing* (*wuqing ren*), regardless of their sexual orientation or socio-economic status. Literati enjoy viewing themselves as those with *qing*, and the targets of their *qing* could cover a wide range, including a *luanton* (catamite or good-looking boy). Zhang Dai (1507–1684), the famous essayist of the late-Ming era, illustrates such a literati mode in his auto-epitaph writing:

> When I was young, I was a dandy (*wanku zidi*). I was addicted to a sophisticated lifestyle. I was fond of exquisite houses, pretty servant girls, beautiful catamites (*luantong*), fine and extravagant clothes, gourmet food, ... drama, music, antiques, flowers and birds.[61]

Zhang Dai's individualistic self-expression reflects the fashion of late-Ming literati lifestyles. His openness about his enjoyment of boys reveals the vogue of homoeroticism. An educated man's *qing* or fondness for young men could be one of many interests signifying his refinement. There is no sense here of anything negative or unseemly. Zhang Dai in his collection of miscellaneous notes writes about his friend Qi Zhixiang, an artist and dramatist, having various obsessions, among them calligraphy, painting, drums, and opera. He then highlights Qi's obsession with Abao, a beautiful young man, in these lines: "Face to face with death his own life would have been expendable, but not his treasure, Abao. ... Leaving his wife and children was for Zhixiang as easy as removing a shoe, but a young brat was as dear to him as his own life."[62]

---

61. Zhang Dai, *Langhuan wenji* (*Langhuan Anthology*), vol. 5; Wu, *Homoerotic Sensibilities*, 38.

62. Zhang Dai, *Tao'an mengyi* (*Dream Reminiscences of Tao'an*) (Shanghai: Shanghai shudian, 1982), 35–36; Wu, *Homoerotic Sensibilities*, 43.

Qing was a central theme of late-Ming culture, in which homoerotic literature became increasingly popular. Homoerotic references were abundant in late-Ming literary works and in Qing literature as well.[63] Much homoeroticism can be detected in *Caps and Hairpins* (*Bian er chai*) and *Fragrant Essences of Spring* (*Yichuan xiangzhi*),[64] two late-Ming novels, each composed of four novelettes by the same author, Zui Xihu Xinyue Zhuren (the heart-moon master of the drunken West Lake), apparently a romantic pseudonym. The author attempts to present same-sex relations as a matter of heart rather than as "merely" sexual stimulation. He transforms mainstream social values, such as loyalty, social justice, and intellectual scholarship, into key elements in male same-sex relationships, which then appear congruent with social morality of *qing* and *yi* (righteousness), as shown in the four titles of the first novel: "*Qing* Fidelity," "*Qing* Chivalry," "*Qing* Sacrifice," and "*Qing* Marvel." These are idealized love stories of male intellectuals who encounter similar-hearted males with whom they share intimacy and genuine *qing*. In another novel the author creates a utopian land for the male lovers entitled "A Land Favorable to Men" (*Yi'nan guo*), where all the citizens (men only) are free to love passionately and openly. In this utopia male desires are no longer frustrated under the regime of heterosexual norms but have free rein to be fully expressed. Such literary works manifest the depth of homoerotic sensibilities, unveiling the desires and values of the literati class. This "male fashion" (*nanfeng*) associated with *qing* expressed a libertine trend of sensuality in the late-Ming era. One late-Ming writer even proclaims: "There is a saying that 'the beauty of boys is the death of old men.' Lately there is no one who would not fall in love with a male beauty."[65] The fashion of male homoerotic desire continues to the Qing dynasty although the cult of *qing* and libertine trend no longer prevail because of the Qing

---

63. See, for instance, the classic Chinese masterpieces like *Mudan ting* (*The Peony Pavilion*), *Jinpin mei* (*Golden Lotus*), and *Hongloumeng* (*Dream of the Red Chamber*).

64. For more details regarding these two works, see Chou, *Tongzhi*, 31–32; Wu, *Homoerotic Sensibilities*, 49.

65. Taoyuan Zuihua Zhuren, *Bieyouxiang* (*An Exotic Fragrance*), vol. 6. See also Wu, *Homoerotic Sensibilities*, 38.

government's stricter rules and prohibition of courtesan quarters, which actually makes male prostitutes even more popular. In the Qing dynasty homoerotic indulgence goes further and is transformed into an aesthetic expression, such that many Qing literati view love between men as the highest romantic ideal.[66]

Apart from the homoerotic trend of the literati class, one also finds non-literati examples of male same-sex relations in the coastal towns and villages of Fujian province. As noted by Wu Cuncun, among the three regions of Beijing (the capital), Jiang-Zhe (surrounding Suzhou and Hangzhou), and the coast of Fujian — each popular with male homosexuality — the practices in Fujian were far more equal and formalized.[67] In Fujian, male homosexual relationships were locally termed *qi xiong-di* (contract brothers), in which *qi* refers to a contract or agreement between a *xiong*, elder brother, and *di*, younger brother. It is a local custom for *qixiong* and *qidi* to engage in ritualized marriage, similar to a heterosexual union and accepted by their parents, relatives, and friends. The literatus Shen Defu (1578–1642) offers a vivid description:

> Fujianese deeply treasure male homoerotic desire (*nanese*). Whether rich or poor, beautiful or ugly, they find a companion of their own kind. The elder one is *qixiong*, the younger one *qidi*. When the elder enters the younger's home, the younger one's parents welcome him as son-in-law. *Qidi*'s plans for the future, including the expenses for taking a wife, are all managed by *qixiong*. Some among them are so devoted to each other that even past the age of marriage they still sleep on the same bed like husband and wife.[68]

---

66. Wu, *Homoerotic Sensibilities*, 39. Wu argues that homoerotic indulgence in the late-Ming era centered on refinement and adventure — an expression of power — and only became romantic within the discourse of beauty, love, and companionship in the Qing dynasty.

67. The male homosexual relationships in Beijing mainly existed between officials and catamites, while in the Jiang-Zhe area they existed between literati or merchants and catamites. See Wu, *Homoerotic Sensibilities*, 45.

68. Shen Defu, *Wanli yhehuobian* (*Unofficial Gleanings on the Wanli Reign*) (Beijing: Zhonghua shuju, 1959), 902. The English version is adapted from Chou, *Tongzhi*, 37.

It is noted that *qixiong* would maintain *qidi*'s upkeep throughout the marriage, and some wealthy couples even adopted boys to be raised as sons. Such marriages usually had to be dissolved after one or both reached the age of thirty in order to enter a conventional marriage to fulfill familial responsibilities of procreation, although they might still be erotically involved as a couple after each took a bride.

The Fujian practice of male same-sex marriage is best illustrated in Li Yu's (1611–80) story, *A Male Mencius's Mother Educates His Son and Moves House Three Times* (*Nan Mengmu jiaohe sanqian*), which is set in Fujian. The story emphasizes the traditional virtues associated with heterosexual marriage, such as filial duties, fidelity, motherhood, and chaste widowhood. Li Yu tactfully uses the homophone of *nanfeng* (a southern wind or southern mode that carries the same sound of male wind/male mode) to combine the meaning of male practices and this southern region. The opening lines read: "People do not know when the southern custom (*nanfeng*) arose or who created it. Nevertheless it has come down to the present age."[69] He explains that his setting is in Fujian, "the region foremost in passion for men," and he emphasizes that "in Fujian the male-mode/southern custom (*nanfeng*) is identical to the practice with women,"[70] including the wedding ritual. The story tells how the scholar Jifang, after the death of his wife, decides to pursue his true passion by marrying a handsome youth, Ruiji, with whom he falls in love. Jifang sells his land to pay the bride price and to help Ruiji fulfill his filial duties by burying his mother and inviting his father to live with them. To reciprocate Jifang's devotion, Ruiji voluntarily castrates himself to avoid heterosexual marriage and remains with Jifang forever. He dresses as a woman and acts as if he is a virtuous wife and caring mother. After Jifang's death, Ruiji tries his best to provide the most accepting environment for his son's education and even moves to Guangdong because in Fujian "boys without fathers esteem the southern

---

69. Li Yu, *Li Yu quanji* (*Complete Works of Li Yu*), ed. Helmut Martin (Taipei, 1970), 5382. For the English version, see Hinsch, *Passions of the Cut Sleeve*, 124.

70. Li Yu, *Li Yu quanji*, 5406. The English version is adapted from Hinsch, *Passions of the Cut Sleeve*, 127; and Wu, *Homoerotic Sensibilities*, 46.

custom, whereas in other places they do not."[71] The story ends with the son passing the imperial examination and Ruiji being honored as "Mencius's mother," the paragon of motherhood totally devoted to the son's education. In this story, Li Yu assumes the prevalence of the "male mode" in Fujian areas and goes a step further to contextualize male same-sex marriage as part of the familial-kinship cultural imperative, making such relationships even more justifiable.

At the same time, one should note the power relation in male same-sex relations. David F. Greenberg codifies the social expression of homosexuality outside the modern West into four categories: trans-generational, trans-gender, class structured, and egalitarian.[72] The first three fit the Chinese male homosexual tradition especially well. The majority of male homosexual relationships in China were closely related to status, power, and money although more egalitarian ones existed, such as the practices of *qi xiongdi.*[73] Despite the homoerotic love between the emperor and his favorites, the wealthy and their catamites, and the literati and good-looking boys displayed in literature and history, the class and age gaps are obvious, especially between the powerful and wealthy and youth. Interest in boys cannot be extracted from the expression of power and control. Underlying the "male fashion" is an unequal power relation and system of dominance in which the wealthy and powerful exploit the poor and less powerful, a subordinate class of males. In the framework of the Chinese gender system, the emperor, the wealthy, and the literati are yang, that is, masculine and dominant, while the catamites or young boys are yin, that

---

71. Li Yu, *Li Yu quanji,* 5442. The English version is from Hinsch, *Passions of the Cut Sleeve,* 129.

72. David F. Greenberg, *The Construction of Homosexuality* (Chicago: University of Chicago Press, 1988), 25.

73. "Egalitarian" homosexuality here is viewed as the relationship between two persons based more on mutual love than on active/passive roles, which are less essential in such a relationship. Song argues against Hinsch's inclusion of adolescent love in *Honglou meng* as egalitarian and tends to view egalitarian homosexual relationships as nonexistent in premodern China. I am more on the side of Hinsch. I consider that since all the relationships in premodern China were more or less hierarchical, a relationship could be viewed as egalitarian as long as mutual love was dominant in the relationship. See Song, *The Fragile Scholar,* 135; Hinsch, *Passions of the Cut Sleeve,* 11.

is, feminine and submissive. These young boys are kept by powerful men and are often treated as if they were women; the "kept class" boys act like women, as well.

Ironically, the most egalitarian form of same-sex relations is found in women who, due to social negligence, are largely free from the hierarchical social constraints governing men's behavior. As Dorothy Ko asserts, "In a society that upheld the doctrine of separate spheres as the ideal, women were left with much leeway to pursue affective bonds of their own without men's interference."[74] Women's same-sex relations were fostered by the fact that they lived in close physical contact with one another within the household, courtesan quarter, or palace. While men were often absent because of their professional pursuits, it was highly probable for erotic or sexual relations to occur among the wife and concubines, courtesans, or palace ladies waiting to meet with the emperor. However, there is no sustained literary tradition of women's same-sex relations. Because men control the world of literacy, the dearth of writings could be due to men's disinterest in women's lives, including their most intimate relationships.

Ko's innovative study of women's culture based on the writings, mainly poems, of seventeenth-century literary women, discloses, in contrast, some remarkably intimate friendships among women that could evoke homoeroticism.[75] The elite woman Shen Yixiu, for instance, detailed her intimate friendship with her cousin Qianqian, including how she was charmed by the latter's glowing feminine beauty at their meetings after each other's marriages, and how they both spent two days, when their husbands were away, at the lake where they parked the pleasure boat to enjoy a moonlit night, drink wine, and enjoy themselves.

While the intimacy between Yixiu and Qianqing may appear more platonic than sensual, the homoerotic spark between the gentry wife Xu Yuan and Lu Qingzi is more revealing. Both Xu and Lu befriended

---

74. Dorothy Ko, *Teachers of the Inner Chambers: Women and Culture in Seventeenth-Century China* (Stanford, CA: Stanford University Press, 1994), 272.

75. Ibid., 166–70, 206–8, 266–73. Ko illustrates, from their poems and prose, that a number of gentry women wrote in sensual terms adoring their daughters, friends, or courtesans, and she uses "love-friendship continuum" to describe such homoerotic sensibility.

courtesans and singing girls, a practice uncommon among women of the gentry class, and they wrote poems using seductive language to describe their bodily charm. Lu, in particular, indicated that she was attracted to women for their feminine beauty and literary resonance. Her intimacy with and longing for Xu are shown in the poems below, written before Xu's departure:

> Our love [*qing*] was already deep when together,
> Our parting brings sadness to my heart.
> If you ask why I became so involved,
> It's for all our resonance.
>
> ... inanimate objects stir up my deep longing.
> I love and adore [*wanlian*] that tender beauty...
>
> Your face is a dazzling crimson...
> I want to pursue the pleasure of my lifetime,
> But the vehicles crowding the road cannot bring me there.[76]

The unabashed language, though poetic and not without allusion, stands out among gentry women's written works. Such poems, by displaying a literary woman's expression of love and desire for another literary woman, suggest the power of shared homoerotic sentiments. While male literati express overwhelming fascination with male beauty, the inclusion of "resonance" in the gentry women's homoerotic *qing* addresses an explicitly spiritual dimension.

The classic literary examples of women's same-sex desire can be found in Li Yu's play *The Loving Fragrant Companion* (*Lian xian ban*), Pu Songling's (1640–1715) short story "Feng Sanniang," and Shen Fu's (1736–?) autobiographical writing *Six Chapters of a Floating Life* (*Fusheng liuji*). In Li's play, a young married woman, Cui, falls in love with a beautiful young woman, Cao, during her visit to a Buddhist convent, and Cao reciprocates her feelings. The two seek union as husband and wife and even invoke the Buddha as their witness: "We could share the same bed and afterwards the

---

76. Quoted in ibid., 271–72, Ko's translation.

same tomb and we would be joined, like two butterflies, flitting hither and thither."[77] They manage to live together, after some hardships, by having Cao marry Cui's husband as a concubine, and hence all are gratified.

Pu's story line coincides with Li's in that two young women meet in a Buddhist nunnery and fall in love with each other at first sight. The gentry lady, Fan, who appears disinterested in marriage as the story unfolds, is enchanted by a young woman, Feng, of unknown background. Fan invites Feng to visit her. During Feng's visit they swear sisterhood, and Fan has Feng stay in her inner chamber, sharing the same bed for about six months before they are discovered by Fan's mother, who is pleased to find that her daughter has a nice female companion. Feng's departure causes Fan to cry "bitterly on the bed as if she had lost her spouse."[78] Feng later finds a promising husband, Meng, for Fan, who begs Feng to marry the same man so the two women can stay together forever. Upon Feng's rejection Fan even plots with Meng to rape Feng in her drunken state. Feng thus reveals herself as a fox spirit whose cultivation with Tao could have allowed her to ascend the primary Heaven but whose inability to resist the enchanted love with Fan has now led to breaching the taboo of sex. She laments all as destiny and departs. Though the story ends with a heterosexual marriage, it vividly depicts the intensity of a lesbian love and attests to a non-homophobic, even approving, attitude toward female-female intimate relationships.

Li and Pu's literary imagination about a wife initiating a concubine for her husband due to her own homoerotic feeling is not without grounds. It can be further verified in Shen's writing. Shen's work is one of China's earliest autobiographical writings about conjugal joy, in which he details his loving relationship with his wife, Yunniang. In one of their venturous trips, not too common for the time, Yunniang finds herself deeply attracted to a courtesan, and she urges her husband to take her as a concubine.

---

77. The English translation is from Michel Beurdeley, *Chinese Erotic Art* (Hong Kong: Chartwell books, 1969), 175.

78. "Feng Sanniang" is a story from *Liaozhai zhiyi* (*Liaozhi's Tales of the Strange*). It is translated by Tze-lan D. Sang and attached as appendix in her book. See Tze-lan D. Sang, *The Emerging Lesbian: Female Same-Sex Desire in Modern China* (Chicago: University of Chicago Press, 2003), 281–87. The quotation is from page 283.

The rejection of her husband's family and the subsequent marriage of the courtesan dash her wish. Yunniang is so dejected that she falls sick and eventually passes away. Yunniang's erotic sensibility to the courtesan, however, should be viewed more as a literary woman's exemplification of *qing* since Yunniang is portrayed as a sensible woman who has aesthetic taste for all the beautiful and refined. Again, the story depicts homoeroticism without stigma.

There is also a proliferation of literary works in late imperial China with the common theme of "the blissful union of a man with two women endeared to each other."[79] These works focus on heterosexual romances; the friendship or mutual attraction between women takes a secondary position. In the well-known *Liaozhi's Tales of the Strange (Liaozhai zhiyi)* by Pu Songling, one finds dozens of stories about two women who become attached to each other as "sisters" and who marry the same man happily without any hint of jealousy. Female homoerotic bigamy is even more apparent in so-called scholar-beauty (*caizi jiaren*) romances popular in the early Qing period. The cult of *qing* from the late-Ming era continues and expands in such romances, in which the ideal women sought by literary scholars as lifelong partners are those endowed with beauty, talent, and *qing*. Once two such women marry the same scholar, their mutual affection, appreciation, or admiration is rather explicit. As is proclaimed by Li Yu and often cited by the scholar, the male protagonist, in the "scholar-beauty" romances: "A true beauty is never jealous of another beauty. And only true talent is capable of sympathizing with talent."[80] These idealized writings could be part of male fantasy or "the literary fantasy of utopian polygamy," as Sang claims.[81] Nonetheless, they reflect social tolerance and

---

79. Ibid., 50.

80. Ibid., 51. This is Li Yu's opening statement in his play *Lian xiang ban*. Li Yu himself has a number of concubines who constitute the major performers of his family troupe, which performs the plays he writes. His writings project his ideal/wish — to replace jealousy among women with mutual love in order to avoid family disputes — and reflect many literati's wishful thinking of his time. His claim that truly beautiful and talented women would cherish and love each other is vividly shown in early Qing's *caizi-jiaren* fiction. See, for instance, Tianhuazang zhuren, *Yu jiaoli (Jade Tender Pear)* (Shenyang: Chunfeng wenyi, 1981), 158, 177–78.

81. Sang, *The Emerging Lesbian*, 49.

even encouragement of female homoerotic relations in the polygamous household.

Apart from the elite gentry women and the literary world, women's homosexual relations are best illuminated in the development of marriage-resistant sisterhoods from the nineteenth to the early twentieth centuries in Canton areas,[82] often characterized by a hybridization of the Han Chinese culture with the indigenous minority culture. One such sisterhood is *zishu nu* (women who comb up their hair), women who reject marriage or after marriage refuse to live with their husbands. They would comb up their hair and make vows to the deity as signs of their unavailability for marriage. With this ceremony a *zishu nu* moves out of her parents' house to live with other *zishu nu* in a spinster house. Interestingly, if two of them develop intimate relations, the rites of marriage would be performed, and they would then live as husband and wife. The couple could even adopt female children who would inherit their property. Such practice is unlike that of *qi xingdi*, who were obliged to enter heterosexual marriages in order to fulfill patriarchal familial duty. To the contrary, *zishu nu*, either in singlehood or female-female unions, would be left alone for life. Another type, *bu luojia* (the bride's delayed transfer after marriage), features a woman's refusal to join the husband's family by returning to her parents' house after the wedding night. These women visit their husbands only at certain important festivals although some also return to complete their childbearing duty. They live together in close relationships, often intimate and sexual. Speculations on such an unconventional practice often point to these women's homosexual inclinations, as well as their economic autonomy occasioned by the silk industry in the region.[83]

One more rich resource of a similar kind, but even more revealing, is found in *nushu* (women's writings), circulated around Hunan prov-

---

82. Chen Dongyuan quotes from Zhang Xintai's *Yueyou xiaozhi* (*Notes from Canton Journey*) and records such practice under "special custom." See Chen Dongyuan, *Zhongguo funu shenghuoshi* (*The History of Chinese Women's Life*) (Taipei: Shangwu, 1980), 300. For more detailed discussion in this regard, see Chou, *Tongzhi*, 40–41; Sang, *The Emerging Lesbian*, 52–54.

83. See Sang, *The Emerging Lesbian*, 52–53; Chou, *Tongzhi*, 40.

ince's Jiangyong county, a secluded place noted to be mixed with Yue minority and Han Chinese. *Nushu* was discovered in 1982 and has since received worldwide attention because of its unique writing style, created and used by women.[84] However, homosexual or homoerotic relations in this women's culture often escape attention. In *nushu*, the cultural medium among the sisterhood, one finds intimate relations among women, called *hangke* (the frequent visitor), who frequent each other's houses and even live together as husband and wife. Homosexual behaviors appear common among *hangke*. "The Songs of *Hangke*," considered among the most touching and significant sections in *nushu*, feature women's self-expression of love and homoerotic desires. These songs, written exclusively for and by women, are passionate and sensual:

> In my dream I feel as if I am at your house bonding intimately with you and so full of joy. . . . Every night I dream about going to your house living and sleeping with you day and night. Are you aware of my affection? . . .
>
> I am really fond of you and I open my heart to you first. I hope you do not feel me unworthy and would come soon to bond with me by heart. We shall let go of those worrisome matters and be romantically together. It is like hibiscus flower matching tender green leaf; we would have such joyful moments in our attic.[85]

Instead of the poetic allusions abundant in gentry women's poems, such writings are straightforward and unabashed. Lu Qingzi's "explicit use of seductive expressions" is deemed "rare in the written works of other

---

84. This women's culture differs from the one featured by Dorothy Ko in a number of ways. First of all, *nushu* authors are village women who are influenced more by local culture than mainstream Confucian culture and who are trained to read and write the special form of writing passed down by local women, while gentry women are embedded in Confucian education and are well versed in the male literati's tradition. Second, *nushu* circulate only among women, and men have no entry to their content, while the poetry of gentry women, though circulated mainly among women, could be shared with their husbands or literati friends, who often sponsored the publication of their works.

85. "Gong Zhebing jiang *nushu*-8," author's translation.

women,"[86] to use Ko's terms. Without the concern of male judgment, *nushu* authors had no reservations about writing what was in their heart; their songs thus appear daring, flowing with direct outpourings of homoerotic feelings and emotions. In addition to women's culture, *nushu* could be viewed as evidence, as well, of a Chinese lesbian culture.

The practices of *hangke*, *zishu nu*, and *bu luojia* provide important information for female homosexual relations outside the Confucian norm of heterosexual marriage. Whether they find the Confucian institution of heterosexual marriage oppressive or simply follow their natural inclination, such practices occur in the areas where minority local cultures interact with mainstream Confucian culture, and the local customs sometimes dominate. The practices of *zishu nu* and *buluo jia*, in fact, demonstrate a compromise of Confucian dictums, seen in the ceremonial marriage between two *zishu nu*, their adoption of children, and the completion of the childbearing obligation before living with other *buluo jia* women. However, these female-female lifestyles exist only within a limited geographic region. More important, they all occur in southern regions, noticeably distinct from the conventional social ethos and considered to be the originating site of Taoism. Taoist culture has certainly been a liberating influence.

Concluding Remarks

This analysis shows the absence of homophobia and the coexistence of heterosexual and homosexual relations in premodern China. A heterosexist reading of Confucianism and Taoism may hint at a longstanding legacy of homophobia, but any detectable bias is readily offset, and dissipated by, Chinese yin-yang discourse and other rich resources, including the Confucian concern for human dignity and Taoist stress on the natural. At the same time, it is clear that homosexual relations constitute no threat to established Chinese gender ideology and social order. The hierarchical power relations between the emperor/the wealthy/the literati and

---

86. Ko, *Teachers of the Inner Chambers*, 272.

the catamites/actors/young boys, though not ideal in Confucian ethics, only reinforce the yin/yang or feminine/masculine gender paradigm. The more egalitarian female-female erotic or sexual relations in the polygamous household actually help to facilitate the stability and harmony of the family.

It is interesting to note that non-literati homoerotic expressions, such as *qi xiongdi, zishu nu,* or *hangke,* perhaps due to similar social status (middle or lower class) and, therefore, with fewer burdens of Confucian norms, tend to go beyond heterosexual marriage and are more egalitarian. The majority of the men and women engaging in same-sex pleasure appear to be bisexual, and their sexual behavior causes no harm to the Confucian priority of family and reproduction. Hinsch assesses the Chinese homosexual tradition in these terms: "In many periods homosexuality was widely accepted and even respected, had its own formal history, and had a role in shaping Chinese political institutions, modifying social conventions, and spurring artistic creation."[87]

When and how, then, does homophobia come on the scene and the cultural tolerance for same-sex eroticism come to an end? As mentioned earlier, the key event focuses on the twentieth and twenty-first centuries and China's modernization or Westernization. This view may sound simplistic, but it largely holds true. Since the late nineteenth century the humiliating encounters between a weakening China and Western powers not only forced China to shift its identity from "universal empire" (*tianxia*) to "nation-state" (*guojia*),[88] but also spurred a series of reform movements along with a sense of urgency about national survival. These dynamics culminated in the New Culture movement of the early twentieth century when Chinese intellectuals advocated modernization/Westernization and the dismissal of age-old Confucianism. A hetero-homo dualism and recognizably Christian homophobia were in vogue with the import of Western science and sexology. The notion that each person is both yin and yang was replaced by a biologized gender dichotomy that makes

---

87. Hinsch, *Passions of the Cut Sleeve,* 4.
88. Chou, *Tongzhi,* 43.

homosexuality appear unnatural and even pathological. Even more, the Confucian familial-marital institution, which has become allied with the prevailing scientific discourse of a binary gender construct, has become fertile ground for an explicitly homophobic construction of sexuality;[89] Confucianism, especially as a cultural system that supports procreative marriage, has been heterosexualized and used to support homophobia. So-called enlightened (Westernized) Chinese scholars hence began treating homosexuality as a mental illness or pathological condition.[90]

The gap between Chinese tradition and modernity appears radical. As Barlow remarks, "In the last hundred years Chinese construction of subjects has changed.... Writers take over 'international' truths of experience — class, race, gender, modernity, scientific objectivity and so on — and make the great narratives of Western modernism part of the modernity of non-western civilizations."[91] In the past century, especially the early period, Chinese largely bypassed their own tradition and embraced Western culture with open arms. After the change of language from classic (*wenyan*) to vernacular (*baihua*) occurred during the New Culture movement, the majority of Chinese became unable to read classical texts and were thus further alienated from their own tradition. Their understanding of Confucian and Taoist tradition has become superficial or partial, and many could easily be led to believe that Confucian culture is inherently homophobic, based on popular misunderstandings about the compatibility of the Confucian familial-marital system with Western sexological assumptions.

The appropriation of Western sexology and a heterosexualized Confucian familial-marital system foster homophobia in modern/contemporary Chinese society. Although the West seems to elevate the "pleasure principle of sexuality over procreation,"[92] Chinese still place primary emphasis on procreation even though the concept of modern marriage, based on

---

89. Ibid., 47.
90. Modern scholar Chen Dongyuan, the widely known author of *Zhongguo funu shenghuoshi*, for instance, after quoting the female homosexual custom in Canton, comments that it is against nature and rather harmful to women's health.
91. Tani Barlow, "Introduction: Gender, Writing, Feminism, China," *Modern Chinese Literature* 4 (1988): 4.
92. Chou, *Tongzhi*, 48.

love between two individuals, differs considerably from past notions. Mencius's line *"buxiao yousan, wuhou weida,"* singled out from the rich repertoire of Confucian tradition and made large by conventional-minded parents and elders, is frequently cited to reinforce the necessity that all adults engage in heterosexual marriage. It is reported that Chinese *tongzhi* are often forced to get married by tremendous social pressure. And even though the concept of homophobia is a Western import, contemporary Chinese *tongzhi* suffer perhaps even more social oppression than their Western counterparts insofar, as noted by Chou Wah-Shan, the Western world has gradually departed from an earlier attitude of ostracism and condemnation and moved toward "greater respect for differences and individuality. Yet China abandoned its traditional tolerance of [homosexuality] for the now outdated Western mental illness model at the turn of the [twentieth] century."[93] A majority of Chinese, oblivious of their traditional past, uncritically presume that the twentieth- and twenty-first-century homophobia is a longstanding cultural legacy from within. Chinese *tongzhi* mistakenly romanticize the Western world as non-homophobic and liberating. Despite some liberalizing trends in some Western countries, homophobia remains dominant worldwide, the result of the global hegemony of Western modernity.

Under the discourse of post-colonialism, every culture is unique and has its value. Honoring the diversity of gender and heterosexual/homosexual relations in traditional China, largely influenced by Confucianism and Taoism, may help to expand the prevailing modernist paradigm. Reconnecting with premodern China's homosexual tradition, as well as the rich

---

93. Chou, "Homosexuality and the Cultural Politics of *Tongzhi* in Chinese Societies," 31. Since the 1950s and 1960s, the Western world has undergone a change of attitude and discarded the mental-illness model, and yet China still held this model and prosecuted those engaged in homosexual activities since 1949; state intervention could be seen in the 1970s, 1980s, and even 1990s. The 2001 award-nominated homosexual movie *Lanyu* (Blue Cosmos), directed by Guan Jinpeng of Hong Kong and based on gay stories in Beijing, cannot be shown in China. See Chou, "Homosexuality and the Cultural Politics of *Tongzhi* in Chinese Societies," 31–32; Wan Yanhai, "Becoming a Gay Activist in Contemporary China," *Gay and Lesbian Asia*, 47–48, 55; *Lianhe zaobao* (Singapore morning newspaper), January 27, 2004.

resources in Confucianism and Taoism, may offer support to contemporary *tongzhi* and facilitate a change of mind-set and public policy. In fact,
recent studies regarding male-male bonding have enabled many Chinese
gay men to claim as their heritage a great male homosexual tradition from
the past.[94] Chinese lesbians, perhaps not as aware of the cultural traditions of sisterly bonding, sworn spinsterhood, and sister unions found in
the stories of *zishu nu, buluo jia*, and *hangke*, still tend to look to Western
models for outside assistance.[95] Further studies on female same-sex practices from the past could perhaps provide inspiration and empowerment
for Chinese lesbians, as well.

---

94. Since Hinsch's *Passions of the Cut Sleeve*, there have been a number of studies
relating to male homosexual relations in the past. In the 1990s Beijing gay men manifested
a longing to retrieve their cultural tradition. See Lisa Rofel, "Qualities of Desire: Imagining
Gay Identities in China," *GLQ* 5, no.4 (1999): 451–74.

95. Sang, *The Emerging Lesbian*, 54. Sang's work is perhaps the first systematic study on
Chinese female homosexual relations though her focus is on modern China.

Chapter Five

Reconstructing Buddhist Perspectives on Homosexuality
Enlightenment from the Study of the Body

YU-CHEN LI

Professor Hui-nan Yang, recently retired from National Taiwan University, has published *Love and Belief: The Movement Devoted to Equality and Ecology by the Taiwanese Homosexual Buddhists.*[1] In addition to bringing to light the existence of a Buddhist homosexual community — the Private Abode of Brahma Youth — this book also discusses whether being identified as homosexual conflicts with Buddhist monastic law (*vinayā*). Furthermore, and significantly, Professor Yang promotes the establishment of a "Third (-sex) Monastic Community."

The public responded to Yang's presentation so politely that one might have concluded that the subject of homosexuality in Buddhism was in no way controversial. The indications are, however, that the general public was simply too shocked by such a topic. People had never questioned Yang's lifelong celibacy and academic commitment as one of the most influential Buddhist scholars in contemporary Taiwan. What shocked the audience was Yang's choice of topic. On April 16, 2005, the date of its publication, Yang's book turned a new page in the complex history of homosexual relations within the Chinese Buddhist community. In his study Yang states that sectarian monastic law prohibits homosexuals from full ordination. According to Buddhist texts, he claims, these homosexual

---

1. Hui-nan Yang, *Love and Belief: The Movement Devoted to Equality and Ecology by the Taiwanese Homosexual Buddhists* (Taipei: Shangzhou, 2005).

men (in Sanskrit, *pandka*; in Chinese, "Yellow Door," a term that often means eunuch or an impotent male) are defined as having abnormal sexual organs. However, he agrees with Leonard Zwilling that a certain type of *pandka* in the early Buddhist scriptures is equivalent to the modern definition of homosexuals.[2]

This chapter explores this contemporary issue in light of traditional Buddhist texts about religious celibacy and homosexuality found in the Chinese Buddhist canon (*tripitaka*). Unlike Yang, who focuses on monastic law, I prefer to investigate the issue of homosexuality by looking at the relationship between body and desire, the essential concern of Buddhist practice. Since no equivalent terminology for homosexuality exists in ancient Buddhist texts, I examine homosexual enlightenment in Buddhism in the following contexts: (1) the ambiguous sexual identity problem found in Early Buddhist sectarian texts, (2) bodily transformation in Mahayana Buddhism, and (3) the social niche of homosexuals and lesbians in Chinese history and contemporary Taiwan. This chapter proposes the usefulness of a complementary bipolar model of body and desire for analyzing the issue of sexual differences in Buddhism.

Buddhist Perspectives on the Body

Buddhist doctrine denies a permanent subjectivity of self (the idea of self-lessness) and regards the body as a result of complex interactions between consciousness and the functions of organs. The organs carry the feelings of pain and comfort that produce the false sense of physical integrity but lack essential subjectivity and eventually decline. From a Buddhist perspective, our sense organs deceive us regarding the surface beauty of the body.[3] Distinguishing between beauty and ugliness in physical appearance is related

---

2. Leonard Zwilling, "Homosexuality as Seen in Indian Buddhist Text," in *Buddhism, Sexuality, and Gender,* ed. Jose Ignacio Cabezon (Albany: State University of New York, 1992), 203–14.

3. Yu-chen Li, "Fojiao Piyu wenxu zhongde nannv meise yu qingyu — zhuiqiu meili de yihan (Religious Desire and Religious Beauty: Gender Difference and Sensual Beauty as Represented in the Buddhist Avadana Literature)," *New History* 10, no. 4 (1999): 31–65.

to the attitudes toward male and female beauty, and this also eventually generates sexual desire and emotional attachment. In order to conquer the temptation of sexual attraction, monastic law describes the female body as being composed of filthy and bloody organs with subjectivity, and monks are sometimes taught to meditate in graveyards on the decaying process of female corpses.[4] In this way, the male-oriented monastic community very often pictures women as bodies that produce distracting sexual desires.[5] At the same time, Buddhism bases the sexual identity of people, whether male, female, non-male, or non-female, primarily on their genital organs.

Even with these efforts to distance and discipline the body, Buddhism also has to recognize the body as the basic tool of religious practice. The Buddhist founder Sakyamuni Buddha proposes a "Middle Way" to treat the human body: neither to torture the body with ascetic practices, nor to corrupt the body with pleasure. Buddhist law regulates the appropriate treatment of the body in great detail, involving controlling one's desire for good food, sound sleep, beautiful clothing, comfort, musical amusement, and so on. Among these physical enjoyments, sexual intercourse for monks is completely forbidden, and those who engage in it are severely punished by being expelled from the monastic community forever.

Celibacy (*brahmacarya*) is essential to keep the Buddhist monastic practitioners on the correct path of freedom. The male-oriented monastic community particularly feels threatened by sex because the sexual impulse endangers the continuity of monastic community. Entering the Buddhist order means departing from marriage, family life, and parenting. Affection for wives and children and the responsibility of supporting household life tie men to family demands. It is sexual intercourse that begins this endless chain of *samsāra* (the suffering cycle of birth and death). The folly of lust itself hinders Buddhist practitioners from preserving celibacy. Since the

4. Lize Wilson, *Charming Cadavers: Horrific Figurations of the Feminine Indian Buddhist Hagiographic Literature* (Chicago: University of Chicago Press, 1996).

5. Sue Hamilton, "From the Buddha to *Boddhaghosa*: Changing Attitudes toward the Human Body in Theravada Buddhism," in *Religious Reflections on the Human Body*, ed. Jane Marie Law (Bloomington: Indiana University Press, 1995), 46–63.

nature of the Buddhist monastic life is homeless and wifeless, managing lust constitutes the central and lifelong discipline of monastic members.[6]

Ironically, as members of the monastic community (*sangha*), monks and nuns learn not only how to discipline their decomposable bodies, but also how to cultivate their physical appearance according to certain ideals. Buddhism emphasizes that the clerical bodies of monks and nuns are significant symbolic representatives of the Three Jewels in Buddhism (Buddha, Dharma, and Sangha). As the heir of Sakyamuni Buddha, every monastic member is regarded as a precious carrier of the Buddha Dharma, one who has taken on the role of "a guide for all human and heavenly beings." It is believed that the benefit of receiving ordination requires innumerable previous lifetimes accumulating good karma. As long as monks and nuns observe monastic law, heavenly beings will safeguard them. Therefore, the Buddhists reprimand those who hurt the bodies of the Buddha, including Buddha images or statues, as well as the bodies of the monks and nuns. It is believed that people who injure monks or nuns, causing even a drop of blood to be shed, are doomed to fall into hell forever. In order to show the privileged blessings awarded to monks and nuns, the highly symbolized clerical body must be well cared for.

The "Abnormal" Yellow Door in Buddhist Law

In order to emphasize the exemplary status of the precious body of monastic members and to prevent those belonging to the Yellow Door from taking the robe, monastic law goes into great detail in defining people with abnormal sexual organs.[7] These allegedly abnormal people are addressed as *pannddka, ssannddha', and kannddāka* in early Buddhist literature. These terms originated in Sanskrit and Indian culture, but Chinese Buddhists

---

6. It is believed that erotic lust is especially an ordeal for monks. Here I do not mean that women do not have sexual desire, but I *am* regarding the issue of sex from the perspective of the male-dominated monastic community in the founding period of Buddhism.

7. The monastic community does not expel monks whose sexual organs are injured after receiving ordination.

translated them as the Yellow Door (in Chinese *huang men*, meaning eunuch) and "the Impotent Male" (in Chinese *bu neng nan*, meaning "not able man"). The definitions of these terms, involving very detailed physical and psychological traits, are as follows in the various traditions (see the table on the following page).

Given this stress on bodily integrity, Buddhist law also does not allow female "Yellow Doors" to receive full ordination. The Mahasanghiga Vinaya introduces five types of female Yellow Doors,[8] again going into remarkable detail.

1. Two-sex women: Women with both sets of sexual organs who can engage in sexual activity either way, according to the sexes of their companions. They look like women, but Buddhist texts sometimes regard them as "neither male nor female."

2. Two-path Women: Women with abnormal urinating habits. This refers to women who are incapable of holding stool while urinating.

3. Small-path women: Women who have difficulty urinating.

4. Bloodless women: Women who do not menstruate.

5. Frequently bleeding women: Women whose menstruation continues for a long time or who cannot stop bleeding.

Why this preoccupation with blood and urine? The female Yellow Door appears to offer the threat of potential pollution, which may contaminate the monastic robe. Moreover, the sources of pollution, such as urine, stool, and blood, are also seen as related to difficulties in giving birth. Not only does irregular menstruation damage the function of reproduction, but damage to urinary organs may also hinder child-delivery. All this is in contrast to male Yellow Doors, who are considered incompetent because they lack functioning sexual organs to consummate sexual intercourse. The male Yellow Door is distinguished from his female counterpart by a capacity for sexual performance rather than by a capacity for reproduction.

---

8. T 24: 364a–c.

People with Abnormal Male Sexual Organs
as Recorded in Chinese Tripit Aka

Sanskrit and Definition	Textual Origin			
	Dharmagupta[9]	Sarvāstivāda[10]	Māhāsamghika[11]	Abidharma-kośaśāstra[12]
jāti-pannddaka: Born without sexual organs	The Yellow Door by birth	The Impotent Man by birth	The Impotent Man by birth	The *Ssannddha* by birth
āpat-pannddaka: Sexual organs cut off after birth	The Injured Yellow Door	The Impotent Man due to illness	The Impotent Man due to injury in childhood	The Injured *Ssannddha*
			The Impotent Man due to injury after childhood, usually refers to eunuch	
īssyya-pānnddaka: Erectile only by seeing sexual intercourse	The Jealous Yellow Door	The Impotent Man only ERECTILE DUE TO jealousy	The Impotent Man ONLY ERECTILE DUE TO jealousy	The Jealousy *pannddaka* or *kannddāka*
			The Impotent Man ERECTILE only DUE TO caressing by others	The *pannddaka* ERECTILE/sexually AROUSED only through special tricks
Asaktaprādurbhā or *vipannddaka:* Premature ejaculation	The Transforming Yellow Door	The Impotent Man due to premature ejaculation		
pakssa-pannddaka: Physically weak and sexually incapable	The Half-Month Yellow Door	The Man impotent during one-half the month	The Man impotent during one-half the month	The *pannddaka* impotent during one-half the month

---

9. T 22: 812c.
10. T 23: 153b–c.
11. T 22: 417c.
12. T 29: 80b, 13b.

To sum up, Buddhism identifies female and male Yellow Doors based on whether their sexual/genital organs function appropriately, but the differentiation also implies conventional expectation of genders. The description of the standardized clerical body, as mentioned previously, aims to screen unqualified people from ordination, and the emphasis is on women's reproductive function and men's sexual competence or incompetence.[13]

Buddhist ordination includes a noteworthy procedure to exclude unqualified candidates by examining the function of their sexual organs. During ordination, the presiders ask the candidates whether they are a Yellow Door, but they do not conduct a physical examination. However, the master is responsible for preparing his disciples for the final ordination. It is not necessary for the master to conduct a physical examination of his disciples because the intimate interaction in the novitiate period leaves the monastic authorities enough time to detect problems. For instance, it takes some time to detect irregular menstruation, but female novices are required to spend two years preparing for full ordination. Whether or not candidates were familiar with the Yellow Door, the master would systematically transfer knowledge about the Yellow Door to the next generation.

Detecting Homosexuality

Most physical features in male and female Yellow Doors can be identified through physical examination, but sexual orientation is another matter. Homosexual orientation is not defined by genital characteristics, and an additional complication is that homosexuality as a category has never been recognized in the Buddhist monastic community. Buddhist texts do not refer to such a thing as a "homosexual body." We must, therefore, investigate Buddhist views of homosexuality in a different way and according to a different context. The most efficient way to trace homosexuals in Buddhism, I believe, is to observe how Buddhist texts have recorded

---

13. As for the Unbeatable Virgin and the Yellow Door with difficulty in urination, these may be indirect references to the chastity of women.

the Yellow Door's violation of monastic law and the sentences that monastic authorities impose as punishment. Fortunately, Buddhist literature preserves detailed descriptions of those actions that are considered violations. There is also discussion of witnesses, sentencing, motivation, and the religious explanations for all this.

If someone behaves inappropriately, monastic authorities will take action and pronounce judgment. In other words, the monastic community has accumulated considerable experience in dealing with people with abnormal sexual organs and sexual misbehavior, leading to the development of the category of Yellow Door, along with measures to prevent damaging the discipline of monastic community through sexual misbehavior.

Sakyamuni Buddha plays an important role in identifying the misconduct of the Yellow Door. For example, it was reported that some monks entered the rooms of other monks and fondled them at night. After being caught, they claimed they were princesses or "neither male nor female" who took the robe in order to be the wife of the celibate monks. Sakyamuni Buddha seems to have identified these monks as Yellow Door and classified them into two groups. The first group includes those Yellow Doors without complete sexual organs by birth who should not be allowed to take the robe. Even though they were already ordained, they should be expelled from the order (*nāsanīyam*) right away. As for the second group of Yellow Doors, those who are impotent but with completely shaped sexual organs, Buddha prohibited them from taking the robe but allowed those already ordained to continue their clerical membership unless they violated the law.[14]

It is interesting that the Buddha defined the Yellow Door only by physical deficiency and offered a very simple reason for expelling Yellow Doors from the monastic community. Certain characteristics, physical and behavioral, disqualified a person from being a monk. In the commentaries (*abhidharma*) three things are specified regarding Yellow Door persons: (1) they have more cankers than ordinary people, (2) they are incapable

---

14. T 22: 417c–418a.

of making right decisions, and (3) they do not feel strong shame like ordinary people.[15] The commentator concluded that these mental and physical shortcomings disqualified a Yellow Door from being chosen as an exemplary vessel of Buddhist law. (Sometimes it was felt that serious violations of monastic law were attributable to the karma from previous lifetimes.) The Yellow Door might be punished by being returned to the lay state until being reborn in a normal body. In contrast, the Yellow Door without completely shaped sexual organs was likely to be expelled from the early Buddhist community.

Buddhist law also prohibits lay members from consummating "wrong sexual intercourse." Paying attention to the physical distinction between normal and abnormal sex in the Buddhist literature may provide a meaningful context for identifying Buddhist attitudes toward homosexuality. Modern interpretations tend to define "wrong sexual intercourse" as engaging in affairs with people who are not one's legal spouse. Some use an even stricter standard, which prescribes that married couples should not have any sexual life unless for the purpose of producing offspring. However, the description of Buddhist legal cases shows that Buddhism judges sexual intercourse not by the relation between the two people, but by the object the sexual organs touch. The objects for sexual intercourse range from people to animals (for instance, the mouth of fish), to equipment (such as the hollow inside bamboo), and to a beautiful heavenly goddess. This long list of improper sexual acts includes people with damaged sexual organs. It is prohibited to have sexual contact with those who are Yellow Door.[16]

Beyond actual sexual activity, Buddhist law is most concerned with diminishing sexual desires. According to monastic law, at the very moment that people desire to consummate sexual intercourse, they have already committed a "crime," and such "misconduct" cannot be purified through confession. In contrast, people who have been able to stop having sexual intercourse and have conquered their sexual desires are allowed to confess

---

15. T 41: 243a.
16. T22: 5a; 571c.

their "misconduct." Confession plays a significant role in Buddhism, and the monastic community usually makes judgments on the nature of the crime and then decides on the consequent punishment after the offender makes a public confession. The cases mentioned above show that Buddhist law views sexual desire as being as serious as, if not more serious than, sexual intercourse itself because unabated desires may eventually generate obstacles to people's religious discipline.[17]

Given the composite nature of the body in Buddhist teaching, the boundaries between genders are flexible, and sexual transformations can occur. This shows that not only sexual orientation but also gender itself is relative and not of primary importance in identifying what a person is. There are many examples in early Buddhist literature describing how men's bodies suddenly change into female bodies because of their obsession with sexual desire toward monks or nuns. In one case, a beautiful male monk was mistaken as a nun and raped. During the sexual attack, however, the rapist found out that "she" was actually a "he." The rapist felt so ashamed that he transformed into a female immediately. Since the rapist could not explain this bodily sexual change, he had to escape into the mountains to hide from all his relatives. At last, his wife heard about him and came to the raped monk asking forgiveness. She begged the monk to accept her husband's confession in person, and the monk agreed. As soon as the rapist gave his confession, he received his male body back and happily returned home with his wife.

In another case, a young boy named Soreyya experienced a sexual transformation.[18] Soreyya met the monk Mahākaccāyana at the public bath and could not stop admiring his beautiful blond nude body. At the very moment that Soreyya wanted to marry Mahākaccāyana, he transformed into a female. The female Soreyya married a rich husband and procreated two sons. Years later, "she" met Mahākaccāyana again and blurted out the secret. Soreyya immediately received his male body back. This

---

17. There are similar cases involving nuns and their sexual obsession.
18. Here I am using the Sanskrit name. Soreyya is Xuli in Chinese, which literally means "Must Leave."

time, he followed the monk Mahākaccāyana and entered the monastic order.[19]

In these cases the change of bodies seems to transgress dramatically the boundary between physical appearance and sexual identity. Gender is relativized. In particular, a change in sex occurs right at the moment one realizes one's offense. The change occurred when the rapist knew about his mistake and was ashamed, as well as when he received forgiveness from the victim face to face. Otherwise, he would have had to wait until his next life to repair the damage because he had already been transformed into the female body, the very body he was so eager to "take over" earlier. In other words, one's attitude is paramount in shaping one's future and in saying who one is.

As for Soreyya, the bodily transformation happened not at the moment he was attracted by Mahākaccāyana's body, but at the moment that he wanted to possess Mahākaccāyana's love. After experiencing intimate re-lationship as a wife, Soreyya realized the burden of love and finally left the household life as a male. The message here is that sexual desire can enmesh a person in the cycle of suffering. Regardless of whether Soreyya was homosexual or not, monastic law presumes that a sexual relationship should be between a male and a female. Nevertheless, the issue is not so much homosexual desire as sexual desire of any kind. Even though heterosexuality is presumed as the standard, that is not the main con-cern. Controlling sexual desire is the concern. It would seem in all of this that sexual desire is on trial, regardless of the gender of the lover or the beloved. Again, this contrasts with the Western habit of stressing sexual orientation in deciding who someone is.

Other stories show changes in a woman's body, including the record of the beautiful nun of the Mango basket.[20] A bully stopped the beautiful nun and asked for her love. With no way to escape, the nun asked him why he picked her. "By your beauty," he answered, "I am attracted." She tried to convince him that all worldly beauty was impermanent, but she

---

19. Dharmmapada-atthakathā, T 2: 831b.

20. Susan Murcott, *The First Buddhist Woman: Translations and Commentary on the Therigatha* (Berkeley, CA: Parallax Press, 1991).

failed. "So then," she asked, "which parts of my body are beautiful and attractive to you?" "Your eyes," he answered. At hearing the answer, the nun dug out her eyes with her own fingers and offered them. "Now you can have my beauty." The astonished bully cried out for her forgiveness. There are two versions of Sakyamuni Buddha's response to this event, one in which Sakyamuni Buddha began to prohibit nuns from walking alone in the forest, as well as traveling to other places, in order to keep them safe. In the other version Sakyamuni Buddha praises the nun's chastity and uses magical power to cure her eyes. It is again sexual desire, not sexual orientation, that is at issue.

Bodily Transformation in Chinese Mahayana Buddhism

The flexibility of the mind-body boundary becomes more significant in Mahayana Buddhism, which enlarges the scope of the body from a set of decomposable organs to the multiple forms of sentient beings. Based on the great compassion of the Bodhisattvas who vow to help all living beings, Mahayana discipline has developed more equalitarian attitudes toward physically and socially disadvantaged people, such as women and Yellow Doors. On the one hand, Mahayana Buddhism still recognizes the body as decomposable and impermanent. On the other hand, Mahayana Buddhism does not put as much stress on bodily differences.

The most famous case of bodily transformation is in the Lotus Sutra where the dragon king's eight-year-old daughter exemplifies its principle of universal equality.[21] In this sutra, the young dragon girl makes a vow to achieve Buddhahood in her female body. The wisest senior monk in the sectarian Buddhist literature, Uāriputra, comes to challenge her out of the conviction that it is impossible for women to attain Buddhahood. In response, the eight-year-old girl changes Uāriputra's body into a female and then asks him, "Are you still yourself now?" Of course, Uāriputra is still

---

21. Miriam Levering, "The Dragon Girl and the Abbess of Mo-Shan: Gender and Status in the Ch'an Buddhist Tradition," *Journal of International Association of Buddhist Studies* 5, no. 1 (1982): 19–35.

aware of himself, even with a female body. Then the dragon girl returns him to a male body and immediately gains Buddhahood in her own female body. This story shows that gender itself is of no major importance, again in contrast with much of Western culture.

According to Buddhist history, Sakyamuni Buddha made the revolutionary move to ordain slaves and women, and the Buddha claimed that nuns are just as capable of attaining *arhant* (liberation) as their male colleagues. However, most early Buddhist schools tried to inhibit this egalitarian impulse by requiring women to wait for another life to gain the male body. They attributed gender inequality to karma out of the conviction that it takes five hundred more lifetimes of religious cultivation to be born into a male body. In contrast, the mechanism of bodily transformation in Mahayana Buddhism provides an appropriate doctrinal base for sexual transformation. The miracle of women changing their bodies into male bodies in this present life symbolizes the strong possibility of women's achieving spiritual freedom.

The case of the dragon girl's transformation exemplifies the dramatic contrast between Mahayana and the earlier sectarian Buddhist schools. Try to imagine the debate between the old male human body of a senior monk and the young, nonhuman, and female body of the dragon girl, and imagine that the latter changes the body of the former into the same female form. This ironic bodily transformation powerfully illustrates the impermanence of any physical form and of any sexual difference or sexual orientation. Most important, as the dragon girl points out, body transformation cannot change one's consciousness because physical characteristics are impermanent parts that function only through our own awareness. Thus, characteristics such as sexual orientation are also relativized due to their radical impermanence.

Mahayana Buddhism, though not always consistent, refuses to evaluate people by their physical appearance and social status. These external conditions are simply various "empty" (*sunya*) forms. This also explains why Chinese Buddhist monastic communities since the fifth century have allowed eunuchs to establish their own monasteries. In earlier sectarian monastic law, eunuchs are definitely disqualified as monks because of their amputated sexual organs. Eunuchs are also viewed as an untouchable group in Chinese society because of their abnormal sexual organs. Ironically, the physically disadvantaged eunuchs saw the Buddhist order as their refuge. It was believed that becoming a eunuch resulted from bad karma in a previous life, which offered a strong motivation for their religious piety in searching for salvation so as to be reborn without this impairment.

Chinese eunuchs established a Third Sex *sangha* in Buddhist history. Yellow Doors were permitted to receive ordination and establish their own monastery. Eunuchs served in the imperial household and lived a double life. On the one hand, people were afraid of (or perhaps jealous of) them for their position in the court because they were the servants of the imperial household and controlled access to the core figures of the political order. On the other hand, some believed that eunuchs were doomed to be reborn into the realm of hell because they lacked complete body parts, and, therefore, the fate of being a eunuch in this life represented punishment as a result of bad karma from a previous life or lives. To a great degree, eunuchs were also stigmatized for their ambiguous sexual identity. In a system that values ancestor worship as much as the traditional Chinese family does, people tend to look down on eunuchs for being incapable of continuing the family line. However, some rich and powerful eunuchs adopted male children to carry on their family names. Another popular trend was that the imperial household took care of elderly eunuchs by establishing a Buddhist monastery to care for them. This development was quite reasonable in light of the fact that eunuchs were the most important agents in assisting the religious activities of royal women.

After Buddhism was introduced into China, Chinese courts began to send their widowed princesses and the court ladies of ex-emperors to Buddhist nunneries in order to preserve their chastity. Throughout history, many Chinese empresses donated their personal money to build Buddhist monasteries and nunneries where religious rituals were offered, especially upon the request of children who wished to hold memorial services for deceased family members. Taking Buddhist law into consideration, the nunneries were usually located at a short distance from male monasteries.

Generous empresses might allow eunuchs to establish their private monasteries nearby in order to allow them to continue their guarding service. In addition to praying for the prosperity of the court, these eunuchs also accumulated religious merit for themselves with the hope of being reborn in a complete body in future lives.

Eunuch monasteries show that Chinese Mahayana Buddhists developed a more flexible attitude toward the bodies of marginalized sectors of society than that exhibited by earlier sectarian Buddhism. This development also indicates that Chinese Buddhists were most concerned about sexual desire and sexual activity. They valued the chaste celibacy of monks and nuns, but were not preoccupied or even troubled by their sexual orientations.

Chinese Ch'an (Zen) Buddhism has undoubtedly inherited the Mahayana view of bodily transformation. Similar to the case of the dragon girl, Ch'an Buddhism urges the eradication of discrimination against the female body. Nun Moran scolded a young monk: "I am neither god nor ghost! Why should I change my body!?" Nun Moran was famous for her skillful teaching, and many monks came to ask for her guidance. A young monk visited her for that purpose but then felt hesitant to receive teachings from a woman. Therefore, he cited the case of the dragon girl and asked Nun Moran to show her superior transformative power. The nun was not trapped by his game. Instead, she shouted out the answer given above.[22] Again, gender, and by implication sexual orientation, was not an issue of importance.

Moreover, in the tradition it is emphasized in various ways that the monks themselves have hindered their own understanding of the Dharma by holding on to conservative and conventional views about physical forms, genders, and so on. Only by transgressing such exterior differentiation, as Nun Moran points out, can one hope to find one's true self (that is, the inherent Buddha Nature). The Ch'an case not only criticizes the stereotypical understanding of gender, but also explores the great potential of the mind. By rising above conventional concerns with sexual identity,

---

22. Levering, "The Dragon Girl and the Abbess of Mo-Shan," 19–35.

a woman can take pride in exploring her intelligence and self-identity, which is the true sense of identity required for enlightenment.

If Mahayana developed universal egalitarianism by introducing a change-able relationship between body and consciousness, the Chinese Ch'an schools accepted the flux and reflux of desire as the appropriate understanding of the construction of subjectivity. However, the purpose of spiritual practice is to explore the impermanent nature of conscious attachment in order to reveal the Buddha nature. In other words, only when we recognize and understand our false subjectivity can we find the path to true freedom. Such freedom requires moving beyond concern with one's own so-called abnormal sexual orientation, an important step in the improvement of meditation discipline. Sexual orientation simply does not define one's true nature.

This concern with false subjectivity emerges, for example, in a famous Ch'an story. An old monk helped to carry a young and attractive woman on his back across a river. A young monk, who was traveling with him, felt troubled and finally, after they had walked thirty miles from the river, asked the older monk whether touching a female body was a violation of monastic law. The old monk answered in surprise, "I have already forgotten this matter, but you have been carrying the woman in your mind over these thirty miles."

As Mahayana and Chinese Ch'an Buddhism show, neither physical nor psychological sexual identity need hinder people from pursuing the Dharma and achieving Buddhahood and Enlightenment.[23] Therefore, it is important to point out that the Buddhist teaching on the relative importance of physical organs and the function of consciousness opens a free space for the homosexual. Rather than focusing on classifications of the normal and abnormal due to sexual orientation, the main concern is on consciousness and enlightenment. This freedom is quite remarkable, given the fact that in many cultures homosexual identity is demeaned and stigmatized because of a heterosexual hegemony and often becomes a

---

23. Miriam Levering, "Lin-chi (Rinzai) Ch'an and Gender: The Rhetoric of Equality and the Rhetoric of Heroism," in Cabezon ed., *Buddhism, Sexuality, and Gender,* 137–56.

continuous source of suffering. The antipathy felt toward the homosexual may be parallel to the indescribable fear exhibited toward many types of physically handicapped people, including the Yellow Doors. But Ch'an Buddhism views obsession with homosexual identity as a matter of false identity from the perspective of religious cultivation. In order to explore the real self, one must first accept oneself. In order to realize the nature of this universe, one should distinguish among different phenomena, but treat them equally rather than remain obsessed by perceived differences or attempt to control or even distort them. In short, the path of the Dharma should not exclude homosexuals or discriminate against them in any way.

Monastic Members' Transcending Sexual Identity

Recently Taiwanese Buddhists have been receptive to homosexuals insofar as they have been able to remain celibate. The issue of homosexuality is rarely discussed in public. Many Taiwanese Buddhists have a very vague understanding of homosexuality, perhaps reflecting the lack of hetero-sexual/homosexual dichotomizing in Chinese culture, but there has been speculation as such issues are often discussed in private. It is interesting that most Buddhists judge misconduct of both heterosexuals and homo-sexuals according to the same standards. The issue of concern is not sexual orientation but proper conduct. Especially for monks and nuns, the homo-sexual relationship is described as a relationship similar to that between husband and wife. Not all lay Buddhists feel this way, of course. Most Buddhists also presume that it is easier for homosexual monks to be-come involved in improper sexual relations. Since Taiwanese Buddhism has not established a central church or any system authorized to deal with homosexual issues, the monastic community in private usually iso-lates members suspected of misconduct, but leaves them alone in public in order to keep the face of Buddhism. Lay Buddhists often have shown anger toward misbehaving homosexual monks and threatened to cut off their financial support.

There is more criticism of male homosexuals than of lesbians; the latter are more easily tolerated insofar as they are perceived as "more personal and private." The custom of religious sisterhood also protects lesbians, who can use the ideal of religious celibacy to refuse marriage if they have the education and money to gain access to the established religious orders and ordination. This explains the spinster houses practicing the cult of Guanyin (in Sanskrit, Avalokiteśvara, the Bodhisattva of Compassion) in Southeastern China and Taiwan.[24] The lack of official ordination involves the risk of being left out of the religious lineage and monastic hierarchy, but people have become accustomed to, and accepting of, this kind of supportive sisterhood. Today, Buddhist nuns' ordination is popularly recognized although many nuns live in private retreat homes and urban *dharma* centers, which are often smaller than monasteries and nunneries in scale and size. If the number of monastic residents is less than five, the nunnery is considered a private hermitage and run independently, both economically and disciplinarily.

The male bias and preference for masculinity are still very much in evidence, however. No religion perfectly lives out its best ideals, and this is also true for Buddhism. The discipline of nuns emphasizes the fact that men and women are potentially equal, but masculinity (exemplified by the Sakyamuni Buddha) is still lifted up as the higher paradigm. This creates problems of ambiguous identity among nuns. Although Buddhists may defend the identity of nuns as transcending conventional gender roles, the bodily discipline and self-identity of nuns continue to reproduce an idealized masculine identity. With their shaven heads and robes identical to those of monks, and their observation of almost the same set of monastic laws (except for additional requirements that subordinate them to monks), it is difficult to distinguish the nuns from the monks by physical appearance and apparent behavior. The terms that female monastic members use to address each other are also male, so that the terms for master and disciples become "fathers" and "sons," and senior and junior nuns address each other as elder and younger "brothers." Buddhists also value highly "the

24. Hon-min Yip, "Lineage and Sisterhood in South China," *Modern Chinese History Society of Hong Kong Bulletin* 8 (December 1996): 43–57; Helen F. Siu, "Where Were the Women? Rethinking Marriage Resistance and Regional Culture in South China, *Late Imperial China* 11, no. 2 (1990): 32–62.

tradition of the Great Man," and some ordained nuns still have as their religious salvation the goal to be reborn into a male body for their next life. Some nuns even adopt radical means to stop their menstruation.[25]

Conclusion

This chapter has explained how earlier sectarian Buddhist monastic communities expelled men and women with abnormal sexual organs and punished sexual misconduct to better symbolize monastic ideals and maintain celibate purity among monastic members. However, the Bodhisattva precepts of Mahayana Buddhism have offered more equal opportunity for every sentient being to take the robe, and on these grounds it is possible to argue that homosexual men (as well as lesbian nuns) should be allowed to be ordained and to organize their own communities. For those homosexuals who enter the order and keep the vows of celibacy, it is not necessary to establish a special community. Celibacy, not homosexuality, is the issue, insofar as intercourse, even between heterosexual couples, is prohibited by monastic law. Most important, Mahayana Buddhists view all kinds of body, including male, female, human, and animal, as impermanent forms. Therefore, obsession with sexual desire hinders the path to enlightenment for both homosexuals and for heterosexuals.

In sum, what concerns the monastic community is not one's sexual orientation as such, but rather one's sexual conduct. Therefore, I believe that there is no need to establish special monastic communities for homosexuals. The separation of the homosexual members from the heterosexual community would only strengthen the negative stereotype of homosexuality among the orthodox monastic community. Controlling sexual desire constitutes a great discipline for Buddhists, both heterosexual and homosexual. Both heterosexuals and homosexuals can enter and follow the path of enlightenment. In this fundamental way Buddhism can transcend prejudice against people who are homosexual.

---

25. Yeshe Choekyi Lhamo, "Transforming Instead of Slaying the 'Red Dragon,'" in *Bridging the Worlds: Buddhist Women's Voices across Generations*, ed. Karma Lekshe Tsomo (Taipei: Yuan Chuan Press, 2004), 268–71.

Chapter Six

Eradicating the Sin of Heterosexism

MARY E. HUNT

Countless Catholics and others whose lives are influenced by Catholic teaching have committed the sin of heterosexism, perhaps without realizing its name. Parents who disown or dishonor their same-sex loving children; lawmakers who vote against same-sex marriage; employers and landlords who discriminate in hiring and housing against lesbian, gay, bisexual, and transgender people; priests and ministers who teach and counsel against same-sex love; and even same-sex loving persons who engage in self-hatred commit a sin against a Divine who created sexually diverse people and a community of people pledged to love one another.

In their gound-breaking book Catholic ethicist Patricia Beattie Jung and Lutheran liturgy professor Ralph F. Smith define heterosexism as "a reasoned system of bias regarding sexual orientation ... that denotes prejudice in favor of heterosexual people and connotes prejudice against bisexual and, especially, homosexual people."[1] This system of privilege accorded to those who love persons of a sex/gender not their own to the detriment of those who love persons of their same sex/gender is deeply woven into the social fabric of laws, customs, ethics, and commerce. While misguided kyriarchal church officials condemn the "problem" of homosexuality, in a justice-centered religion like Catholicism it is the evil of heterosexism that

1. Patricia Beattie Jung and Ralph F. Smith, *Heterosexism: An Ethical Challenge* (Albany: State University of New York Press, 1993), 13.

requires exploration and eradication, the twin goals of this essay.[2] I write as a Catholic lesbian feminist theologian in the United States, indebted to colleagues around the world who are moving the debate on homosexuality to new anti-heterosexist ground.[3]

Methodology

I explore heterosexism in its Catholic structural and personal dimensions and propose how to eradicate it as part of an inter-religious strategy to bring about relational justice. My method is not to revisit the many excellent Catholic biblical, theological, and ethical treatments of same-sex love that are persuasive in their pro-lgbt arguments even if they do not deal explicitly with heterosexism.[4] To do so would simply reinscribe homosexuality as the primary theo-ethical concern. After all, homosexuality is a phenomenon that, absent heterosexism, is no more ethically interesting or relevant than heterosexuality. It is a descriptive category that is morally neutral. Rather, I will demonstrate how shifting the focus from homosexuality to heterosexism, what others have called "reframing the issue,"

---

2. Elisabeth Schüssler Fiorenza coined the term *kyriarchy* to describe interstructured forms of lordship that are oppressive. The Catholic all-male hierarchy is quintessentially kyriarchal. See Elisabeth Schüssler Fiorenza, *But She Said: Feminist Practices of Biblical Interpretation* (Boston: Beacon Press, 1992), 117, 123.

3. I am grateful to colleagues in the Heterosexism Project of the Religious Consultation for Population, Reproductive Health, and Ethics, especially Judith Plaskow and Marvin Ellison for helpful suggestions on this essay. I am also grateful to Diann L. Neu for her careful reading.

4. Among the most useful treatments of homosexuality in Catholic literature are John Boswell, *Christianity, Social Tolerance, and Homosexuality: Gay People in Western Europe from the Beginning of the Christian Era to the Fourteenth Century* (Chicago: University of Chicago Press, 1980); Bernadette J. Brooten, *Love between Women: Early Christian Responses to Female Homoeroticism* (Chicago: University of Chicago Press, 1996); Robert Goss, *Jesus Acted Up: A Gay and Lesbian Manifesto* (San Francisco: HarperSanFrancisco, 1993); Mark D. Jordan, *The Silence of Sodom: Homosexuality in Modern Catholicism* (Chicago: University of Chicago Press, 2000); and John McNeill, *The Church and the Homosexual* (Boston: Beacon Press, 1976). For scriptural arguments, see also Daniel Helminiak, *What the Bible Really Says about Homosexuality* (San Francisco: Alamo Square Press, 1994). An excellent contemporary resource that includes both theology and scripture is an anthology edited by Patricia Beattie Jung with Joseph Andrew Coray, *Sexual Diversity and Catholicism: Toward the Development of Moral Theology* (Collegeville, MN: Liturgical Press, 2001).

results in new insights that can transform Catholicism and contribute to other religions' efforts to transform themselves.[5]

A compelling reason for taking this approach is because debate in Catholic circles on the morality of homosexuality has resulted in a complete impasse and a lot of damage. Those who consider homosexuality a sin and those who consider it healthy, good, natural, and holy simply disagree. Kyriarchal church teaching favors the former. The *sensus fidelium*, the sense of the faithful, or what most people believe, is moving in the other direction. Joseph Cardinal Ratzinger in his capacity as the prefect of the Congregation for the Doctrine of the Faith was the theological proponent of the most heterosexist of teachings and policies.[6] As Pope Benedict XVI he has additional powers of persuasion and enforcement. Official Catholic teaching is virtually silent on the sin of heterosexism despite its heavy prohibitions against homosexuality.

If there were no consequences to the impasse, I would ignore it and let the consensus develop in favor of sexual diversity in its own time, as seems to be happening. However, the Roman Catholic Church causes untold spiritual and psychological damage to its billion-plus members throughout the world and others by promoting heteronormativity. It is, however unintentionally, complicit in the gay-bashing violence that occurs in cultures where same-sex love and lovers are despised. The Vatican influences public policy in many countries to make heterosexuality the only legitimate sexual practice, to prevent same-sex couples from accessing the legal rights of marriage, and, in some places, to criminalize consenting sexual

---

5. George Lakoff has popularized this approach in *Don't Think of an Elephant! Know Your Values and Frame the Debate* (White River Junction, VT: Chelsea Green Publishers, 2004). However, feminist theologians have been doing this for decades in their refusal to respond to cultural givens and in the construction of new paradigms. One classic example is Elisabeth Schüssler Fiorenza, *In Memory of Her: A Feminist Theological Reconstruction of Christian Origins* (New York: Crossroad, 1983).

6. Among the most damaging documents that were published while Joseph Cardinal Ratzinger was prefect of the Congregation for the Doctrine of the Faith are *Letter to the Bishops of the Catholic Church on the Pastoral Care of Homosexual Persons*, October 1, 1986, and *Some Considerations concerning the Catholic Response to Legislative Proposals on the Non-Discrimination of Homosexual Persons*, July 23, 1992.

behavior between adult persons of the same sex. The stakes are too high to ignore the theo-political dimensions of a heterosexist religious institution.

The old argument, as framed by church officials, is whether homosexuality is morally acceptable or not. This framing puts the onus on those who love to defend their love, an odd and unjust demand in a religious tradition that teaches love as its highest value. It also allows those who reject social-scientific and theological data to ignore it since what is problematized is an abstraction, "homosexuality," rather than the concrete reality of human beings loving and expressing their love regardless of the sexual constellation of the lovers. At issue is not the morality of anyone's sexual orientation. Putting the focus there obscures the fact that heterosexism harms all persons regardless of sexual orientation and prevents many people from achieving what I describe as "sexual integrity." Only after heterosexism has been dismantled can Catholics revisit the question of homosexuality with any objectivity. It is to be hoped that at that point it will not be necessary to do so since the irrelevance of sexual preference for any moral debate will be obvious.

Exploring Heterosexism

Heterosexism is the attitude and ability to enforce the notion that heterosexuality is normative to the exclusion of the full flowering of same-sex possibilities. It is not to be confused with homophobia which, as a psychological approach to the same phenomena, deals with fear of same-sex love and lovers. Nor is it to be conflated with "homo-hatred," which is the explicit articulation of disdain toward homosexuals that often leads to violence. Rather, heterosexism is an increasingly disputed assumption that sexual difference (or what may be thought of as mixed-gender bonding or heterosexual pair-bonding) is normative and necessary for "good sex," that is, for morally acceptable physical expression of love.[7]

---

7. See Patricia Beattie Jung, Mary E. Hunt, and Radhika Balakrishnan, eds., in *Good Sex: Feminist Perspectives from the World's Religions* (New Brunswick, NJ: Rutgers University Press, 2001).

Catholic theological heterosexism takes many subtle and overt forms. Some are seemingly benign, such as the incessant insipid mantra of the Christian Right that "God did not create Adam and Steve." Others are more clearly harmful, such as the prohibition on same-sex activity that results in religious censure. These negative messages tell people they are not good, holy, or natural because of their sexuality. In addition to being detrimental to the psychological, spiritual, and sometimes even physical health of lesbian, gay, bisexual, transgender, and queer people, these assertions contradict basic Catholic teachings on the dignity of the individual.[8] None of these teachings specifies that the individual whose rights are guaranteed because of her or his personhood must be heterosexual.

Heterosexism, rooted in an outdated anthropology that claims sexual complementarity between males and females as natural law, is perhaps easiest seen on the macro or structural level by the Vatican ban on same-sex marriage. International discussion of and progress toward the legalization of same-sex marriage in countries such as Belgium, Canada, the Netherlands, and Spain occasioned *Considerations regarding Proposals to Give Legal Recognition to Unions between Homosexual Persons,* one of the documents signed by Joseph Cardinal Ratzinger, now Pope Benedict XVI.[9] The document concludes:

> The Church teaches that respect for homosexual persons cannot lead in any way to approval of homosexual behavior or to legal recognition of homosexual unions. The common good requires that laws recognize, promote, and protect marriage as the basis of the family, the primary unit of society. Legal recognition of homosexual unions or placing them on the same level as marriage would mean not only the approval of deviant behavior, with the consequence of making it a model in present-day society, but would also obscure basic values which belong to the common inheritance of humanity. The Church

---

8. See for example, Vatican Council II, *Gaudium et Spes (Pastoral Constitution on the Church in the Modern World)* (1965), par. 26.

9. Congregation for the Doctrine of the Faith, *Considerations Regarding Proposals to Give Legal Recognition to Unions between Homosexual Persons,* June 3, 2003.

cannot fail to defend these values, for the good of men and women and for the good of society itself. (par. 9)

Three common features of the Ratzinger theological method are evident in this statement. First, the teaching is rooted in a worldview which assumes that (1) "marriage" means heterosexual marriage; (2) "the common good" excludes all but those who are heterosexual; and (3) homosexual activity is "deviant behavior." While one can hold these opinions, they are by no means "given" in any objective sense, nor are they universally held. They emerge from a static worldview that upholds mixed-gender coupling as normative, heterosex open to procreation as the only moral option, and same-sex activity as morally evil. Competing worldviews held by other Catholics result in the conviction that coupling is not gender dependent and, further, that sexual morality is dependent on intention and results, not biology. Such worldviews are difficult to reconcile.

A second feature of the Ratzinger method that is apparent here is a reliance on natural law to explain why certain behaviors are acceptable (heterosexuality) and others are not (homosexuality). This, too, is a matter of philosophical proclivity and not received truth. Indeed, the data of the social sciences are ample to prove that heterosexuality is only one of several ways to be sexual in the world.

The third feature of this method is that there is always a public policy component, in this case an effort to stem the tide of same-sex marriages. As more and more countries throughout the world and more states in the United States move toward same-sex marriage as a matter of justice, this effort looks increasingly weak. Nevertheless, it is a way for the Vatican to stay in the moral conversation at a time when it is all but ignored on matters of war, economics, and the environment.

What the writers of the document call "basic values" are now obviously heterosexist assumptions in need of exploration and eradication. They are not universally shared. Behavioral scientific and anthropological data on same-sex love show that what was once a diagnostic category of mental

illness is now considered a common and healthy lifestyle.[10] This is not
new information and cannot be passed over by those who claim to speak
theologically in postmodernity. When such discoveries and shifts are ignored, it is not only that the Vatican is in disagreement with progressives,
but that Catholics live out of different worldviews that may indeed be
irreconcilable.

It is doubtful that Catholics will come to consensus on the morality
of same-sex love anytime soon. While polls do not make theology, it
is impossible to ignore that just as Catholics have changed their views
on slavery, the place of women, and the role of science, so, too, many
Catholics have changed their views on homosexuality. They are morally
mature enough to recognize that same-sex relationships, like mixed-sex
ones, come in all sorts of packages. The ethical focus is on the quality of
the love, not the quantity of each gender involved. As a pragmatic matter,
it is useful to locate many such points of contact among the diverse faithful
in an effort to limit the damage the kyriarchy does, especially to young
people.

Changing the Focus

Changing the conversation from the morality of homosexuality to the
sin of heterosexism is an effort to move from a non-conversation about
homosexuality, where agreement eludes us, to a productive conversation
on eradicating heterosexism, where widespread agreement may be a real
possibility. The starting point is the common acknowledgment that there
are many lesbian, gay, bisexual, transgender (henceforth lgbt), and queer
Catholics. In fact, there are many more than most people know. For example, some conservative estimates indicate that at least half of U.S.
Catholic priests are gay. My own observation is that the percentage is

---

10. For a good summary of the social scientific data on this question, see Isaiah Crawford
and Brian D. Zamboni, "Informing the Debate on Homosexuality: The Behavioral Science
and the Church," in *Sexual Diversity and Catholicism: Toward the Development of Moral
Theology,* ed. Patricia Beattie Jung with Joseph Andrew Coray (Collegeville, MN: Liturgical
Press, 2001), 216–51.

even higher, though reprisals against openly gay priests prevent anyone from having accurate data.

Regarding lgbt people the *Catechism of the Catholic Church* states: "They must be accepted with respect, compassion, and sensitivity. Every sign of unjust discrimination in their regard should be avoided" (par. 2358). This statement can be taken generously as openness to eradicate heterosexism. However, as we have learned painfully in the abortion debate, common ground is hard to come by, so when found, it can be useful in moving the question along. Catholics, including some in the Vatican, are beginning to see the damaging effects of heterosexism, especially its impact on children, and hence the need to refocus the discussion.

The extent of the problem is clear in the document on same-sex marriage (*Considerations Regarding Proposals to Give Legal Recognition to Unions between Homosexual Persons*) in a section on adoption: "Allowing children to be adopted by persons living in such unions would actually mean doing violence to these children, in the sense that their condition of dependency would be used to place them in an environment that is not conducive to their full development. This is gravely immoral" (par. 7). This statement alone illustrates the pernicious intent and destructive impact of Catholic heterosexism. Have the people who wrote and approved such a statement ever been up in the night with a sick child or held one of the hundreds of thousands of children who are orphaned because of sexist population policies or the HIV/AIDS pandemic? Many lesbian and gay families include such children, welcoming them with love and affection, reasoning that a child's life with one parent or with two parents of the same sex is far better than languishing in an institution or, worse, dying from neglect.

Either Vatican officials are abysmally ignorant of the world or, more likely, pathologically focused on the need for one parent from column A and one from column B to keep their worldview in its hegemonic place. That is, they are so concerned to have a biological man and a biological woman, regardless of what other dimensions those persons bring to the relationship, that they cannot imagine or prioritize the well-being of children. Thus, it is Vatican officials, not same-sex parents, who do violence to children through the ruthless demand for heterosexual normativity. This is the kind of classic reversal that feminist philosopher Mary Daly named in *Beyond God the Father* more than thirty years ago.[11] A variety of studies have shown that children of same-sex parents do just fine.[12] If anything, they are a little more open to experimenting with same-sex dating than their peers, but in fact about the same percentage of them turn out to be heterosexual. The violent shoe is on the Vatican's foot.

Teaching children to find and share love is a basic responsibility of their adult caretakers. In Catholic circles this has traditionally meant teaching that friendships are multiple, but that a love relationship resulting in marriage, the only legitimate setting for sexual expression that must be open always to procreation, is a singular experience possible only with a person of a different sex.[13] Experience has increasingly contradicted this approach. The sexual revolution of the last century, the women's liberation movement, the widespread use of effective and economical birth control, and the rise of same-sex lovers daring to speak their love's name have made the contradictions explicit. In fact, heterosexual marriages end in divorce as often as in death. Most heterosexual women now have sex with the intention of procreating only a few times in their lives. Same-sex love is a common and delightful experience for many people, sometimes to their great surprise. These new realities demand a new catechesis for Catholic children for which a new Catholic theology of sexuality is necessary.

Shifting Understandings

Catholic ethicist Christine Gudorf contributes to a new theology of sexuality by clarifying the "postmodern shift from human sexual dimorphism to human sexual polymorphism."[14] A careful look at biology is enough to

---

11. Mary Daly, *Beyond God the Father* (Boston: Beacon Press, 1973), 95–97.

12. Psychologist Charlotte Patterson has done major research on children of lesbian and gay parents. For a summary and bibliography see the American Psychological Association's 1995 study "Lesbian and Gay Parenting: A Resource for Psychologists," *www.apa.org/pi/parent.html*, accessed August 15, 2005.

13. For a critique of this position, see Mary E. Hunt, *Fierce Tenderness: A Feminist Theology of Friendship* (New York: Crossroad, 1991).

14. Christine E. Gudorf, "The Erosion of Sexual Dimorphism: Challenges to Religion and Religious Ethics," *Journal of the American Academy of Religion* 6 (2001): 863–91.

indicate that human beings are created in a rich variety of ways for which a dimorphic paradigm is simply inadequate. Moreover, sex is not viewed as biologically given while gender is socially constructed. Rather, as Gudorf observes, "both sex and gender are socially constructed categories; both sex and gender must be interpreted."[15]

The assumptions that there are only two sexes and two genders and that we know what it means to be a man or a woman, and, consequently, what it means to be a lesbian woman or a gay man, can no longer be taken for granted. In concrete terms, "polymorphous sexuality means that we may be attracted to a person only to find out that the person does not have a body sexed in the way we thought, or may have a body sexed the way we thought but not the sexual identity we thought would accompany that body, or may have a body sexed the way we thought and the sexual identity we thought would accompany it but not be interested in the sexual acts we are interested in."[16] At present there is no Catholic theology adequate to respond to this new reality. The old heterosexist model is in no way adequate.

The hierarchically dualistic way of thinking about sexuality in general is itself outmoded. This habit of thinking in twos, such that one is always better than the other (male over female, white over black, heterosexual over homosexual) rather than in multiple (poly) possibilities is deeply in-grained in Catholics. Feminist theorist Catherine MacKinnon described the problem as the inability to see difference without discrimination.[17] The dualistic insistence on viewing the world in either-or terms with one always better than the other undergirds heterosexuality and places it in a kyriarchal (lordship) relationship over homosexuality. One form of sexual expression is regarded as normative, the other as sinful. This dynamic is a reflection of the Vatican's effort to keep in place a top-down, male-only clerical power model. Decision-making is restricted to a very few, and

---

15. Ibid., 876.
16. Ibid., 887.
17. Catharine MacKinnon, "Difference and Dominance: On Sex Discrimination," in *The Moral Foundation of Civil Rights*, ed. Robert K. Fullinwinder and Claudia Mills (Totowa, NJ: Rowman and Littlefield, 1986).

those must be members of the ordained clergy, effectively constructing a two-tiered system of rulers and ruled. Given the difficulty in defending its sexual theology in light of twenty-first-century experiences and sources, I submit that power rather than certain forms of sexuality is what the Vatican seeks most to protect.

Heterosexist assumptions are the basis of the Vatican's teaching that homosexual orientation "is a more or less strong tendency ordered toward an intrinsic moral evil; and thus the inclination itself must be seen as an objective disorder."[18] Likewise, the Vatican holds that "homosexual acts are intrinsically disordered and can in no case be approved of."[19] However, once such analysis is stripped of the notion that persons of different sexes are required for morally ordered sex and relieved of the burden of proving that there is only one good way of being sexual, the teaching falls apart and slips away.

Likewise, the teaching that all same-sex sexual activity is wrong in every case looks dubious without heterosexism. What could possibly be wrong with loving, mutual, safe, consensual, and community-building sex between committed male or female partners? How tragic to think that Catholic teaching would deem "intrinsically evil" something so obviously good. Many Christian ethicists have offered creative, feasible alternatives to heterosexist options, sketching what healthy relationships look like and how to achieve them.[20]

The Vatican's construction of homosexual sex as wrong in every case passes over the data of anthropology that show same-sex love lived out (as healthily as heterosexism allows) in virtually all human cultures. It is heterosexism, the barriers erected to keep same-sex love from flourishing, that needs to be eradicated in order to recognize this reality. The same

---

18. Congregation for the Doctrine of the Faith, *Letter to the Bishops of the Catholic Church on the Pastoral Care of Homosexual Persons*, par. 3.

19. Congregation for the Doctrine of the Faith, *Declaration on Certain Questions concerning Sexual Ethics*, December 29, 1975, par. 9.

20. See, for example, Kelly Brown Douglas, *Sexuality and the Black Church: A Womanist Perspective* (Maryknoll, NY: Orbis Books, 1999); Marvin M. Ellison, *Same-Sex Marriage? A Christian Ethical Analysis* (Cleveland: Pilgrim Press, 2004); and Marie Marshall Fortune, *Love Does No Harm: Sexual Ethics for the Rest of Us* (New York: Continuum, 1998).

theological view leaves aside the data of sociology that provide countless examples of people in same-sex relationships who function as mature moral agents. Only heterosexism explains why exemplary lives, including those of some lesbian nuns, gay cardinals, and lesbian/gay revered teachers, have to be hidden. Bracketed altogether in the Vatican's approach to love are the claims of transgender people that gender is a much more fluid category than previously understood.[21] Heterosexism obscures the significant theological consequences that flow from this insight.

More heterosexist assumptions lurk. Priestly celibacy until quite recently was assumed to mean that the priest would not marry, nor engage in heterosexual sex outside of marriage. Homosexual conduct was not discussed. The vow of chastity taken by women and men in religious orders was assumed to mean that persons would abstain from sexual (read heterosexual) relations. Many priests and/or religious have justified their same-sex experiences on this basis, arguing correctly that they engaged in no heterosexual conduct and certainly did not marry. However, as the priest pedophilia and episcopal cover-up scandals have demonstrated, such confusions or jesuitical sleights of hand have led to serious problems and the erosion of trust within the Catholic community. The Vatican and some U.S. bishops have sought to link clerical sexual misconduct with homosexuality.[22] But it was duplicity about sexuality in general and not homosexuality specifically that encouraged illegal sexual activity and its cover-up.[23]

The heterosexist bias has sacramental implications, as well. In fact, there are seven sacraments for heterosexual Catholics and only six for homosexual Catholics until same-sex marriage is approved. The parallel with sexism is clear since the sexist ban on the ordination of women results in seven sacraments for Catholic men and only six for Catholic women.

---

21. See Virginia Ramey Mollenkott, *Omni-Gender: A Trans-Religious Approach* (Cleveland: Pilgrim Press, 2001).

22. See Patricia Beattie Jung, "Sexual Diversity and Ordained Ministry," *Union Seminary Quarterly Review* 57, nos. 1–2 (2003): 67–87.

23. See Mary E. Hunt, "Duplicity Writ Large," in *Gay Catholic Priests and Clerical Sexual Misconduct: Breaking the Silence*, ed. Donald L. Boisvert and Robert E. Goss (New York: Haworth Press, 2005), 113–21.

Heterosexist bias even reaches to the choice of godparents for baptism. If the parents choose to have two godparents they must select one of each sex, even if two women or two men would do quite well in a given case.

The personal damage of heterosexism is widespread and stunning, as a few examples demonstrate. A young lesbian woman saw the contradictions of her faith when she confronted her Catholic mother, a well-educated mental-health professional, on why her mother had not presented same-sex love on a parallel with heterosexuality during her formative years. A revered gay priest sold thousands of books on healing as a wounded person without publicly disclosing a major source of his own wounds. A Catholic nun with a woman lover counseled many people on relational issues without feeling safe enough to share her own. In addition to the tragedy for the individuals involved, these cases and legions like them signify a loss of integrity for the whole community.

On the macro level, the United States Conference of Catholic Bishops and many diocesan offices lobby against same-sex marriage in national and local settings. They help keep the more than 1,138 federal rights that accrue to married couples from those in same-sex partnerships.[24] The Vatican does the same at the international level, putting pressure on governments like Spain (to no avail) to keep marriage heterosexist. One wonders why in the face of so many international problems, including war, racism, ecocide, and poverty, a religious organization would spend its symbolic capital on sexuality unless it were the lynchpin in its hierarchically dualistic worldview. Paired with the sexism that always accompanies it, heterosexism plays a key role in Catholic kyriarchal thinking, both to discriminate against lgbt people and to prevent especially women from exercising moral and spiritual agency.

Heterosexual people are damaged by Catholic heterosexism, as well. The pressure to partner with someone of a different sex has led to many a short marriage. One can speculate that it has occasioned many a missed

---

24. The Human Rights Campaign website reports: "An update to the 1997 GAO report (1,049 Federal Benefits for Married Couples) found that 120 new statutory provisions involving marital status were enacted since the last report, and 31 were repealed or amended to remove marital status as a factor. The new total is 1,138."

love, as well. Those who are taught that heterosexual nuptial imagery best describes the relationship between Jesus and the church are impoverished spiritually and disenfranchised intellectually. All these failures of religious imagination are preventable by eradicating the heterosexist bias that undergirds them.

Fortunately, feminist scholars are addressing this problem. Ethicist Christina L. H. Traina examines heterosexual marriage, concluding that "the ultimate fruitfulness and durability of any union — heterosexual or homosexual — have nothing to do with gender complementarity or lack thereof. But they have everything to do with faith, friendship, generosity, communal support, the serendipity of personalities, sexual and verbal affection, and the hard work that goes into mutual formation of a working partnership."[25] Dr. Traina's reflections rejecting heterosexist assumptions and placing all relationships on a level moral playing field demonstrate that the implications of changing views on homosexuality will have a broad and positive impact on views of sexuality in general, more motivation for the task at hand.

Eradicating Heterosexism

The process of eradicating a deeply entrenched habit such as heterosexism is complex. I suggest four constructive approaches to begin the work: sacramental, philosophical, theological, and pastoral. Each is rooted in the Catholic tradition but extends it in a non-heterosexist direction. Of course, such suggestions need to be fleshed out in future work, but by naming them, I seek to set an agenda for Catholic scholars, activists, and pastors that will replace the current unproductive impasse on homosexuality with more dynamic options for the whole community.

A Sacramental Approach

A first step toward eradicating heterosexism in Catholic circles is to use the traditional language and sacramental theology of sin and forgiveness.

---

25. Cristina L. H. Traina, "Papal Ideals, Marital Realities: One View from the Ground," in Jung and Coray, *Sexual Diversity and Catholicism*, 269–88.

The impact of heterosexism is to cut off relationships and possibilities, a contemporary definition of sin. Such alienation needs to be remedied, for which the traditional formula for the Catholic sacrament of penance is useful. It is a process Catholics recognize instantly and trust to work.

In order for forgiveness to be granted in this sacramental schema, one begins by acknowledging the sin. Catholics need to name their heterosexism in the same way that some acknowledged holding slaves and others acknowledged their sexism and racism by specific reference to behaviors and beliefs that are unacceptable. It is not a cheap or easy way out, but rather a first step toward change, to say that what one was taught — and has taught the next generation — was simply wrong.

Next comes the request for forgiveness, often done in personal terms from those who have been wronged, but also needing institutional or corporate acknowledgment. The parallel here is to anti-Semitism, of which individual Catholics and the kyriarchal church have been guilty over millennia. The institutional church has made only small gestures in this regard in comparison with the gravity of the sin, but there have been notable examples of individual Catholics changing their views and begging forgiveness from their Jewish colleagues, all according to the sacramental model they were taught. As Catholics realize the error of their ways with respect to heterosexism and reflect on the incalculable damage done to lgbt people over the years, one can expect both individual confession and corporate acknowledgment of guilt.

The third part of a Catholic reconciliation process is the resolution not to commit the sin again. This will require concrete proof that the old ways of thinking, no longer adequate for ethical work, are rejected. Individuals will find ways to express their newfound wisdom about love in its many packages, assuring their families and students, their neighbors and friends that what matters is the love, not the package. A revision of the *Catechism* and an institutional acknowledgment of the importance of lgbt theology will be good first steps for a church that wishes to eradicate the sin of heterosexism. Though seemingly impossible under the present pope, these are the kinds of institutional changes needed to signal the embrace of a variety of ways of loving as authentically Catholic.

Finally, there is penance or providing some restitution for the harm done as the process of reconciliation is brought to closure. So many lgbt people, some long dead, are due restitution from the Catholic Church and its members that almost any gesture in this direction will be helpful. Educational programs, parish gay-straight alliances, celebrations of same-sex committed love, and the like will begin to repair centuries of damage. Apologies to and support for lgbt people and programs will be welcome next steps.

This is the traditional penitential formula. It has a proven track record. It is easy to understand, regardless of what one thinks of homosexuality. Given the harm done by the sin of heterosexism on the personal and corporate levels, there is no time to waste implementing this strategy.

A Philosophical Approach

Terminology remains a thorny problem on issues of sexuality. Despite decades of research, little is known about the causes of heterosexuality, whether homosexuality has a genetic component, or if bisexuality is common. Likewise, there is little evidence to prove or disprove that human beings choose their sexuality. The range of ways in which human beings are transgender (including cross-dressing, bi-gender, and transvestitism) presents even more challenge to the terms used to describe a person. For example, is a male-to-female transgender person who loves a woman a lesbian? What if the other woman considers herself heterosexual? The permutations are as endless as human variety.

One thing certain in the sexological research is that for many people sexuality and gender are not only fluid but changing realities over time. This is obvious in young people whose dating may include persons of various sexes and genders. Many young people are reluctant to label their own sexuality for fear of precluding possibilities or buying into categories they find restrictive. They sometimes use the term "gender queer" to describe themselves. All of this remains to be sorted out as experiences deepen and new understandings of the complexity of human sexuality emerge.

In terms of moral discourse and ethical decision-making, it is useful to name the task at hand as the search for "sexual integrity," which means finding a certain fit between what one sees and what one gets or a correspondence between word and deed.[26] By focusing on sexual integrity rather than preference, orientation, or even identity, I mean to pass over the answerless question of why people love as they do. I propose that we move on to affirm that most people do the best they can to love well. The fallible human condition results in the fact that our best is usually not good enough. But insofar as our efforts to love are often quite enough to sustain human community and invite human greatness, I observe that it is integrity, not preference, orientation, or identity, with which we ought to be concerned.

This philosophical shift makes moral sense since preference, orientation, and identity make no ethical difference if heterosexism is no more. What does matter is whether a relationship is mutual and consensual and whether good flows from it that has an impact on other people and the world. Integrity has an individual dimension — a feeling of wholeness in oneself. It also has a communal dimension — the sense that one's self in its totality is experienced in community. Many parents on hearing of their children's sexuality may bemoan the specifics but rejoice in the fact that their children were honest with them. This is integrity in a way that "don't ask, don't tell" will never be. It is a solid basis for a new Catholic moral theology of sexuality.

A shift in terminology alone is not a magic solution to centuries of heterosexism, but it is a start toward forming new habits of thinking about sexuality and new conversations about sexual morality. Other religious traditions may take it up, as well, or offer their own alternatives to the restrictive heterosexist tradition.

A Theological Approach

The development of a non-heterosexist Catholic theology is a work of the imagination because it is new under the sun. It requires both historical sources and constructive offerings. Among the historical sources, there are

---

26. Mary E. Hunt, "Sexual Integrity," *WATERwheel* 7, no. 3 (Fall 1994): 1–3.

virtually none that is predicated on an explicit anti-heterosexist approach, but many lay the groundwork for it.

Among the prime sources that pave the way is historian John Boswell's case for the occasional tolerance of homosexuality in the Christian community over the centuries.[27] His work, though disputed by some scholars, opened the possibility that same-sex love had a place in the Catholic community long before the contemporary period. Heterosexism kept many relationships from seeing the light of day before Dr. Boswell's explorations.

Scripture scholar Bernadette Brooten focuses on lesbians in the early Christian community.[28] Her research has led her to conclude that they were considered problematic not so much for the sharing of sexual pleasure between women as for the fact that they lived out sexual equality between partners rather than sexual inequality between a man and a woman or a man and a boy. Lesbians, she argues, transgress the kyriarchal model that demands that one partner always be dominant and the other submissive. Her work has opened many eyes to see lesbians in scripture at all, something that heterosexism has obscured.

John J. McNeill, whose book *The Church and the Homosexual* resulted in his being dismissed from the Society of Jesus, wrote in 1976: "Homosexuals within the Church have an obligation, and therefore a right, to organize and attempt to enter into dialogue with Church authorities. Church authorities in turn should show an example in terms of just behavior ... by displaying an active willingness to hear, to enter into dialogue, and to seek ways to resolve whatever injustice becomes clear as a result of dialogue."[29] He opened a door that made it possible for many Catholic lesbian and gay people to imagine themselves Catholic, lesbian/gay, and good all at the same time, something ecclesial heterosexism rendered nearly impossible.

---

27. John Boswell, *Christianity, Social Tolerance, and Homosexuality: Gay People in Western Europe from the Beginning of the Christian Era to the Fourteenth Century* (Chicago: University of Chicago Press, 1981).

28. Bernadette Brooten, *Love between Women: Early Christian Responses to Female Homoeroticism* (Chicago: University of Chicago Press, 1996).

29. John J. McNeill, *The Church and the Homosexual*, 4th ed. (Boston: Beacon Press, 1993 [1974]), 195.

Indebted to these insights, I have claimed that Catholic lesbian feminist theology is no longer an oxymoron, even though it is just beginning to be articulated.[30] The experience of lesbian nuns and other Catholic lesbian women provides the experiential grounding for such a claim.[31] Today, lesbians have the option of motherhood, share the human call to holiness, and respond to "the invitation to break bread and do justice," hallmarks of a common Catholic spirituality.[32] In this prolegomenon to a Catholic lesbian feminist theology, I argue that lesbian sexual expression, like all sexual expression, "is part of a larger relational constellation, and how that relationship is conducive to community. The rest, as the rabbis say, is commentary."[33] Much more needs to be done to develop such a theology, but eradicating the heterosexist bias is a necessary precondition to its development.

Catholic historian Mark D. Jordan, has provided some of the most salient treatments of church life, in which he dismantles the heterosexist structures. He offered a brilliant analysis of "the invention of sodomy" in medieval Catholicism.[34] Then he went on to look at how the modern church was at the same time so homoerotic and so homophobic.[35] He offered a look at a postmodern Christianity and the debated focus on same-sex marriage.[36] His work provides resources for eradicating heterosexism, as well as some initial forays into a post-heterosexist Catholicism.

These sources point the way beyond gender-based heterosexism and open the way to sexual justice, toward what I have labeled "just good sex" as a basic human right.[37] "Just good sex" is a play on words used

---

30. Mary E. Hunt, "Catholic Lesbian Feminist Theology," in Jung and Coray, *Sexual Diversity and Catholicism,* 289–304.

31. Rosemary Curb and Nancy Manahan, eds., *Lesbian Nuns: Breaking Silence* (Tallahassee, FL: Naiad Press, 1985); Barbara Zanotti, ed., *A Faith of One's Own: Explorations by Catholic Lesbians* (Trumansburg, NY: Crossing Press, 1986).

32. Hunt, "Catholic Lesbian Feminist Theology," 302.

33. Ibid., 300.

34. Mark D. Jordan. *The Invention of Sodomy in Christian Theology* (Chicago: University of Chicago Press, 1997).

35. Mark D. Jordan, *The Silence of Sodom* (Chicago: University of Chicago Press, 2000).

36. Mark D. Jordan, *Blessing Same-Sex Unions: The Perils of Queer Romance and the Confusions of Christian Marriage* (Chicago: University of Chicago Press, 2005).

37. Mary E. Hunt, "Just Good Sex: Feminist Catholicism and Human Rights," in Jung, Hunt, and Balakrishnan, *Good Sex,* 169.

to emphasize a starting point in the larger, longer, and richer Catholic social justice tradition that takes, as an imperative of faith, engagement in social change to bring about equality. Developing sexual relationships that are safe, pleasurable, community building, and conducive of justice is part of a larger social agenda focused on the eradication of sexism, racism, economic oppression, colonialism, and, of course, heterosexism. This is the basis for a renewed Catholic theology of sexuality that emerges "from Catholic feminist theological insights, commitments and struggles that are in themselves extensions of the tradition and a new source of Catholic teachings."[38]

A Pastoral Approach

The Catholic sacramental, philosophical, and theological approaches need to be applied in pastoral settings if they are to succeed as received teaching. I suggest the most practical, though challenging, approach is to begin with the longtime pro-lgbt advocacy groups because they, too, will need to reshape their missions to reflect the non-heterosexist future.

For example, New Ways Ministry, founded by Sister Jeannine Gramick and Father Robert Nugent in 1977 to provide "a gay-positive ministry of advocacy and justice for lesbian and gay Catholics and reconciliation within the larger Christian and civil communities," helps many Catholics deal with the spiritual dissonance the kyriarchal church has created around being gay/lesbian and being Catholic.[39] It is well positioned to rethink its programs and writings using non-heterosexist presuppositions because it has done so much to bring them about.

Dignity, the Catholic lesbian and gay organization founded in 1969 under the leadership of Father Patrick Nidorf, OSA, has as its mission to work "for respect and justice for all gay, lesbian, bisexual, and transgender persons in the Catholic Church and the world through education, advocacy and support."[40] It will eventually be able to reposition itself as

---

38. Hunt, "Just Good Sex," 173.
39. New Ways Ministry website.
40. Dignity USA website.

a church reform group with a broader social justice agenda when the heterosexist assumptions that led to its founding are eradicated.

The Conference for Catholic Lesbians, founded in 1983 "to promote Catholic Lesbian visibility and community" and now a virtual community on the Internet, can focus on the fundamental contradictions of being female in a sexist church once the problems of being a lesbian in a heterosexist church are eradicated.[41] Feminist Catholic women are deeply concerned about the rank discrimination against all women on issues of reproductive health, ordination, and the like, prompting a commitment to substantive changes in church structure rather than "merely" inclusion of some women in what already exists.

These are the "first responders" to a non-heterosexist approach in Catholicism. Even they will find this a challenge because it will require that they change some of their ways of operating from defensive to offensive approaches. It is relatively easy to react and respond when one is attacked, a posture these groups have had to develop. It is much harder to offer new, creative ideas, in this case to imagine the post-heterosexist future, but I am confident that they are up to the challenge. Of course, some groups may at least initially prefer to operate out of heterosexist presuppositions, since those make the need for their work so obvious, but in time the inevitable changes presented by transgender people and the growing number of young people who see their sexuality in postmodern polymorphous terms will, I believe, make it impossible to operate out of the old models. Because they have prepared for a different future, such groups are the best hope for moving in that direction.

The kyriarchal church will have its own opportunities, whether it welcomes them or not, to move in this direction. I am less optimistic about its potential than I am about the groups that have already shown valuable leadership. Nonetheless, seminaries, theological schools, and Catholic universities need to incorporate this new approach into their teaching, assuring that the next generation will be equipped to handle the pastoral needs of its day. Changes in canon law are also in order so that the rights

---

41. Conference for Catholic Lesbians website.

of all are assured. Catholicism may seem far from this posture, but at least now there is a trajectory for moving in the right direction.

Conclusion

Eradicating heterosexism from Catholic circles will have many positive effects. The gains for lesbian, gay, bisexual, transgender, and queer people are obvious as we stand to live and love on a level moral playing field for the first time in human history. Some lives may even be saved as hate crimes decrease for lack of Catholic theological support.

Just as undoing racism has been helpful to white people, and undoing sexism has given men more freedom, heterosexual people will gain, as well. They can question the strictures on love that they received and perhaps even notice some love missed along the way. They can leave aside a distorted sense of self that heterosexism confers, something that can be a barrier to authentic human connections. They can affirm their love, more confident than ever that it is good because it is not mandatory.

As heterosexism is dismantled, I predict that Catholicism will move into the twenty-first century with increased intellectual and moral integrity. While there will not be immediate agreement across the board on homosexuality, at least the Catholic community will be debating the right issue, heterosexism. Removing the moral focus from homosexuality will mean an implicit "normalization" of same-sex relationships and, therefore, an opportunity to reflect on how ordinary most of them are. The tired old polarizations will go by the wayside. New alliances will form among those who seek "just good sex." There will be little need to parse either homosexuality or heterosexuality because, after all, what will matter is the love and commitment, not the body parts.

I hope this proves a useful Catholic contribution to the interreligious discussion on sexuality, since Catholics have not been alone in focusing on same-sex love and ignoring the larger heterosexist framework. As the interreligious conversation unfolds on inclusive and unbiased ground, Catholics now have something sex-positive to offer.

Chapter Seven

Heterosexism and the Black American Church Community

A Complicated Reality

KELLY BROWN DOUGLAS

The issue of sexuality, especially non-heterosexuality, is a complex matter within the Black Church community. Even with all their diversity, Black Church people are regarded as strikingly similar in their attitudes toward non-heterosexual sexualities. They are viewed as not only homophobic, but more homophobic than other segments of society. Recent polls suggest that while various constituencies of American society are becoming more supportive of gay and lesbian rights, African Americans are not. In fact, the African American community appears to be moving in the opposite direction. A September 2004 Pew Forum poll indicates that although support for gay and lesbian rights has grown in American society from 35 percent to 45 percent (since 1992), there is an exception: the African American community. This poll indicates that a plurality of African Americans now oppose gay and lesbian rights, whereas four years prior, 56 percent of African Americans had favored those same rights.[1]

Probably no issue better highlights Black Church views toward non-heterosexuality than that of same-sex marriage. Another Pew study indicates that the Black Church community is more opposed than other communities to these marriages. The study reports that 64 percent of African Americans oppose same-sex marriages, a percentage that has

---

1. See the Pew Forum on Religion and Public Life website.

held steady for several years while the overall population has become less opposed to these marriages (from 41 percent in 1996 to 30 percent in 2003).[2]

The Black Church community's obstinate stance in regard to gay and lesbian rights is most striking when one considers the historical black struggle for social equality and the Black Church's prominent role within that struggle. It appears inconsistent, if not hypocritical, for the Black Church to be in the forefront of racial justice concerns yet resistant, if not repressive, when it comes to the rights of non-heterosexual persons. How are we to account for this close-mindedness? Is it possible to move the Black Church community toward a more equitable view, and if so, how? These questions are addressed in this chapter. To be sure, Black Church people's responses toward same-sex marriage reflect the complicated nature of their attitudes toward homosexuality in general. As earlier stated, the Black Church community's views toward non-heterosexualities are not a simple matter, but rather the result of a complex interaction of socio-political, historical, and theological realities. In order to understand the heterosexism of the Black Church community, as well as move this community toward greater justice, this complex socio-political, historical, and theological interaction must be apprehended. Before doing so, however, two things must be recognized.

First, any analysis of the Black Church community must recognize that neither black people nor the Black Church itself is monolithic. This church is a disparate collective of churches that reflects the diversity of the black community. These churches are diversified by origin, denomination, doctrine, worshiping culture, spiritual ethos, class, size, and other less obvious

---

2. This study is cited on the Religious Tolerance.org website. It should be noted that various polls are constantly being conducted, with some suggesting that the gap in opinion between the overall population and that of African Americans is closing. For instance, a study in November 2003 revealed that opposition to same-sex marriage within the general population had grown to 59 percent, even as the African American population remained steady at about 60 percent (The Pew Research Center for the People and the Press, "Religious Beliefs Underpin Opposition to Homosexuality"; November 2003 (*www.people-press.org/reports/display7.php3?PageID=765*; accessed June 28, 2005).

factors. They may be within white denominational structures or independent of them. They may reflect congregational, connectional, or episcopal polities. They may be urban, suburban, or rural. They range in size and structure from storefronts to mega-churches. Yet, as disparate as Black churches are, they share a common history and play a unique role in black life, both of which attest to their collective identity as the Black Church.

Black churches emerged as a central part of black people's culture of resistance to white racist tyranny. They have played a decisive role in black people's survival and overall well-being throughout their history in American society. W. E. B. Du Bois aptly described the Black Church as both the religious center and the social center of the black community.[3] At the same time, a discussion of the Black Church in general must appreciate Black churches in particular. While certain attitudes may prevail in the Black Church community, there are always exceptions. Although this chapter focuses on pervasive homophobic sentiment within the Black Church, it recognizes that various Black churches have more progressive views toward sexual expression and even same-sex marriage.[4]

Second, before proceeding I must clarify the vantage point from which I speak as a black female Episcopal priest and womanist theologian. Thus, I represent that aspect of the Black Church community that is part of a white denominational system, but even as a black Episcopalian, my story of faith is inextricably linked to the story of Absalom Jones, a former slave, who was co-founder of the Free African Society, co-initiator of the independent Black Church movement along with Richard Allen, and the first black Episcopal priest. Jones signifies a persistent black presence within the Episcopal Church that constantly advocates for racial justice

---

3. W. E. B. Du Bois, *Souls of Black Folk* (1903; reprint, New York: Alfred A. Knopf, 1993), 153.

4. One such prominent Black church is Covenant Baptist Church in Washington, DC, with co-pastors Reverends Dennis Wiley and Christine Wiley. This church was featured on a July 16, 2004, PBS documentary (episode 746) titled "Black Churches and Gay Marriage." Covenant was highlighted as a church that not only welcomes gay and lesbian persons but also performs same-sex marriage blessings.

within the denomination and whose primary identification is with the wider black community in the struggle against white racism.

Furthermore, even though the denominational system of which I am a part might be considered more progressive in its views because it allows the blessing of same-sex unions, ordains self-identified non-heterosexual persons, and recently consecrated a gay bishop, the black Episcopal community with which I identify tends to mirror the prevailing attitudes of the wider Black Church community.[5] While there are black episcopal voices supportive of gay and lesbian rights within the church, there are also significant black voices that are not. Interestingly, the most strident opposition to the recent consecration of a gay bishop has been from the African continent, suggesting perhaps a consistency of passion throughout the African diaspora when it comes to non-heterosexual sexualities.[6] Nonetheless, it is from out of — and to — the wider black faith community, of which black Episcopalians are a part, that I speak.

I also acknowledge that my Episcopal denominational affiliation undoubtedly provides me with more of a protected ecclesiastical space from which to speak about sexual issues than is typically available to those in historically black denominational systems. Unlike many who are members of black denominations, within my denomination there is an ecclesiastical platform from which to advocate for gay and lesbian rights. While there are those of my denomination who may disagree with my theological position, advocacy for gay and lesbian rights does not necessarily marginalize me within my denomination (or congregation) in a way that it might those within black denominational structures. Denominational affiliation

---

5. In November 2003 Gene Robinson, an openly gay priest, was consecrated as ninth Episcopal diocesan bishop of New Hampshire.

6. It should be noted that at the Third International Conference on Afro-Anglicanism held in Toronto, Canada, July 20–27, 2005, an accord was agreed upon that addressed, among several issues, the topic of human sexuality. In regard to sexuality the accord states: "We have wrestled with deep sincerity with the complex issues of human sexuality. . . . The vast differences of approach have been evident in our dialogue. Nevertheless, we have not departed from the sacred truths of our common humanity. We have all been created in God's image. God's compassion and love are extended to all whom God has created. . . . We yearn together for the day when the human body will become the symbol, and source, and sacrament of unity among us an no longer a cause of division or an instrument of strife."

notwithstanding, my womanist identity further compels me to speak about matters of sexual injustice.

As a womanist theologian I am "committed to the survival and wholeness of entire people, male and female."[7] Therefore, I am obliged to speak against any form of injustice whether it is present within the black community or in the wider society. More specifically, womanist scholars are compelled to question homophobic attitudes and heterosexist structures as they exist within the church in an effort to debunk and dismantle them.[8] These attitudes and systems have negatively infringed upon the lives of many black women and men and have contributed to the Black Church community's slow response to the HIV/AIDS crisis, now ravaging the black community.[9] Thus, if for no other reason, the womanist commitment to survival and wholeness compels a discerning theological response to issues of sexuality. Womanist theologians also cannot ignore that aspect of the womanist definition which states that a "womanist loves other women sexually and/or non-sexually."[10] An inherent task of womanist theologians is to work toward creating a church and community in which non-heterosexual persons are able to love themselves, as well as those whom they choose to love, without fear of social, political, or ecclesiastical penalty, all so that they, along with all other black men and women, may enjoy life and wholeness. It is explicitly from my commitments as a womanist theologian that I address the homophobia and heterosexism of the Black Church community.

The Black Church and Same-Sex Marriage

The Black Church community and its leaders have not been silent about same-sex marriage. In April 2004 the Church of God in Christ, a predom-

---

7. See Alice Walker's four-part definition in *In Search of Our Mothers' Gardens* (New York: Harcourt Brace Jovanovich, 1983), xi–xii.

8. Womanist theologian Katie G. Cannon used the term *debunk* on various occasions, speaking of the womanist task to "debunk" the methods and notions of white patriarchal ethical and theological systems.

9. See my discussion of this in *Sexuality and the Black Church: A Womanist Perspective* (Maryknoll, NY: Orbis Books, 1999).

10. Walker, *In Search of Our Mothers' Gardens*, xi.

inately black denomination of 5.5 million members, issued a proclamation that states that marriage should be reserved only for heterosexual couples. Furthermore, the statement reads, marriage as ordained by God is meant for procreation, homosexuality is sinful and a "direct violation of the law of God," and regardless of whether same-sex unions gain social acceptance or legal legitimacy, the Church of God in Christ "will stand resolutely firm and never allow the sanctioning of same-sex marriages."[11] Several months later, the African Methodist Episcopal Church expressed similar sentiments. In July 2004, delegates to the AME convention voted unanimously, and reportedly without debate, to forbid its clergy from performing same-sex marriages or civil-union ceremonies. This vote by a denomination that claims about 2.5 million members was the first vote of its kind by a predominately black denomination.[12]

Black pastors have also been very vocal within their local communities in rallying support against same-sex marriage. For instance, in February 2004, three major associations of black clergy within the Boston, Massachusetts, area joined together to issue a statement against nonheterosexual marriage. The Black Ministerial Alliance, the Boston Ten Point Coalition, and the Cambridge Black Pastors Conference, all primarily made up of clergy from historically black denominations, stated that they believe "marriage to be a unique covenant established between a man and woman" and support "the call for a Constitutional Amendment to define marriage as a covenant between a man and a woman."[13] In that same year, Reverend William Owens, a sixty-five-year-old black pastor in Memphis, Tennessee, established the Coalition of African-American Pastors. This nationwide coalition has joined with several white "pro-family" groups in the fight against same-sex marriage.

All across the country black clergy have come to the forefront to "defend" heterosexual marriage and vehemently to oppose same-sex marriage.

---

11. "Marriage: A Proclamation to the Church of God in Christ Worldwide," available on the Christianmemorialchurch.com website.

12. See "AME Rejects Same-Sex Unions," July 8, 2004; available online.

13. "Black Clergy Statement on Marriage," February 6, 2004; available online.

With some measure of success they have pressured local black elected officials to abandon the agenda of the Democratic Party, of which they are members, in order to "defend" marriage as a "union between a man and a woman." Indeed, Republican Party leadership has seized upon the heterosexist passions of many black clergy in order to garner black electoral support and to pressure members of the Congressional Black Caucus to support a constitutional marriage amendment. Various black leaders acknowledge that the Republican party used same-sex marriage as a "wedge issue" during the 2004 presidential campaign to divide the black community and erode black support for the Democratic presidential ticket. Polling data from the 2004 presidential election suggest that to some extent this strategy worked. President Bush garnered 2 percent more of the black vote than he received in 2000, and many analysts attribute this gain to the Bush campaign's efforts to block gay marriage.[14]

What has stirred the passions of the Black Church community with respect to this issue? What has provoked so many black pastors to speak out when the Black Church community has typically remained silent on issues of this nature? Even though it has long been understood that the Black Church community, for the most part, considers homosexuality to be sinful, this community has never before issued official proclamations or public statements on the topic. Even when the Supreme Court ruled against the Texas Homosexual Conduct Statute in June 2003, declaring it unconstitutional to infringe upon the rights of homosexual persons to engage in consensual sexual activity, the Black Church community remained virtually silent. Therefore, what has prompted such a public display of emotion and opinion in regard to this particular topic?

Even minister and social rights activist Jesse Jackson, an avid supporter of gay and lesbian rights, has acknowledged that this topic should not be of special concern to black people, given the other socio-political and economic challenges that threaten black well-being. Throughout the 2004 presidential campaign season, Jackson repeatedly reminded black church

---

14. See, for instance, the Pew report entitled "The American Religious Landscape and the 2004 Presidential Vote: Increased Polarization" by John C. Green et al. (February 3, 2005); available online.

members that the issues over which they should be most concerned related to social and economic justice, not sexuality. Jackson pointedly said that issues like same-sex marriage "didn't make the Top 10 with Moses, and Jesus didn't make mention of them."[15] Given the historical lack of priority granted to sexual issues within the Black Church community, why has the idea of same-sex marriage pricked the social/theological consciousness of this community?

The issue of same-sex marriage came into national prominence in 1996 when President William Clinton signed into law the Defense of Marriage Act (DOMA), defining marriage as a "legal union between one man and one woman" and granting states the right not to recognize the validity of same-sex unions from other jurisdictions. However, this topic did not capture the public imagination until seven years later, in November 2003, when the Massachusetts Supreme Judicial Court determined that the state ban against same-sex marriage was unconstitutional. This court decision was the catalyst for cities across the country, most notably San Francisco, to begin issuing marriage licenses to gay and lesbian couples. With this, the battle was joined between supporters and opponents of gay and lesbian couples' right to state (if not church) sanctioned marriage.

The nationwide debate that quickly ensued over same-sex marriage formed a "perfect storm" in relation to the Black Church community. This debate struck several chords within the black political, historical, and theological psyche that brought to the surface long and deeply held sentiments concerning homosexuality, in general, and the fight for gay and lesbian equality, in particular. Donna Brazile, black political operative and 2000 campaign manager for Al Gore, has described it as the "mother of all wedge issues" for the black community,[16] but what are the specific factors of this perfect storm that compelled the Black Church community to respond and thus expose the complicated reality of Black Church heterosexism?

---

15. Jesse Jackson quoted in Neela Banerjee, "Black Churches Struggle over Their Role in Politics," *New York Times*, March 6, 2005; available online.

16. Donna Brazile, quoted in Candi Cushman, "Pastors Provoked," *Citizen*; available online.

An Issue of Civil Rights

Much of the public discourse surrounding the fight for same-sex marriage has framed it as a struggle for civil rights. One of the central claims of the gay, lesbian, bisexual, and transgender community is that the fight for social equality is a civil rights issue. This point was underscored, for example, through lgbt participation in the fortieth anniversary celebration of the March on Washington. Even though the lgbt participants had been invited by the planning committee of the event, many Black Church leaders, especially those who had previously participated in the 1960s civil rights movement led by Martin Luther King, Jr., were incensed when the National Gay and Lesbian Task Force brought several busloads of mostly white people to the Lincoln Memorial to join the celebration. One black minister said, "[Gay and lesbian persons] know nothing about what we went through.... How can they even compare that? They've hijacked the civil rights movement."[17] The Reverend Jesse Jackson surprised many when he criticized gay-marriage advocates for equating their battle with black people's historical struggle for civil rights. Speaking at Harvard Law School, he said, "The comparison with slavery is a stretch....Gays were never called three-fifths humans in the Constitution."[18] Even a leading member of the National Gay and Lesbian Task Force in Washington, Matt Foreman, recognized that equating the gay and lesbian movement with the civil rights movement can "rightly [be] seen as offensive." He, too, acknowledged that the oppression of gay and lesbian persons does not "compare to state-sanctioned centuries of oppression" that black people have faced.[19]

Black Church leaders' vehement resistance to viewing the gay and lesbian struggle for social equality as a civil rights issue is about more than homophobia, despite what some would suggest. It is also more than a chauvinistic response to black people's marginalized status in America. Rather, it speaks to a profound awareness of racialized oppression in American

---

17. Quoted in Cushman, "Pastors Provoked," 1.

18. Jesse Jackson, quoted in Cushman, "Pastors Provoked," 3.

19. Matt Foreman, quoted in Eric Deggans, "Gay Rights and Civil Rights," *St. Petersburg Times Online*, January 18, 2004.

society. The fact remains that social and economic privilege and penalty
are predicated on skin color. As many have long pointed out, the lack
of economic resources, jobs, and educational opportunities; the dispro-
portionate numbers of black people, especially men, in prison; and the
inadequate funding for HIV prevention and AIDS treatment in certain
communities are all matters of race. Because the "colorline" remains such
a pressing problem within contemporary society,[20] many black leaders re-
sent the equation of the gay and lesbian movement with the civil rights
movement, not solely because of their aversion to homosexuality, but because to do such a thing obscures the complex and persistent reality of
black oppression as part of the fabric of American society in ways that,
arguably, the oppression of gay and lesbians is not. The Reverend Irene
Monroe, an openly lesbian African American theologian, points out that
black people's reluctance to affirm the lgbt rights movement stems from
the fact that "civil rights gains have come faster for queer people" than
for black people. "From the Stonewall Riots of 1969 to May 17, 2004,
the LGBTQ movement," she writes, "has made some tremendous gains
into mainstream society, a reality that has not been afforded to African
Americans."[21] Others have observed that the gay and lesbian movement
itself, reflecting the racialized character of America, is not free from its
own racism. As one black gay man pointed out, even as the Human Rights
Campaign was pushing to equate gay civil rights with black civil rights, this
mostly white gay organization had "no visible black leadership or tangible
support from black leaders."[22] Monroe acknowledges that "racism is as
rampant in the white queer community as it is in the larger society."[23] She
further argues that because the LBGTQ movement "persistently [dons]
a white face," it marginalizes those people of color who are part of the

---

20. In his book *Souls of Black Folks* W. E. B. Du Bois, in discussing racism in America,
argued that the problem of the twentieth century was the problem of the "color-line."

21. Irene Monroe, "No Marriage between Black Ministers and Queer Community," *The
Witness Magazine*, available online (*www.thewitness.org.*)

22. Kenyon Farrow, "Is Gay Marriage Anti Black???" *Chicken Bones: A Journal*, available
online.

23. Monroe, "No Marriage between Black Ministers and Queer Community," 2.

movement and makes claims appear legitimate that assert that the lgbt movement is "pimping" the civil rights movement.

Given the whiteness of the mainstream gay and lesbian movement, it is interpreted as a sign of white privilege and arrogance when any white gay and lesbian organization glibly usurps the language of, and attempts to "piggy-back" on, the black civil rights movement, especially when it is not more aggressive in eliminating racial discrimination within its own organization. One gay black man put it best when he said, "While the anger of black heteros is sometimes expressed in ways that are in fact homophobic, the truth of the matter is that black folks are tired of seeing other people hijack their [stuff] for their own gains, and getting nothing in return. Black non-heteros share this anger of having our blackness and black political rhetoric and struggle stolen for other people's gains."[24]

Though it should be noted that notable black ministers and/or civil rights advocates, such as Congressman John Lewis, Reverend Al Sharpton, and the late Coretta Scott King, have recognized the gay and lesbian struggle as a matter of civil rights, no constituency within the black community would be more outraged by the equation of gay and lesbian rights with civil rights than the Black Church community. As mentioned earlier, much of Black Church history and identity are tied to black people's struggle for rights. The Black Church has been the institutional center of black people's struggle for freedom from slavery to the present. Moreover, the 1960s civil rights movement emerged out of the Black Church community and was sustained by black churches. For many Black Church people, the civil rights battle was more than a social or political issue. It was, more significantly, a matter of faith. Martin Luther King, Jr., Baptist minister and leader of the civil rights movement, made plain the connection between black faith and the black struggle for civil rights in his first speech during the Montgomery bus boycott, when he stressed the inextricable link between being Christian and being involved in the battle against racial injustice. He said, "We are not wrong in what we are doing.... If

---

24. Farrow, "Is Gay Marriage Anti Black???" 6.

we are wrong God Almighty is wrong. If we are wrong Jesus of Nazareth was merely a utopian dreamer who never came down to earth."[25]

Moreover, many Black Church leaders have made personal sacrifices to the civil rights struggle, and many black lives were lost. It is no doubt for these reasons that black ministers felt compelled to respond so passionately when the fight for same-sex marriage was framed as a civil rights issue. For them, it is not a matter of blind homophobia but of legacy. Homophobia and heterosexism notwithstanding, to frame the struggle for gay and lesbian rights as a civil rights issue appears to many within the Black Church community as a sign of disrespect and disregard for black people's historical struggle against white racist oppression and, most important, an attempt to marginalize black people within the very movement for which black lives were lost.

The fight for same-sex marriage and gay and lesbian rights is considered an affront to black people's history for yet another reason. Support of homoerotic relationships, in the minds of many, only reinforces the destructive consequences of white racist oppression upon the black community and family. In general, the issue of homosexuality becomes an issue of the black community's survival under historical oppression, particularly as that oppression has affected the black family. Again, no issue made this link clearer in the Black Church than that of same-sex marriage.

An Issue of Oppression

No black leader has been more vocal in proclaiming same-sex marriage a threat to the black family than long-time civil rights activist Reverend Walter Fauntroy. In testimony before Congress in support of the Federal Marriage Amendment, Fauntroy argued that the legalization of same-sex marriage would have a detrimental impact on society and especially on black families. He stated, "For most black Americans who know our history, we do not want any further confusion about what a marriage and

---

25. Martin Luther King, Jr., "Address to the Initial Mass Meeting of the Montgomery Improvement Association," Holt Street Baptist Church, December 5, 1955 (King Center Archives).

family happen to be." He went on to say, "We have not yet recovered from the cruelties of slavery which was based on the destruction of the family."[26] Various Black Church people have expressed similar sentiments. Another black pastor noted that because the black community has witnessed firsthand the havoc wreaked by the destruction of the family unit through slavery and welfare it is poised to lead a rebellion against any further destruction gay marriage would cause."

While casting gay marriage as a threat to black families is misguided, especially given the actual social and political threats of the lack of employment, educational, housing, and healthcare opportunities, this argument points to the reality of black oppression that shapes black people's attitudes toward sexual issues. White racist oppression of black people, as defined by the slavocracy, did not respect the black family. Typically, black people were not permitted to marry. As chattel, they had none of the rights of human beings, of which marriage was one. In addition, the slavocracy viewed marriage as a threat to the slavocracy's re-productivity by interferring with the enslaved people's ability to be good breeders. Most significantly, the very notion of enslaved marriages ran counter to the white supremacist ideology that undergirded the slavocracy and projected black women and men as hypersexualized beasts controlled by lust. They were, therefore, deemed suited for breeding but not for intimate, loving relationships. However, even if enslaved men and women were allowed to marry, such permission did not require their masters to respect their unions. The exigencies of the slavocracy prevailed over the marriage commitment. Thus, the master retained the right, and typically exercised it, to use the husband and wife as breeders and then to sell them away from one another. Any children that issued from the marriage were also likely to be sold away from their parents. In short, black marriages, and hence families, were not respected within the slavocracy. Marital rights were simply not granted to those viewed as hypersexualized beastly chattel.

---

26. Quoted in Phuong Ly and Hamil R. Harris, "Blacks, Gays in Struggle of Values: Same-Sex Marriage Issue Challenges Religious, Political Ties," *Washington Post*, March 15, 2004.

Restrictions upon black marriage rights did not end with the slavocracy. Long after slavery, black-white marriage unions were prohibited. It was not until June 12, 1967, in *Loving v. Virginia,* that the U.S. Supreme Court ruled to lift restrictions on interracial marriages. Prior to this decision, at least sixteen states maintained laws forbidding blacks from marrying whites. The lifting of miscegenation laws did not, however, indicate respect for black families, which have been consistently under siege by the interlocking social, political, and economic systems of white racism.

Black people's persistent history of racially sexualized oppression, especially with its attack on the family, has shaped their responses to social and sexual matters. To a great extent, in an effort to offset white racist hypersexualization of them, black people have adopted, perhaps unwittingly, a *hyper-proper sexuality* in a effort to mitigate if not sever the link between blackness and "deviant" sexuality. This hyper-proper sexuality is characterized by a strident determination to engage sexuality only in a "proper" manner and to present the black community as an exemplar of proper sexuality. The meaning of *proper* is shaped by social-cultural narratives of power and thus is defined in terms of heterosexist, patriarchal notions of correct sexuality. Accordingly, within a society defined by white patriarchal heterosexist standards of acceptability, non-heterosexuality is viewed as immoral. Thus, the Black Church community's responses to issues of sexual difference, including homosexuality and gay and lesbian rights, are significantly shaped by a heterosexist sensibility.

Furthermore, the history of white racist attacks upon the black family has compelled the black community to become hyper-vigilant in protecting the well-being of the black family. This vigilance is also influenced by white heterosexual patriarchal norms, and, therefore, *family* is defined accordingly. Despite the fact that it has developed effective models of extended family, and despite socio-economic pressures, the black community has consistently struggled to conform to white patriarchal standards of family by maintaining a male-centered nuclear family.[27] Ironically, the end

---

27. One should note, for instance, the 1965 Moynihan Report, which opens by stating that the "deterioration of the Negro family," is the "fundamental source of the weakness of the Negro community." The report further argues that the Negro family is at the heart

result is that its history of oppression has compelled the black community to adopt standards of sexuality and notions of family that are consistent with the very (white, patriarchal) ideologies that have served to oppress them. Hence, the Black Church community as a whole has adopted sexual values that are non-accepting of homoerotic sexuality and, most certainly, of same-sex marriage. Both are seen as affronts to proper black family structures as well as to black sexual propriety.

At the same time, it has not only been black people's history of sexualized oppression that has shaped their sense of proper sexuality. As important, black people's views on family and sexual values have been shaped by their religious tradition. In fact, black people's history of oppression and their faith have come together in such a way as to create an almost impregnable position on same-sex marriage. As theologian Imani-Sheila Newsome-Camara explains, "Marriage was traditionally undervalued in slave communities, not by slaves, but by owners, so the black religious institutions sought to give African-Americans legitimacy as human beings, and that history has been woven together with the theology that God created man and woman for marriage."[28] Let us now examine the faith that informs Black Church views on same-sex marriage.

An Issue of Faith

Reverend Fauntroy again makes the issue plain when he says that his church teaches him that same-sex marriage is an "abomination." His view is echoed by numerous black ministers as they assert that the Bible condemns not only same-sex marriage but also homosexuality. The bottom

---

of the "tangle of pathology" that perpetuates poverty and antisocial behavior within the black community. The report identifies the centrality of the black mother as opposed to the father within the black family, erroneously identified as a "black matriarchy," as the root cause of the Negro family's deterioration. It cannot be emphasized enough, however, that this report is just one example of the way in which the black family has been attacked for not conforming to white patriarchal standards at the same time that it provides a scapegoat for the white racist system and structures that actually contribute to the poverty and social problems within the black community.

28. Quoted in Michael Paulson, "Black Clergy Rejection Stirs Gay Marriage Backers," *Boston Globe*, February 10, 2004.

line, according to many Black Church people, is that the Bible says homosexuality is wrong. In fact, whether they are churchgoers or not, black
people often argue that the Bible makes it clear that homosexuality is a
sin.[29] Invoking biblical authority places a sacred canopy over their views
toward gay and lesbian persons. This canopy renders homophobia and
heterosexism within the Black Church community practically intractable
and certainly renders same-sex marriage an intolerably sinful deed.

The irony is, however, that the Bible does not present as clear a position
on homosexuality as is often asserted. The meaning of the biblical stories
customarily referred to as proof against homosexual practices has generally been misconstrued or distorted. Biblical scholars have painstakingly
shown that the Leviticus Holiness Codes (Lev. 18:22; 20:13), the story of
Sodom and Gomorrah (Gen. 19:1–9), and Paul's Epistle to the Romans
(Rom. 1:26–27) do not present a compelling case against homoeroticism.[30]
These scholars have also pointed out that neither the words nor the actions of Jesus, as recorded in the New Testament Gospels, suggest an
anti-homosexual stance. To be sure, the New Testament does not portray
Jesus as making any pronouncements about homosexuality. In this regard,
Jesse Jackson is right to point out that issues of homoerotic sexuality were
not of concern to Moses or Jesus.[31] However, regardless of "nonacademic"
readings of the Bible by many Black Church people, it would take more
than insights from biblical scholars to create a significant shift in black
people's thinking in relation to the sanctity of homosexuality. At stake is
not what scholars may say about the biblical witness, but a hermeneutic approach to the biblical witness that is grounded in black people's
experience of struggle.

---

29. See the November 18, 2003, Pew Study, "Republicans Unified, Democrats Split on
Gay Marriage: Religious Beliefs Underpin Opposition to Homosexuality." This study states
that three-quarters (74 percent) of black Protestants consider homosexuality sinful. The
only group with a higher percentage of persons considering homosexuality sinful was white
evangelicals (88 percent).

30. See for instance, John McNeill, *The Church and the Homosexual* (Kansas City, KS:
Sheed, Andrews, and McNeel, 1976); Daniel Helminiak, *What The Bible Really Says about
Homosexuality* (San Francisco: Alamo Square Press, 1994).

31. See Banerjee, "Black Churches Struggle over Their Role in Poltics."

The prevailing hermeneutic within the black faith tradition emerged as black people struggled to maintain life and dignity in a society hostile to their blackness and degrading to their humanity. This hermeneutic grants authority to texts and stories that black people consider compatible with their own struggles for life and freedom. Hence, the events and heroes of the Exodus story have become normative within the black faith tradition insofar as they confirm black people's own experience of God as being on the side of the oppressed. This hermeneutic also grants authority to those texts that project a standard of behavior suitable for a godly, chosen people. It cannot be said enough that white dehumanization of black people involved a sexualized attack upon their very character, and one way black people countered this attack was by adopting a code of hyper-proper conduct that defied their sexualized beastly characterization. Such a code was consistent with what they found in the Bible as it related to holy behavior. In short, the biblical hermeneutic prevalent within the black faith tradition grants authority to those texts that resonate both with black people's aspirations for freedom and with their defiance of their oppression.

As a result, the authority granted to certain texts and readings has far less to do with the canons of biblical scholarship and far more to do with the struggle against white racist oppression. To be sure, it is difficult to alter any interpretative tradition that has served people well. In essence, as long as the biblical strategy continues to sustain black life and well-being, there is no perceived need to change. What, then, does this suggest about arresting black people's use of the Bible as a sacred canopy for their homophobic and heterosexist responses to gay and lesbian persons? While a full answer falls beyond the parameters of this essay, clearly Black Church people must be led to understand that a hermeneutical approach to the Bible that sanctions any form of human oppression and tyranny, including heterosexism, does not in actuality serve the black community's interests and must be changed.[32]

---

32. See Douglas, *Sexuality and the Black Church*, esp. 94–96.

As central as the Bible is to the black faith tradition, another key ele-
ment of black faith also informs black people's responses to homoerotism: a
platonized theology, which has shaped an influential strand of the Christian
tradition. This theology emerged as early Christian apologists integrated
into their Christian theologies the most prominent Greek philosophies of
their day. In so doing, they established within mainstream Christian thinking a platonic and Stoic view toward the body. Specifically, the platonic
belief in the world of forms as different from, and superior to, the world of
the senses coalesced in Christian thought with the Stoic regard for reason
and disregard for passion. In the process, a significant strand of Christian
thinking adopted a theology that esteemed the immaterial world, regarded
as the world of reason, spirit, and soul, while it renounced the material
world, regarded as the world of passion, flesh, and body. This split between
the two realms resulted in the body-devaluing theology and tradition of
platonized Christianity.

Platonized Christianity invariably places the body in an antagonistic
relationship to the soul. The soul is divinized; the body is demonized. The
soul is revered as the key to salvation; the body is condemned as a source
of sin. The locus of bodily sin is human passion and sexual pleasure or lust.
This sacred disdain for the sexual body pervades the Christian theological
tradition, particularly as it has given way to a definite sexual ethic. The
writings of the apostle Paul, especially as they are refracted through an
Augustinian reading, are most responsible for this body-denouncing theo-
ethical tradition. Specifically, platonized Christianity advocates a dualistic
sexual ethic that offers only two ways in which to engage in sexual activity,
one that is tolerable and not inherently sinful, and another that is intol-
erable and sinful. Procreative use is tolerably good; non-procreative use
is intolerably evil. Characteristic of platonized Christianity, a third possibility is not permitted. A platonized sexual ethic does not allow sexual
activity as an expression of an intimate, loving relationship. For all intents
and purposes, platonized Christianity severs intimate sexuality from loving
relationality.

The implications of platonized Christianity are grievous. First, platonized Christianity makes clear that the site for procreative sexuality is

marriage, even as marriage is viewed as a privileged context for procreative sexuality. Second, platonized Christianity provides theological shelter for the denigration of certain human beings. Inasmuch as certain people are thought of as hypersexualized, which is a presumed characteristic of any marginalized people, then those people can be deemed sinful by nature because sexualizing them denotes that they are unavoidably given to lustful sexual behavior.

Platonized Christianity became an influential part of the black faith tradition during the eighteenth-century religious revivals. During these revivals a significant number of black men and women were converted to evangelical Protestant thought, the principal conduit of platonized Christianity in America. Black Church people most affected by this platonized tradition tend to affirm Paul's assertions that one should "make no provision for flesh," but if one must engage in sexual behavior, "it is better to marry than to burn" (1 Cor. 7:1, 9). At the same time, reflecting this platonized tradition, Black Church people tend to view all homoerotic behavior as lustful and sinful. Since homosexuality is not procreative, it is not considered a proper form of sexual expression and thus not deserving of the shelter of marriage. In this respect, Black Church people's concept of a hyper-proper sexuality is driven not only by white patriarchal heterosexist norms but also by a platonized Christian theology, even as the two narratives coincide when it comes to homosexuality and same-sex marriage. It is also noteworthy that these narratives coincide about women. Both define women's sexuality in terms of their capacity to procreate and, thus, in relation to men while denying the possibility of non-procreative and, therefore, non-male-centered sexual expression. While white patriarchal heterosexist social narratives and platonized theology disavow the propriety of non-heterosexual expressions of sexuality, they also uphold the center of patriarchal power: a heterosexual male-centered family where women's primary role is to procreate.

In sum, Black Church people's vehement responses to homosexuality and same-sex marriage reflect a *theo-historical dynamic* grounded in a platonized theology and propelled by a history of racial sexualized oppression. The issue of same-sex marriage is experienced as a direct affront to black people's sense of struggle, experience of oppression, and faith tradition. As such, this issue exposes the social, historical, and, most important, theological factors that coalesce to provide a perfect storm for bringing to the surface prevailing black attitudes toward non-heterosexuality. While homophobia and heterosexism may be the result of this storm of interconnected issues, these dynamics emerge from the struggle of being black in a society hostile to black humanity. Nevertheless, both must be challenged because they limit the life options of non-heterosexual women and men, including non-heterosexual black women and men. Even while we may appreciate the complexity of black homophobia and heterosexism, it still must be confronted and dismantled.

Toward the Eradication of Heterosexism and Homophobia: Theological Correctives

Two things stand out in regard to Black Church people's intolerance of non-heterosexuality: the primacy of their historical experience and the importance of their faith tradition. Paradoxically, these two factors also come together to suggest a more equitable response to non-heterosexuals.

The black faith tradition emerged in defiant response to a platonized Christian tradition that supported the enslavement and dehumanization of black people. Because of God's embodied presence in Jesus, the enslaved were able to testify that God was an active, affirming reality in their lives. Refrains like "Oh, when I talk with God," "Mass' Jesus is my bosom friend," and "A little talk wid Jesus makes it right" echoed through the songs of the enslaved. Jesus, as God's intimate presence in their lives, was one who understood their pain and tears, walked and talked with them, and provided for their needs. Moreover, the enslaved proclaimed that they, too, were created in the image of God. Their spirituals were filled with lyrics such as "We are the people of God," "We are de people of de Lord," and "I really do believe I'm a child of God."

The sung testimony of the enslaved crafters of the black faith tradition witnessed to a God who is neither remote nor abstract, but rather personal and intimate. Such testimony revealed the enslaved people's rejection of white Christian notions that God sanctioned cruel and inhumane treatment, such as the exploitation of their sexual bodies and the denigration of their families. Central to the enslaved people's understanding of a God who cares about them was a fundamental appreciation that Jesus was God incarnate. It was because God was embodied that God could connect with them, responding to their needs. God's embodiment was crucial to any understanding of God's meaning in human history, specifically their history. No doubt because the enslaved inherited and maintained an African religious tradition in which things of the flesh were not associated with evil, they could fully appreciate the fullness of God's revelation in Jesus. Such an appreciation defied any notion that the human body was bad or an impediment to a relationship with God. Indeed, the theology of the enslaved suggests a high regard for the body/flesh as "the very temple of God," as the medium of God's presence in human lives. The enslaved seemingly understood that it was in becoming body/flesh that God has been significantly revealed in human history, again in their history. They also perceived that it is only via body/flesh that human beings can reach out to God, as well as to one another.

For the Black Church to adhere to a Christian tradition rooted in a repudiation of the body/flesh is for the Black Church to betray its own distinctive theological heritage. Even more, for the Black Church to espouse such a platonized tradition is to affirm the very theological claims that allowed for the compatibility of Christianity and slavery, along with the persistent disregard for the black sexual body. Platonized Christianity has sustained a theological tradition that has sanctioned white supremacist notions of innate black inferiority, sustained by characterizations of black people as hypersexualized beings. For Black Church people to profess a dualistic split between body and soul or to condemn the sexual body and repudiate non-procreative loving sexuality upholds the foundation of the very tradition that justified slavery and impugned enslaved marriage and families. Thus, it is imperative for the Black Church to connect firmly to its own enslaved religious heritage, one that defied the body-soul split and protected the sanctity of loving sexuality while proclaiming God on the side of the oppressed in their quest for liberation. Moreover, the Black

Church must allow itself to be critiqued by that liberating, body-affirming tradition.

Specifically, black people's demand that those in the gay and lesbian struggle for justice respect the history of black struggle does not mitigate the need for black people to recognize the parallels between white cultural contempt for them and heterosexist contempt for non-heterosexual persons. Just as white racist culture has historically refused to admit the humanity of black women and men and denied that black people are created in the image of God, so, too, does heterosexist culture repudiate the humanity of non-heterosexual men and women and thereby disavow their creation in God's image. Indeed, the Black Church often mimics white cultural contempt for humanity by asserting that God did not create human beings to be gay and lesbian and speaking of non-heterosexuality only as sinful. Once again, Black Church people must recognize the similarity between white racism and heterosexism, even as that heterosexism is perpetuated within the Black Church community itself.

In this regard, while black people may be unable to acknowledge the gay and lesbian struggle as a civil rights issue, their own history of oppression compels them at least to admit that it is as a *human rights* issue.[33] In so doing, the Black Church community is further obliged by its own faith claims to affirm the divine worth and inalienable rights accorded to all human beings, including gay and lesbian persons. These rights include life, dignity, and the freedom to live out their full potential as divinely created beings. Most significantly, and again in accordance with black people's own history of struggle, these rights include the freedom to marry.

To reiterate, the black enslaved were routinely denied the freedom to marry. Marriage was considered a right granted to human beings capable of loving relationships. Because black people were considered less than human, that is, beastly chattel, they were thought incapable of loving relationality. Consequently, they were not granted the right to marry. Thus, for them, marriage became an important marker of their humanity and,

---

33. This notion of human rights is taken from the Universal Declaration of Human Rights adopted by the General Assembly of the United Nations on December 10, 1948.

therefore, highly valued. Many enslaved men and women pursued marriage despite the oppressive conditions that mitigated against it.[34] In his nineteenth-century novel *Clotel*, black novelist William Wells Brown, in speaking of enslaved marriages, poignantly depicts the inextricable link between marriage and humanity:

> Marriage is, indeed, the first and most important institution of human existence.... It is the most intimate covenant of heart formed among mankind; and for many persons the only relation in which they feel the true sentiments of humanity.[35]

Essentially, if black people are to take seriously the meaning of their own history of struggle for their humanity, particularly as that struggle has been informed by their faith, then they must realize the rightness of non-heterosexual women's and men's struggle for full affirmation of their humanity. Most important, as Black Church people witness to a God who enters into compassionate solidarity with the black oppressed in their struggles, they must also recognize that this God is no respecter of persons when it comes to the oppressed. That is, just as God has revealed God's self on the side of black people as they strive toward freedom and justice, so is God on the side of non-heterosexuals as they do the same. Perhaps Reverend Kelvin Calloway, pastor of the Second A.M.E. Church in Los Angeles, best describes the mandate for the Black Church by acknowledging: "Oppression is oppression is oppression.... Just because we're not the ones who are being oppressed now, do we not stand with those oppressed now? This is the biblical mandate. That's what Jesus is all about."

Finally, the Black Church is compelled to recognize that platonic Christianity spawns and sanctions structures of oppression. Inasmuch as it

---

34. For more discussion of this, see Angelo Robinson, "The Subject of Romance: Sexual Healing and the Completion of Humanity in Neoslave Narratives," paper presented at the American Studies Association Convention, Atlanta, Georgia, November 12, 2004. See also Kelly Brown Douglas, "Contested Marriage/Loving Relationality," in *Liturgy: Journal of the Liturgical Conference* 20, no. 3 (2005): 51–60.

35. William Wells Brown, *Clotel* (London: Patridge & Oakley, 1853), 83.

deems non-procreative sexuality evil, it provides the theological frame-work for dehumanizing ideologies that routinely caricature the sexuality of their victims. In addition, as platonized Christianity diminishes the sig-nificance of God's *embodied* reality, it permits the degradation of the bodies of others. This tradition must be repudiated as heretical. To be sure, it is only in reclaiming its own non-platonized religious heritage that the Black Church will become more consistent in its justice politics as it addresses issues beyond racial justice, including human sexuality. However, as long as the Black Church is bound to a platonized Christian tradition, it will be vulnerable to the manipulations of white political power, as was the case during the 2004 presidential campaign. In other words, inasmuch as a platonized theology shapes the Black Church community's responses to social justice concerns, then the Black Church is susceptible to upholding the very culture of domination and systems of power that have ensured their very oppression. Not until the Black Church community decidedly frees itself from platonized notions of sexuality will it be able to become liberated from the politics of white patriarchal heterosexist oppression.

The problem of homophobia and heterosexism within the Black Church community is a complicated one, but regardless of the complexity of the matter, it is one that the Black Church must overcome. It is time for the Black Church to reclaim more fully and enthusiastically its justice-affirming political, historical, and theological tradition and, thus, join allies in other religious traditions (and no religious tradition) to eradicate the sins of homophobia and heterosexism from its very midst and beyond.

Chapter Eight

"There Are Many Branches on the Tree of Life"

The Irreconcilability of Hinduism and Homophobia

ANANTANAND RAMBACHAN

In 1998 *Fire,* a film by Canada-based producer Deepa Mehta, was released in India. *Fire* tells the story of two middle-class sisters-in-law, Sita and Radha. Sita, after an arranged marriage, joins her husband and his family only to discover that his affections are centered on his Chinese girlfriend. Radha's husband, on the other hand, is on a spiritual quest and has chosen a life of celibacy. Spurned by their husbands, Sita and Radha turn to each other for support, and a love affair ensues. Although *Fire* is centrally concerned with the themes of patriarchy, repression, and rejection, the portrayal of a lesbian relationship ignited a hostile and violent reaction. Theaters screening the movie were burned to the ground, the life of the producer was threatened, and for a time the Indian government banned the film.[1]

Hindu nationalist groups like the Shiva Sena and Rashtriya Seva Sangh led the agitation against *Fire.* The controversy reached the Indian parliament where a heated debate ensued between opponents of the movie and those who defended the rights of the film maker. Protesters contended that homosexuality was a Western import alien to the culture and traditions of India and denounced the movie as degrading and un-Indian. Shiva Sena leader Bal Thackeray offered to end the agitation if the names of

---

1. For a summary of the controversy generated by *Fire,* see the newspaper articles at the sawnet.org website.

201

the women in the film were changed and they were given Muslim names! Mehta and others responded with the argument that homosexual relationships are part of the ancient heritage of India and condemned protesters for their homophobic behavior. Gay activist Ashok Row Kavi claimed that the criminalization of homosexuality was a legacy of British colonial rule and that the Hindu tradition does not condemn those who have different sexual preferences.

The violent response to *Fire* underlines a trend to disavow the reality of homosexuality in ancient India, represent it as a Western phenomenon, and deny its accommodation within Hinduism.[2] It highlights the sharp divisions that currently exist among Hindus over the status of homosexuals within the tradition. These differing positions are well illustrated in the experiences of Jim Gilman, a gay man and former member of the Chinmaya Mission, a popular neo-Hindu movement founded by the charismatic teacher Swami Chinmayananda (1916–93).[3] As a disciple of Swami Chinmayananda, Gilman found complete acceptance at the feet of his teacher. His gayness was a non-issue. When questioned about his attitude to homosexuality, Chinmayananda's response was sharp and brief: "There are many branches on the tree of life. Full stop. Next question."[4] After the death of Swami Chinmayananda in 1993, Gilman was asked by his successor, Swami Tejomayananda, to relinquish his position as a teacher (*acharya*) and to leave the Chinmaya Mission. There were no criticisms of his work or behavior. Protestations about his observance of celibacy (*brahmacharya*) were to no avail. The issue was his gay identity and his past. Members of the mission, as Gilman discovered, were concerned about his sexual orientation "based in typical erroneous stereotypes of gay people as perverts and child molesters. I must say that it was one of the most painful experiences of my whole life."[5] A recent Hindu account represents homosexuality as

---

2. See Amara Das Wilhelm, *Tritiya-Prakriti: People of the Third Sex* (Philadelphia: Xlibris, 2003), 33.

3. For a life of Swami Chinmayananda, see Nancy Patchen, *The Journey of a Master: Swami Chinmayananda, the Man, the Path, the Teaching* (Bombay: Central Chinmaya Mission Trust, 1989).

4. *Trikone Magazine* (July 1996): 6.

5. Ibid., 7.

"harmful to all parties," "against nature and the natural order of things," and as "known to cause the spread of diseases like AIDS."[6]

Diversity of Hinduism: A Precious Resource

Any attempt to offer a Hindu perspective on homosexuality must acknowledge, at the inception, the diverse and decentralized character of Hinduism. Although the appellation *Hinduism* suggests uniformity, the reality is that it subsumes a multiplicity of traditions and perspectives, reflecting the rich diversity of India and the Hindu diaspora. In addition, these traditions have not found it necessary to designate a common creed or rituals that are stipulated as requirements for belonging or acceptance within the religion. There is no single institutional or personal authority to which Hindus are subject or that issues binding proclamations on matters of belief and practice. The consequence is that Hindus are oriented to accommodate and accept diversity as a natural and inevitable feature of the human condition. There are many names for God, many ways (*margas*) of being religious depending on individual disposition, family, and community traditions, and multiple perspectives about (*darshanas*) reality. Diana Eck contrasts the Hindu attitude to diversity with her own

> distinctively Western habit of thought, grounded primarily in the Western tradition of monotheism: the expectation of singularity and uniqueness, and the valuing of such singularity and uniqueness.... In monotheistic consciousness, the singular is the proper number for questions of Truth: There is One God, one Only-Begotten Son of the Father, one Seal of the Prophets, one Holy Book, one Holy Catholic and Apostolic Church. It might be called "the myth of monotheism": that there is one and only one holy story to be reflected upon by theologians, and to be participated in by the faithful.[7]

---

6. Nawal K. Prinja, ed., *Explaining Hindu Dharma: A Guide for Teachers*, 2nd ed. (Surrey: Vishwa Hindu Parishad, 2001), 169.

7. Diana Eck, *Encountering God: A Spiritual Journey from Bozeman to Banaras* (Boston: Beacon Press, 1993), 59.

The Hindu openness to diversity as necessary in the religious sphere is a precious resource that needs to inform our reflection on matters of human sexuality. Historically, discussions among Hindu sub-traditions were dialogical, and there was a notable absence of efforts to stamp out alternative ways of thinking. The language of engagement was not militaristic, and traditions were seen as members of a single family tree. It would be a tragedy if, like the opponents of Deepa Mehta's *Fire*, Hindus were to privilege a single interpretation of the tradition and hatefully denounce alternative understandings. If Hindus respect and remain faithful to their pluralistic legacy, homosexuals, like heterosexuals, ought to be valued and accepted within the expansive embrace of the tradition.

Recognizing Third-Sex Persons in Hinduism

Literary evidence contradicts the claim that homosexuality is a modern import into Hinduism. There are ancient references to the existence of three sexes in the Hindu tradition. These are males (*pums prakriti*), females (*stri prakriti*), and members of the third sex (*tritiya prakriti*).[8] The term *tritiya prakriti* seems to have been widely employed by the fourth century.[9] In the Kamasutra, persons belonging to the third sex are described as belonging to two types "according to whether their appearance is masculine or feminine."[10] While some may argue that references to a third sex in

---

8. Examples of this classification offered by Wilhelm include *The Laws of Manu* (3.49), and the *Srimad Bhavagatam* (4.17.26, 4.28.61, 8.3.24). *The Laws of Manu* (ca. 200 B.C.E.–100 C.E.) is an authoritative compilation of Hindu law authored by Manu. The *Srimad Bhagavatam* (ca. 800–900) is attributed to the poet-compiler Vyasa and focuses on the life of Krishna, revered by many Hindus as an incarnation (*avatar*) of God. See Wilhelm, *Tritiya Prakriti*, n.4, 178.

9. See Leonard Zwilling and Michael J. Sweet, "Like a City Ablaze": The Third Sex and the Creation of Sexuality in Jain Religious Literature," *Journal of the History of Sexuality* 6, no. 3 (January 1996): 359–84. These authors suggest that the three-sex model originated in the speculation of Sanskrit grammarians who sought to find a connection between grammatical genders (male, female, and neuter) and human gender. See also Leonard Zwilling and Michael J. Sweet, "In Search of Napumsaka," *Trikone Magazine* (July 1996): 14.

10. The Kamasutra (ca. 400 C.E.) is attributed to Vatsyayana. While not an authoritative scripture, it gives us an important glimpse into the sexuality in ancient India. The word *kama*, means "pleasure" and includes both sensual and aesthetic enjoyment. It is

ancient Hindu literature ought not be equated with homosexuals, it is important to note that these references are free from homophobic hatred and bias, and, as will become clearer later, there are no denunciations of the third sex based on theological or religious argument. There appears to have been no need for a sharp either/or dichotomy regarding sex and gender.

Our understanding of the significance of a third sex in ancient Hindu literature is deepened by the specific terms used to designate this group of persons. While *tritiya* (third) *prakriti* is usually translated "third sex," the Sanskrit term *prakriti* does not literally mean sex. Rather, it describes "the original or natural form of anything" and is often used as a synonym for "nature, character, constitution."[11] The use of this term highlights the understanding of the ancient thinkers that important aspects of one's sexuality, whether homosexual or heterosexual, are inherited at birth.[12] For example, *Manusmriti* (3.49) offers a biological explanation for sexual differentiation at birth:

A male child is produced by a greater quantity of male seed, a female child by the prevalence of the female; if both are equal, a third-sex child (*napumsaka*) or boy and girl twins are produced; if either are weak or deficient in quantity, a failure of conception results.[13]

---

one of the four legitimate goals of Hindu life. The other three are *artha* (wealth), *dharma* (virtue), and *moksha* (liberation). Vatsyayana focuses primarily on sexual relationships and defines *kama* as "the mental inclination toward the pleasures of touch, sight, taste, and smell, to the extent that the practitioner derives satisfaction from it." See *The Complete Kama Sutra*, trans. Alan Daniélou (Rochester Park: Street Press, 1994), 2.9.1, 183; and 1.2.11, 28–29. Hinduism emphasizes that the pursuit of wealth and pleasure is subject to the norms of virtue (*dharma*).

11. See Monier Monier-Williams, *A Sanskrit-English Dictionary* (Oxford: Oxford University Press), 654.

12. This interpretation of the meaning of *prakriti* is not meant to suggest that all aspects of sexuality are biologically determined. Today, we understand much better the significance of socialization in the shaping of sexual identity and roles. Wilhelm sees a further significance in the use of the term, *prakriti*. "Generally," he writes, "the word 'sex' refers to biological sex and 'gender' to psychological behavior and identity. The term *prakriti* or nature, however, implies both aspects together as one intricately woven and cohesive unit." See Wilhelm, *Tritiya Prakriti*, 4.

13. The Sanskrit term *napumsaka* (literally, not male), widely used for a homosexual, reflects the patriarchal bias of Hindu society and its emphasis on procreation. Male identity

Ancient Indian medical practitioners took a similar approach and sought their explanations for sexual identity in conception and fetal development.[14] Sexual identity is understood to be determined by the character and respective proportions in which the father's semen and the mother's blood combine at conception:

> Thus, a defect in the mother's seed may result in the birth of a baby that is female in appearance but not a true female (that is, an individual of the third gender), while a defect in the father's seed may result in a similarly defective male birth. A variation is the belief that a third-gender individual is conceived when amounts of the male and female seed are equal, as opposed to a preponderance of one or the other, which results in a child of the respective gender.[15]

Although the medicalization of homosexuality or treating it as an "embryological abnormality" is fraught with danger, including the assumption of heterosexual normativity, it is important to note that ancient Hindu thinkers appreciated the inherent dimension of sexual identity and did not view homosexuality as either deviant or unnatural. This may explain why

---

was synonymous with the ability to procreate. Other terms include *sandha* (half-male, half-female) and *kliba* (non-reproductive). These terms are commonly translated "eunuch," but it must be noted that castration was rare in ancient India and never recommended for persons of the third sex. See Arvind Sharma, "Homosexuality and Hinduism," in *Homosexuality and World Religions,* ed. Arlene Swidler (Valley Forge, PA: Trinity Press International, 1993), 48. In *Tritiya-Prakriti,* Wilhelm argues that the practice of castration became popular with the advent of Islam into India in the eleventh century (49–51). As noted by Sweet and Zwilling, "Castration, either of men or of animals, was regarded with disapproval and at times legally forbidden in Indian tradition prior to Muslim rule. Therefore the use of 'eunuch' as an equivalent translation for terms found in classical texts denoting individuals who are not normative in their sexual or gender-role behavior is rarely appropriate." See Michael Sweet and Leonard Zwilling, "The First Medicalization: The Taxonomy and Etiology of Queerness in Classical Indian Medicine, *Journal of the History of Sexuality* 3, no. 4 (April 1993): 590–607.

14. The most important of these are the manuals of Caraka (*Carakasamhita*) and Susruta (*Susrutasamhita*). Both are dated around the second century C.E. See Priyavrat Sharma, ed. and trans., *Caraka Samhita,* 3 vols. (Varanasi: Chaukambha Orientalia, 1981); and P. Ray, H. Gupta, and M. Roy, eds., *Susruta Samhita: A Scientific Synopsis* (New Delhi: Indian National Science Academy, 1980).

15. Sweet and Zwilling, "The First Medicalization," 604.

no attempts were ever made to treat or confine homosexuals.[16] The appreciation of third-sex orientation as congenital influences significantly the response to such persons. The Hindu tradition, as noted above, has cultivated a remarkable ability to accommodate diversity, and we can surely see third-sex persons as part of this wonderful and enriching diversity of creation. Even as heterosexual persons are not called upon to justify their sexuality, third-sex persons should not be burdened with an obligation to explain or defend their identities or with being mistakenly perceived as disordered expressions of another sex.

One of the finest examples of such acceptance and fair treatment of third-sex persons in ancient Hindu society concerns Arjuna, the Pandava leader, friend, and disciple of Krishna in the Bhagavadgita and the hero of the Mahabharata.[17] The Mahabharata narrates the story of the conflict between two sets of cousins, the Kauravas and the Pandavas. The Pandavas have been cheated out of their rightful share of the family kingdom, treated unjustly, and forced into exile. After losing a loaded game of dice against the Kauravas, the Pandavas were required, under the terms of the wager, to live for twelve years in the wilderness and spend the thirteenth year incognito. If their true identities were discovered during this year, they had to spend another twelve years in exile.

Arjuna, the warrior, chose to spend the thirteenth year in the court of a local ruler, King Virata. He assumed the dress and personality of a member of the third sex, wearing the clothing and ornaments of a woman. Arjuna introduced himself to the king as Brihannada, a teacher of dance and music:

> I sing and I dance and make fine music,
> I am good at the dance and master of song.

---

16. Ibid., 606. Sweet and Zwilling compare the Indian approach to that of Europe and the United States where efforts were made, with medical support, to treat and confine homosexuals.

17. The Mahabharata (ca. 400 B.C.E.–400 C.E.) consists of a hundred thousand verses, and is popularly referred to as the fifth Veda. Within it occurs the Bhagavadgita (Song of the Lord), a dialogue between Krishna (*avatar*) and Arjuna. The Bhagavadgita is one of the most popular scriptures of Hinduism and is regarded as a philosophical pillar of the Hindu tradition.

> Pray give me to Uttara, sire, to serve her,
> I shall be the dance master of your queen.
>
> The reason I have this form — what profit
> Is there in recounting it but great pain?
> Brihannada, sire, is my name, deserted
> By father and mother as son and daughter.[18]

The king was initially skeptical of Arjuna's identity because he could not reconcile Arjuna's muscular build with his femininity. The king tested Arjuna in dancing and music, consulted with his ministers, and had him examined by women. On learning "for sure that he was not a man," Arjuna was allowed to live among the palace women and be an instructor.

> So in his disguise Dhananjaya [Arjuna] dwelled there
> In control of himself and doing them favors;
> And none of the people there found him out,
> Neither those in the house nor those outside.[19]

As a bona fide person of the third sex, Arjuna found acceptance, employment, and safety within the palace walls and among the women in the court. We must assume that Arjuna chose this particular guise knowing well that as a person of the third sex he would not be rejected, humiliated, or demeaned. His choice had to be grounded in a wider social acceptance and role of third-sex persons in Hindu society.[20]

Third-Sex Persons in the Law Codes

Although there is good evidence that Hindu society acknowledged the existence of a third sex and had some appreciation for the biological basis

---

18. J. A. B van Buitenen, trans. and ed., *The Mahabharata* (Chicago: University of Chicago Press, 1978), 4:40–41.

19. Ibid., 4:41.

20. For other summaries of this story see Devadutt Pattanaik, *The Man Who Was a Woman* (New York: Harrington Park Press, 2002), 95–96; and Wilhelm, *Tritiya-Prakriti*, 22–23.

of sexual identity, ancient codes of law specify sanctions against certain kinds of homosexual behavior and exclude homosexuals from ritual privileges and family inheritance.[21] One of the often-quoted texts is from Manu (11:175):

A twice-born man who commits an unnatural offense with a male, or has intercourse with a female in a cart drawn by oxen, in water, or in the day-time, shall bathe, dressed in his clothes.

This is a problematic verse, highlighting many important exegetical issues. First is the accuracy of the translation. The translator, G. Buhler, prejudicially renders *maithunam pumsi* (literally, sex with a male) as "unnatural offense with a male."[22] Second, the text appears to be more concerned with specifying a certain time and place where sexual relations are undesirable since it makes mention of heterosexuality as well as homosexuality. It seems that the verse intends to curb public displays of sexuality. Third, the verse identifies the punishment as applying to the twice-born man.[23] The question of whether this verse should be read as applying to persons of the third sex remains doubtful.[24] Fourth, the punishment, a

---

21. It is very important to note that the law codes in the Hindu tradition fall under the classification of *smriti* texts. These are distinguished from revealed texts, referred to as *sruti*. *Smriti* texts are secondary in authority to *sruti* texts and are explicitly understood to reflect the views of a particular human author and the times when the author lived. The four Vedas are the paramount examples of *sruti* texts in Hinduism, while the law code of Manu is an example of a *smriti* text.

22. See G. Buhler, trans., *The Laws of Manu* (Delhi: Motilal Banarsidass, 1988), 466. Recent translators have shed such prejudices and are more faithful to the original text. See, for example, Wendy Doniger and Brian K. Smith, trans., *The Laws of Manu* (London: Penguin Books, 1991), 268. Sharma, "Homosexuality and Hinduism," offers a comment on this issue of translation. Alain Daniélou, *The Complete Kama Sutra*, points out that the Sanskrit term for lesbians, *svairini* (literally, independent women), becomes "corrupt women" (6).

23. Twice-born refers to the male members of the first three castes — Brahmins, Kshatriyas, and Vaishyas. A twice-born person alone is entitled to the study of the Vedas through the sacrament of being invested with the sacred thread.

24. Wilhelm claims that there are no verses in the law books that forbid sexual relations between people of the third sex. See *Tritiya Prakriti*, 17–18.

ritual bath while fully dressed, must be considered a relatively minor punishment.

Manu (11:68) also prescribes loss of caste for sexual relations between males:

> Causing an injury to a priest, smelling wine or things that are not to be smelled, crookedness and sexual union with a man are traditionally said to cause loss of caste.[25]

Here also we see that sexual relations between males is not treated by itself but included with a variety of actions of varying moral significance. In addition, as Sharma rightly notes, the loss of caste was not permanent and could be recovered by the performance of prescribed rites of expiation.[26] The important point here, as Zwilling and Sweet point out, is that the "rabid homophobia of the Judeo-Christian West is absent — there are no exhortations to burn or to stone to death people who have queer sex, or who are otherwise different in their gender or sexual role. The Hindu law books do contain penalties for same-sex behavior, but these are for the most part minor fines and penances, comparable to similar heterosexual offenses and other violations of ritual purity or social norms."[27] Most significantly, there is no evidence of any hateful persecution of third-sex persons.

In the Laws of Manu, people of the third sex are also excluded from certain privileges accorded to others. These include making offerings to departed ancestors and deities (3:150, 165), receiving family

---

25. The translation is by Doniger and Smith. Buhler again uses the expression "unnatural offense with a male."

26. Sharma, "Hinduism and Homosexuality," 54. Moreover, it is not clear if this verse is referring to third-sex persons or heterosexual men who engage in homosexual behavior.

27. Leonard Zwilling and Michael J. Sweet, "In Search of the Napumsaka," *Trikone Magazine* (July 1996): 15. For the severity of punishments for certain kinds of heterosexual offenses, see Manu (8:359–68). Manu (8:369–70) also stipulates harsher punishment for lesbian sexual relations. We may account for this by reference to the influence of patriarchy and greater concern in traditional Hindu society for female virginity.

inheritance (9:201, 203), and making sacrificial offerings into the sacred fire (4:205–6):

> A priest should never eat at a sacrifice offered by a priest who does not know the Veda by heart, by someone who conducts sacrifice for every sort of person, or by a woman or an impotent man.
>
> Where an oblation is offered by such people there is bad luck for virtuous men; it goes against the grain of the gods, and therefore one should avoid it.

While the gender bias of Manu is revealed in his exclusion of women, some interpreters understand these exclusions to be connected with the fact that third-sex individuals did not fulfill traditional Hindu obligations through marriage and bearing children.[28] The exclusion from inheritance may be a direct consequence of not having children to whom one may bequeath family property. Religious celibates, however, also give up rights to family property and do not participate in traditional rituals that are prescribed for householders. The exclusions that are mentioned in Manu, therefore, do not have to be construed as pertaining to homosexuals merely because of their sexual identity. These have to be seen in the light of the significance of procreation. The Hindu tradition places a very high value on having children, and raising a family discharges what is understood to be a debt to one's ancestors. A son is required for funeral rituals and to perform annual postmortem offerings on behalf of departed parents. Ritual worship in the Vedas presumes a heterosexual family with children. This is an issue to which we will return.

Divine Immanence and the Value of the Person in Hinduism

It is important to acknowledge that although the tradition recognizes the reality of a third sex and has argued for its biological basis, heterosexuality is still treated as normative. Third-sex persons, especially in the

---

28. See Wilhelm, *Tritiya Prakriti*, 18–19.

law codes, are judged differently in relation to married, child-producing heterosexuals.[29] The challenge remains to move from acknowledgment of a third sex to affirmation of equal worth and the justice due to all sexes.

There are important resources in the Hindu tradition for such a movement toward justice and pivotal resources upon which this can be grounded. The ultimate worth of the human person in Hinduism is not located in his or her sexual identity. It proceeds from the claim that the human being embodies the real and infinite divine spirit (*brahman*). The various traditions of Hinduism have characterized the relationship between the divine spirit and the human self (*atman*) in various ways, dependent on their philosophical standpoints. The non-dualists (Advaitins) speak of the ultimate identity of the two while the qualified non-dualists (Vishishtadvaitins) describe the relationship as one of inseparability and not identity. All of them agree, however, on the fact that the divine exists equally and identically in all beings. As the Bhagavadgita (13:27) puts it:

> One who sees the supreme Lord,
> Existing alike in all beings,
> Not perishing when they perish,
> Truly sees.[30]

The profound significance that the Hindu tradition accords this truth may be appreciated from the fact that its discernment is equated with liberation (*moksha*), the highest goal of human existence. *Moksha* is awakening to the identical presence of the divine in all beings. The Bhagavadgita (18:20) commends the wisdom that enables a person to see "one imperishable Being in all beings, undivided in separate beings." This vision does not call upon us to ignore or deny the uniqueness of individuals and communities, but to perceive the unity that underlies all and to realize the value of each one that flows from it. One cannot profess to value the

---

29. As already noted, it is not clear if the verses apply to heterosexual persons who engage in homosexual behavior or if these are applicable to third-sex persons.

30. *The Bhagavadgita*, trans. Winthrop Sargeant (Albany: State University of New York Press, 1984).

divine and then despise the multiplicity of beings into which the divine has willingly entered.

While the social and political implications of this truth are not detailed in the classical texts, the need for egalitarianism in human relationships is unmistakable. When the implications for human relationships are enunciated, these are done in terms of equality. As the Bhagavadgita (5:19) states it:

> Even here on earth, those whose minds are impartial overcome rebirth. God is perfect and the same in all. Therefore, they always abide in God.[31]

Justice, understood as equality of opportunity and treatment, is a consequence of the equal presence of the divine and is a condition for liberation and oneness with God. There is no good reason why this principle should not also be applied to persons who are recognized as members of the third sex.

The Hindu doctrines of the unity of existence through the divine and of the worth of all life are the sources of such cardinal values as *ahimsa* (non-injury), compassion (*daya*), and generosity (*dana*). Belief in divine immanence requires reverence and consideration for all and also relationships characterized by justice and freedom from violence. The divine is identified, especially in the non-dual tradition of Hinduism (Advaita), as the ground of human selfhood, and the divine (*brahman*) is spoken of as non-different from the human self (*atman*) at its most fundamental nature. With this ultimate identity in mind, scriptural texts speak interchangeably of seeing the self (*atman*) in all beings and/or of seeing the divine (*brahman*) in all beings.[32] For example, Isa Upanishad (6) reminds us that the wise person who sees all beings in the self and sees the self in all beings is liberated from hate. The Bhagavadgita (12:13) puts this same point positively and describes such a person not only as free from hate but as friendly and compassionate to all. Freedom from fear is also a mark of wisdom and

---

31. My translation.
32. See, for example, Bhagavadgita 6:29–32.

liberation.[33] Homophobia, characterized by fear, hate, and denigration of third-sex persons, finds no justification in Hinduism and betrays its most fundamental vision and values.

The Hindu ideal of seeing all beings in one's own self and one's self in all beings ought not to be interpreted passively. At heart it is a call to learn to enter compassionately into the lives of others, seeing through their eyes, sharing their emotions, understanding their thoughts, and responding to their needs. It is, as the Bhagavadgita (6:32) explains, identifying with others in joy and in sorrow and learning to own their joys and pains as one's own. The requirement, in the case of third-sex persons, is that through identity with them we know the pain that comes from being demonized, ostracized, excluded, and persecuted because of one's sexual identity. Knowing the pain of the other through an enlarged identity helps us to overcome an important source of homophobia, rooted as it is in the human tendency to devalue those who are defined as different and perceived, consequently, as a threat. As Ervin Staub points out in his seminal study *The Roots of Evil*, devaluation and the relegation of people to outgroups "serve as a basis for scapegoating and a precondition for harming."[34] Devaluation leads to the perception of people as objects and not as fellow beings who feel and suffer as we do. It provides the conditions for guilt-free violence and mistreatment. Humans are less likely to oppress those in whom they see themselves, and the Hindu ideal of seeing oneself in all beings and all beings in oneself is an important antidote to the poison of homophobia and all other prejudices.

Sex and Liberation (*Moksha*)

It is very important to take note of the fact that in relation to the attainment of *moksha* (liberation), the ultimate and highest goal of human existence in Hinduism, there is no difference between heterosexuality

---

33. See Bhagavadgita 17:1 and Taittiriya Upanishad 2.7 and 2.9 in *The Upanisads*, trans. Patrick Olivelle (Oxford: Oxford University Press, 1996).

34. Ervin Staub, *The Roots of Evil: The Origins of Genocide and Other Group Violence* (Cambridge: Cambridge University Press, 1989), 48.

and homosexuality. Sexual identity does not debar a person from life's most desirable end.[35] It is a widely shared view among the traditions of Hinduism that ignorance (*avidya*) of the true nature of the human self (*atman*), God (*brahman*), and the world (*jagat*) is the fundamental cause of bondage and suffering. Freedom or liberation cannot be attained without right knowledge of reality and the transformation of vision and action that this implies.

For three of the great philosophers and traditions of Hinduism, Shankara (Advaita — non-dualism), Ramanuja (Vishishtadvaita — qualified non-dualism), and Madhva (Dvaita — dualism), the self cannot be entirely identified with the mortal physical body or the ever-changing mind. In its essential nature, the self is timeless and full. Consciousness and joy (*ananda*) constitute its essential nature. For Shankara, the self is ultimately identical with *brahman*. For Ramanuja, it is related to *brahman* as body to soul or as part to whole. For Madhva, it is entirely different from but completely dependent on God. Ignorant of its true nature, the self wrongly identifies with the characteristics of body and mind, including sex, assumes the limitations of these, and considers itself incomplete and wanting. *Moksha* is consequent upon the right understanding of the nature of the self. It implies that recognition of the self is more than the psycho-physical composite. The true self transcends the limits of these to be full and complete.

This Hindu understanding of liberation, however, should not be interpreted to mean that the tradition is life-denying or that it despises the body and human sexuality. Pleasure (*kama*) is one of the legitimate goals of Hindu life, so long as it is sought in accordance with the requirements of *dharma* (moral values) and its primary virtue, non-injury (*ahimsa*).[36] One of the recommended ways for contemplating God, in the Taittiriya Upanishad (3.10.3–4), is as joy in sex, and sex is treated in the Upanishads

---

35. This is not to deny that there are patriarchal Hindu traditions that suggest that being a woman is disadvantageous for the attainment of liberation. My contention is that when one looks at the Hindu understanding of the fundamental human problem and the nature of liberation, sexual identity cannot be an impediment.

36. In the Bhagavadgita (7:11), for example, Krishna identifies himself with pleasure that is not in opposition to virtue.

as sacramental in nature.[37] It is ignorance (*avidya*) and the immoderate and uncontrolled life that stand as obstacles to liberation, not sexuality, heterosexual or homosexual. I am not aware of any authoritative (*sruti*) text that excludes a person from Hinduism's highest goal on the basis of sexual identity. As Katha Upanishad (2:24) states it:

> One who has not abstained from evil conduct, whose senses are not controlled and whose mind is not concentrated and calm cannot gain the Self through knowledge.[38]

One of the most remarkable examples of sexual inclusivity in the sacred texts of Hinduism, and perhaps in the religious literature of the world, occurs in the Ramayana (Story of Rama).[39] The context here is a story told by Rama in which he likens God to a parent having numerous children. Although each child possesses a different gift, the parent loves all in the same way. The entire universe, Rama explains, is his creation, and he is equally compassionate to all. The following text is most significant:

> One who worships me in thought, word, and action, relinquishing deceit, whether man, third-sex person, or woman, is supremely dear to me.[40]

It is clear that, in the view of the author of the Ramayana, human sexual identity, as well as other kinds of distinctions, do not matter to God.

---

37. See, for example, Brihadaranyaka Upanishad, 6.2.9–16; 6.4.2–3; Chandogya Upanishad, 2.13.1–2.

38. My translation.

39. Klostermaier refers to the Ramayana as Hindus' favorite book. See Klaus Klostermaier, *A Survey of Hinduism* (Albany: State University of New York Press, 1994), 89–93. First authored by Valmiki (ca. 200 C.E.), the text has been reworked in the various Indian regional languages. The most popular version, the *Ramacharitamanas*, was authored by the poet Tulasidasa (ca. sixteenth century) in a dialect of Hindi. The importance of the Ramayana follows from the widespread Hindu belief that Rama is an *avatar*. His words and teachings in the text are significant and influential. The verse cited comes from the Tulasidasa version. See *The Ramayana of Tulsi Das*, trans. F. S. Growse (Delhi: Interprint, 1983), *Doha* 87, 541.

40. My translation. I translate *napumsaka* as "third-sex person." Some translators render it as "eunuch," which, for reasons already mentioned, is inappropriate. One translator speaks of "one lacking the characteristics of both (man and woman)."

Love and purity of character are all important. While the above verse is the only one in the text referring specifically to third-sex persons, the message about the centrality of love and the inclusiveness of God's love is unmistakable. Earlier in the text, in another remarkable exchange with an outcaste woman who was apprehensive about approaching him because of her sex and caste status, Rama assures her that the relationship of love is the only one that binds God to human beings.

> I recognize no relationship save that of love: neither lineage, family, religion, rank, wealth, power, connections, virtue or ability. A person without love is of no more account than a cloud without water.[41]

Similar passages can be found in other authoritative Hindu texts underlining the impartiality of God and the priority of a loving relationship. One well-known text is Bhagavadgita (9:29):

> I am the same to all beings; I do not favor or despise anyone; those who worship me with love are in me and I am in them.

Other sections of the text (2:55–72; 12:13–20; 14:23–26) describing the character of the wise person and the servant of God make no reference to sex and speak only of virtues of the mind and heart, such as delight in God, self-control, absence of hate and greed, friendliness, and compassion.

Procreation, Marriage, and the Third Sex

Although homosexuality is not regarded in Hinduism as a religious sin (*papa*), one of the principal reasons for stigmatization has to do with non-procreation through inability or disinterest. As Devadutt Pattanaik points out, "All hell breaks loose in a Hindu household not so much when a son or daughter displays homosexual tendencies, but when those tendencies come in the way of heterosexual marriage.... Non-heterosexuality is ignored or tolerated so long as it does not upset the heterosexual world order.[42] While the value of children should not, by itself, be thought of as

---

41. *The Ramayana of Tulsi Das*, 90. Growse translation (amended).
42. Pattanaik, *The Man Who Was a Woman*, 8.

problematic, it becomes so when those who, for various reasons, do not procreate are perceived as defective and of lesser worth.

As already noted, the value and worth of persons in the Hindu tradition do not come from sexual identity or, we must now add, procreative ability or choice. The famous lines of the Kaivalya Upanishad (3) remind us that immortality is attained through renunciation and not by work, progeny, or wealth. Worth comes from the human embodiment of the divine, and liberation (*moksha*) is not contingent on procreation or its absence. The traditional value for procreation must be seen in the context of labor needs in an agricultural economy and a high rate of infant mortality. Today these conditions have changed, and the need for offspring is no longer urgent.

In addition to economic need and high infant-mortality rates, male progeny is required also for the performance of annual postmortem rituals (*sraddha*) for the departed parent. This ritual, it is believed, saves the parent from suffering in the afterlife.[43] The eldest son has the privilege of offering the rice-ball (*pinda*) each year when the rites are performed for the departed ancestors. The role of the son in the performance of postmortem rituals causes preferential regard for male offspring, and families sometimes continue to have children until a son is born. There may be many pragmatic reasons why sons were given the responsibility of making annual offerings on behalf of departed ancestors. Traditionally, the married male child remained a part of the joint household while the daughter left her home and took on a new identity as part of her husband's home. Her obligations after marriage were centered on her husband's family. Today, with the growth of nuclear families, both sons and daughters are leaving the family home, and a married daughter may be more interested and available to perform postmortem rituals. It is necessary now to reconsider the exclusion of Hindu women from such important family rituals.

In addition to challenging the injustice of the preference for male offspring, the Hindu tradition should emphasize the significance of its

---

43. I have addressed the injustice of this practice elsewhere. See Anantanand Rambachan, "A Hindu Perspective," in *What Men Owe to Women*, ed. John C. Raines and Daniel C. Maguire (Albany: State University of New York Press, 2001), 23–25.

teaching on *karma*, which makes each person responsible for his or her own fate after death. As I have argued elsewhere, these rituals persist "in spite of the fact that they contradict the widely accepted worldview of *karma, samsara* and *moksha*. They are based not on the assumption of rebirth, but on the hope of the departed eventually joining the company of ancestors in an ancestral world. The emphasis is not on the moral law of *karma* determining the individual's future prospects, but on the ritual offerings of the descendant."[44] Returning to its philosophic roots will avert the need for this kind of emphasis on ritual in the Hindu tradition.

For reasons already mentioned, progeny and parenthood (*prajapati*) became the central purpose of Hindu marriage. The tradition, however, has identified five purposes for marriage: pleasure (*rati*), parenthood (*prajapati*), companionship (*sakhya*), worship (*yajna*), and spiritual bliss (*ananda*). There are good reasons today for giving renewed emphasis to the goals of friendship and spiritual growth.[45] Hindu couples wishing to be married are not required to give proof of their procreative ability or intent, and older persons, beyond the age of procreation, are allowed to marry. Clearly, the Hindu tradition recognizes that the purpose of marriage is not limited to procreation. Marriage also enhances religious growth and personal development through love, sharing, and control of sensual impulses.

There are ancient traditions in the Hindu world that may be cited and appropriated to point the way forward in transforming attitudes toward marriage and procreation. One ancient text, the *Narada Smriti* (1.12.15), advises against the marriage of homosexual men to women.[46] In addition, the Kamasutra (2.9.36) actually records the practice of homosexual marriage in ancient India:

---

44. See Anantanand Rambachan, "The Hindu Way of Death," in *Handbook of Death and Dying*, 2 vols., ed. Clifton D. Bryant (Thousand Oaks, CA: Sage Publications, 2003), 2:647.

45. See S. Cromwell Crawford, *Dilemmas of Life and Death* (Albany: State University of New York Press, 1995), 196.

46. Cited in Wilhelm, *Tritiya Prakriti*, 20. It is possible that this text may be responding to the social practice of forced marriages, but it is difficult to make sound historical judgments based on this textual evidence.

There are also citizens, sometimes greatly attached to each other and with complete faith in one another, who get married (*parigraha*) together.

The purpose of such marriages would not be procreation but rather the goals of friendship, mutual care, and spiritual development.

Conclusion

Many commentators note that the homophobia that exists today in India and among Hindus is a direct consequence of Western, in particular, British, colonial influence.[47] The criminalization of homosexuality came with British legislation in 1860 and still remains in the law books. For example, Section 377 of the Indian Penal Code reads:

Whoever voluntarily has carnal intercourse against the order of nature with any man, woman or animal, shall be punished with imprisonment for life, or with imprisonment of either description for a term which may extend to ten years, and shall be liable to fine.

Cross-dressing was outlawed, and homophobia was reinforced through prejudicial translation of ancient texts. Indigenous attitudes that recognized and accepted the reality of third-sex persons and accorded them a place and role in society were displaced and replaced by guilt and condemnation. Gandhi, educated in England, sent groups to destroy erotic images on temples and had to be stopped by India's Nobel laureate poet Rabindranath Tagore. Jawaharlal Nehru, India's first prime minister, also British educated, was upset by the publication of photographs by Alain Daniélou of sculptures dating from the eleventh century that depict homosexual relations. Nehru's contention was that such vices were the product of Western influence.[48] Today, the task of identifying authentic Hindu

---

47. See Pattanaik, *The Man Who Was a Woman*, 10; Daniélou, *The Complete Kama Sutra*, 10–11; and Wilhelm, *Tritiya Prakriti*, 47–48.

48. See Daniélou, *The Complete Kama Sutra*, 10.

attitudes to homosexuality involves stripping away the colonial accretions and puritanical attitudes about human sexuality that originated elsewhere.

Although ancient Hindu society stigmatized homosexuals and sought to debar them from certain privileges enjoyed by heterosexuals, there are important resources in the tradition for overcoming injustice and transforming our thinking about human sexuality. The highly decentralized Hindu tradition allows for great diversity of thought and religious choice. At its best, the Hindu approach is essentially dialogical, and proponents of differing viewpoints are not demonized. Moreover, it is one of the earliest cultures to propose the category of a third sex (*tritiya prakriti*) with characteristics different from heterosexual males and females.

It is true that "in the earliest speculations about a third gender there was a wavering between viewing it a true third category 'neither male nor female,' or assimilated to a defective (that is, female) pole of the male gender, erasing its uniquely androgynous characteristics."[49] The defect was primarily associated with the inability or unwillingness to procreate. However, the category of *tritiya prakrit* provides us with a valuable resource that challenges and enlarges our thinking about sex categories that are generally thought to be binary in nature. It helps us to recognize the reality of a third sex different from traditional male and female identities and to accept such sexual diversity as a natural part of the diversity of the tree of life. The use of the term *prakriti* to describe the third sex suggests, importantly, that this category is "not against nature and the natural order of things."[50]

The homophobia now discernible in sections of the Hindu community is absent in ancient texts. While there are certain legal penalties for homosexual conduct mentioned in the law codes, these are fairly mild in nature, and there is no evidence in medical treatises of attempts to convert or cure homosexuals. One text explicitly forbids the compulsory marriage of homosexual men to women. While the stigmatization of homosexuals in Hindu society seems particularly connected with the value of male

---

49. Sweet and Zwilling, "The First Medicalization," 601.
50. Prinja, *Explaining Hindu Dharma*, 169.

progeny, this desire is explicable in the context of labor needs in an agricultural economy and high infant-mortality rates. The need for a male child to perform postmortem rituals that avert the suffering of the parent belies the core Hindu teaching about the doctrine of *karma*. Instead, individual responsibility needs to be emphasized today.

As far as recognition of a third sex is concerned, it is also important to note that, as with heterosexuality, this does not imply a disregard for the necessity of attentiveness to ethical values in human relationships. There are certain common values (*sadharana dharma*) to which all are expected to subscribe. Among these are truth, forgiveness, sense control, cleanliness, and freedom from anger. Hindus are guilty, like people of other religions, of stereotyping persons of the third sex and wrongly equating homosexuality with promiscuity. Such stereotyping includes emphasis on sexual behavior. We need to remember also that the term *homosexuality*, like *heterosexuality*, should not be narrowly equated with sex. The issue, as with heterosexuality, is about preferences in relationships and the values of love, justice, loyalty, trust, caring, and friendship that are at the heart of all good relationships. The emphasis should be on the importance of these values for all relationships.

Ultimately, in Hinduism persons are not valued for their procreative abilities or sex. Human worth is the outcome of the immanence of the divine, and the discerning of this divine omnipresence is equated with liberation (*moksha*). The equality of the divine presence is the ground for human dignity and equal justice. The tradition emphasizes the inclusivity of divine love and the accessibility of liberation. The significance of sexual identity, homosexual or heterosexual, has to be seen in relation to the teaching that the self (*atman*), however related to God, is not bound or limited by sexual or any other specifications. In affirming the sex-transcendent nature of the self, the Svestasvatara Upanishad (5:11) quite significantly lists all three sexes: "It is not woman, man, or third-sex person. It identifies with whatever body it assumes."[51]

---

51. My translation.

This inclusion of third-sex persons in the Upanishad, as in the Ramayana, is a significant recognition in an authoritative text that human sexuality is not limited to heterosexual identities. It is also a challenge for us to reevaluate our contemporary attitudes and assumptions about homosexuality and to realize, appreciate, and enjoy the fact that "there are many branches on the tree of life."

Index